THE BEST SELLER

OR

HOW TO MAKE $100,000 A YEAR IN SALES

Albert Winnikoff
and
Burt Prelutsky

Melvin Powers
Wilshire Book Company

12015 Sherman Road, No. Hollywood, CA 91605

Albert Winnikoff and Burt Prelutsky
The No. 1 Best Seller or How to Make $100,000 a Year in Sales
by Albert Winnikoff and Burt Prelutsky
First Edition.

Edited by Eric Wilinski, B.A., M.A.
Copy-edited and Typeset by Joe Cavella & Carol Cavella.
Cover Design by the Warren Group, Venice USA.

Published by:
Melvin Powers
Wilshire Book Company
12015 Sherman Road
No. Hollywood, CA 91605

Printed in the United States of America

Printed in the United States on acid-free paper
First Edition

Library of Congress Catalogue Card Number: 96-061082
ISBN 0-87980-440-8

WARNING: DO NOT READ THIS BOOK IF YOU ARE AN ATTORNEY OR A PSYCHIATRIST

We dedicate this book

with mixed emotions, to

the most important people in the world:

our customers.

IF

If you can keep your head when all about you
    Are losing theirs and blaming it on you;
If you can trust yourself when all men doubt you,
    But make allowance for their doubting too;
If you can wait and not be tired by waiting,
    Or, being lied about, don't deal in lies,
Or, being hated, don't give away to hating,
    And yet don't look too good, nor talk too wise;

If you can dream - and not make dreams your master;
    If you can think - and not make thoughts your aim;
If you can meet with triumph and disaster
    And treat those two impostors just the same;
If you can bear to hear the truth you've spoken
    Twisted by knaves to make a trap for fools,
Or watch the things you gave your life to, broken,
    And stoop and build 'em up with worn out tools;

If you can make one heap of all your winnings
    And risk it on one turn of pitch-and-toss,
And lose, and start again at your beginnings
    And never breathe a word about your loss;
If you can force your heart and nerve and sinew
    To serve your turn long after they are gone,
And so hold on when there is nothing in you
    Except the Will which says to them: "Hold on";

If you can talk with crowds and keep your virtue,
    Or walk with kings - nor lose the common touch;
If neither foes nor loving friends can hurt you;
    If all men count with you, but none too much;
If you can fill the unforgiving minute
    With sixty seconds' worth of distance run -
Yours is the Earth and everything that's in it,
    And - which is more - you'll be a Man, my son!

—RUDYARD KIPLING
On the occasion of his son's 13th birthday

TABLE OF CONTENTS

INTRODUCTION

by
Albert Winnikoff

My father was a terrible businessman.

But he sure was a swell guy.

He never would have made it as a salesman, but he made it just fine as a survivor. To his family and friends he was a very decent, kind, generous and loving human being. Tenants and customers sometimes posed problems, but my father never held a grudge for long. He was a very religious man and, after his retirement, went off to pray at his favorite house of worship three times a day. While I always suspected he did this in part to get away from my mother (he denied my sacrilegious suspicion), I never questioned the intensity of his belief.

My father's early childhood began on a farm in Grafskoy, Russia, a town that no longer exists. I suspect it was a normal farmboy childhood—until 1905, when my father was eight years old. In 1905, my grandfather, Beryl Vinnikoffsky, died suddenly of unknown causes. My father became a serf.

That year, the Russo-Japanese War was raging. The austerity of the times created terrible problems for my family, and my impoverished grandmother could not afford to raise, clothe, feed and educate her youngest son, the child who was to become my father. According to the custom of the time, my father was sold off to a neighboring farmer. Visitation rights were restricted to four times a year. His first job was that of a shepherd, and although he cried a great deal out of fear and loneliness, he was not permitted to return to his mother. His life was not a bucolic idyll. Nor was tending sheep 365 days a year, outdoors, conducive to good health. The brutality of the Russian winters took its toll. My father developed TB and later, asthma. By some miracle he survived both maladies.

My father saw his mother only during the quarterly bazaar held by local farmers. The bazaar took place four times a year and his mother brought whatever gifts she could. But she could not take him home. Because of his tender years, my father cried a great deal more. During one of the winter bazaars, the local women cursed the mother of the young shepherd boy who lived the life of an animal. Overhearing them, my grandmother replied: "Do not curse the mother. She had no choice."

My grandmother, Leah Vinnikoffsky, was a small, iron-willed woman who determined that her family would not be torn asunder by the vagaries of war, revolution, sickness, death, privation and tragedy. The long-term plan was for the entire family to go to the New World—to Leader, Saskatchewan, Canada—to work as farm-hands for a distant relative.

When World War I broke out, my father, despite a bad cough, was conscripted into the czar's army. He served at the front and was wounded. After the war came the revolution. The Vinnikoffsky family decided it was time to put their long-term plan into action.

The eldest son, his new wife and his younger sister (whom he adopted so they could all get out) were the first to leave. They went to Canada. Over a span of seven years, they brought out the rest of the family.

My father was the last to leave.

Upon his arrival in Halifax, two immigration officers, one French-Canadian and the other Anglo-Canadian, changed my father's name from Moishe Vinnikoffsky to Maurice Winnikoff.

The translator, a Polish man who spoke flawless Russian, advised my father to use the name Morris instead of Maurice. The translator did not like Frenchmen. It was a new life and a new beginning.

So Morris Winnikoff entered the Promised Land thinking that to get a job with the Canadian government you had to be a little crazy.

But he also knew it was a good land. A good country. Full of good and decent and honest and helpful people.

He knew he would never go back to Russia. He never did.

In addition to the great goodness of the Canadian people, our family was helped along by immigrants who had preceded them. When they became established, they in turn helped the next crop of immigrants. It is a family tradition we continue to this day. For our people do not take lightly the Biblical injunction to help the widow, the orphan and the stranger.

Because of his past and the way he was put together, my father was deeply appreciative of the simple things in life. Good family and friends, a good meal, occasional good music, and a deep and abiding religious faith. All these were important to him. He was, at various times in the New World, a farmer, tailor, grocer, laundry owner and, in his retirement, the owner of a 24-unit apartment house with my beloved aunt, Mary Omansky.

My father was not cut out to be a great apartment house owner. He was too nice a guy. In addition, taking care of the apartments cut into his time for religious devotion. But his son Albert (that's me) could fix anything. In the course of a few years, father and son replaced 24 water heaters, replaced a tremendous number of washers and unstopped what seemed to be 24 million drains.

Long before rent control came to Los Angeles, there was a surplus of vacant apartments. And Winnikoff and Omansky certainly had their share of those vacancies.

And so it came to pass that one of my father's tenants (who was also his close friend), Mr. Wolfe, had a heart attack about the same time my father had a heart attack. Mr. Wolfe and his wife lived on in the apartment house, rent-free, for four years.

As the chief handyman whose salary consisted only of

dinners and a lot of parental love, I was a bit miffed by my father's charity towards Mr. Wolfe. If my father collected the rent, he could then afford to hire a plumber instead of imposing all those leaks and stoppages on his good-natured but overworked son. Seeing my plight, my mother and my aunt asked me repeatedly to discuss the matter with my father.

We talked.

The answer was always the same. "But I already have vacancies. So this way I have one more."

After three years of the free-rent-for-Mr.-&-Mrs.-Wolfe-insanity, I took my father aside and said, "Look, Pop, if you want to give Mr. Wolfe free rent, that's one thing. But do you have to buy his groceries?"

My father shrugged.

He was a terrible salesman. He never would have made it as a salesman. He had no sales ability whatsoever.

But he sure was a swell guy.

He said the three most important things in business were honesty, honesty and honesty.

And despite his lack of sales ability, he taught me a great deal about selling. He taught me to be a salesman who can face himself in the mirror.

He taught me that everything we do must relate to human beings and human kindness. That money isn't everything. That people are infinitely more important than money. That it is far better to do something good and fail than to do nothing and succeed. That morality is not a preference but an absolute duty.

In the course of writing this book, Burt and I talked to a lot of people. The ones with pinched souls and twisted minds told us that selling is the art of cheating people. We reject that approach and maintain steadfastly that selling— our kind of selling—is an honorable profession. It always has been and always will be. And we will prove it to you with our words and actions. If you don't believe us, put this book down and go elsewhere for advice.

For the benefit of those who *do* believe us, let us say for openers that we want you to be The No. 1 Best Seller in your own heart and soul. Be the very best and most hard-working person you can be, and success will very likely follow you like a trusting child. Cheat people and the Demon Failure will stalk you like the cold blast of an endless winter.

We have no easy, simple answers. You may not become number one in the sales office, but follow our advice and we suspect you will become number one at home and among those you love and who love you.

And if you ask me how I know all this, I can only defer to a man who taught me a great deal of what I know about selling and life itself.

My father.

—Albert Winnikoff
Malibu, California 1996

INTRODUCTION

by
BURT PRELUTSKY

It may well be that love makes the world go round, but sales keep everything else moving. In fact, the success of America can be traced to the fact that we are a nation of sellers.

It is not just material goods that we have sold in every sector of the globe. It is not just our oats and apples and automobiles that have made us something special in the history of mankind. It is the American Dream. It is democracy. It is free speech and freedom of religion. It is our ability to peaceably remove the most powerful leader in the world from office every fourth November. It is something we have been selling for over 200 years. Which goes to prove that if you have a first-rate product, you don't ever have to worry about gimmicks, trends or the competition.

There are those who believe they are above selling, who regard it as a low trade. When they think of selling, the image they conjure is of a fast-talking huckster trying to unload a '78 Chevy with a bad transmission or some oily con man attempting to pass off parcels of Florida swampland as country club estates.

Nobody would ever suggest that every person who calls himself (or herself) a salesman (or saleswoman) is a saint in clever disguise. But far too often, honest, decent individuals have been tarred with the brush that only a few liars and mountebanks deserve.

This book is not intended to convert the chiselers. We'll leave that matter up to the courts and jails. Our audience consists of hardworking, honorable men and women who need to learn how to do what they do a little bit better. And who need to be reminded that nobody who has ever written a great book, created a life-changing invention or even founded a religion has ever achieved success without the ability to sell.

One way or another, everyone who has shaped the world in which we live has done so through salesmanship. Everything from the music that stirs us to the homes that shelter us to the Golden Rule that guides us is the end result of people selling products, ideas and aspirations to other people.

Whatever it is that you choose to sell, it is our sincere hope that this book will enable you to sell it creatively, profitably and—most important of all—without selling out.

—Burt Prelutsky
North Hills, California 1996

YOUR INTRODUCTION

We want you to be a great success. Not an average or mediocre success. But a great success.

How? By belief.

We are all creatures of belief.

If you believe words like DECENCY, ATTITUDE, ENTHUSIASM, PERSONALITY, DEALMAKING, PROFIT, MONEY, CREDIBILITY, SUCCESS and HONESTY are good words, then chances are that you will discover the magic of good selling. Our kind of selling.

You may wonder why two slightly eccentric—but very successful—salesmen would want to divulge their secrets and hard-earned understanding of the necessary elements of good sales.

Actually, it's quite simple.

We believe that all the good, ethical people of this world belong to each other. If you bought this book, we have made a deal. We wrote it. And you are reading it. At this point, we are together. We have offered information and you are receiving it. We have made an honest deal. We profit from the sale and you profit from the information.

This is the essence of good sales and good deals. And it boils down to this: a good sale is good for both the buyer and the seller.

We are not going to bore you with all the dazzling stories about salespeople making a million dollars a year in commissions. We're realistic. We settle for less. We always try to come in second; we want the customer to come in first. A No. 1 Best Seller cannot lose if the customer wins.

We want mightily to introduce you to one of the greatest sales tools in your arsenal: *credibility*. If you are perfectly honest with the clientele, you will be far, far ahead of your competition. If you enjoy lies, deception, gossip and naysaying more than you love the truth, go into script writing or something like that. But don't go into sales. Your talents are needed elsewhere.

Let us give you an example.

One evening at a real estate sales seminar, when Mr. Winnikoff was invited to speak, he got on the topic of truth-telling. In the audience, one Dirk Sharkey sat next to Mrs. W. Dirk, a disbarred lawyer, leaned towards Mrs. W. and muttered, "Tell them the truth, the whole truth, and nothing but the truth and you're going to lose them."

Mr. Sharkey never did make it as a salesman.

He tried. But he never made it.

He had no credibility.

On the other hand, there is the story of a young sales-man-to-be who attended the Lumbleau Real Estate School many years ago and passed his state exam on the first pass. He was an interesting young man who prefers to remain anonymous. His story: One evening, with dozens of students standing in front of the school building, two young men (totally unrelated to the real estate school) were pushing their stalled car uphill towards the local service station. Behind the wheel of the car was the girlfriend of one of the car pushers. The young men were laughing loudly as they pushed and grunted.

Of the many real estate students drinking coffee and watching the spectacle of the broken-down car, one—and only one—went across the street and helped the laughing, grunting kids push their car to the service station. The other students laughed; some of them clapped, and a few cheered. But none of *them* lent a hand.

The student helper, our anonymous young salesman, certainly received no reward other than a thank you. The good deed did not help his grades. He did come in for a bit of ridicule from his peers. But we know for a fact that he became an extremely successful real estate salesman. Unlike some of his classmates, he *believed* what the Lumbleau Real Estate School taught about ethics.

He suffered indignities and setbacks along the way, but

his rise to the top was never at someone else's expense.

If you believe, as we do, that most people are good and decent and honest, then go into selling. If not, try another line of endeavor. If you believe in doing what is *right* instead of what is immediately remunerative, go into selling.

And if you believe that it's worth that mixture of joy and heartache—and that the two are inseparable—and that you can hang in there with an occasional smile and a sense of wonder, go into selling.

Work hard, tell the truth, set a good example for your kids, do an honest job, sell an honest product, and we promise you the most exciting times of your life.

We all know we deal in an imperfect world with imperfect people sitting at imperfect tables (and wobbly chairs) to try and close less-than-perfect deals. Hey Gang, that's life. But as TNOBS you must make perfection your goal. There is nothing in that jumbled mass of messmaking that says we should not or cannot at least *try* for the perfect deal. Try hard. Make yourself indispensible to your customer by proving that you *try* harder than anyone to give perfect customer satisfaction. Try your hardest and see what happens. If our hunches are right, you will ultimately leave your competitors far, far behind. Why? Because you are TNOBS.

We want your introduction to the toughest game in town to make you a full-time winner. After all, isn't that why you bought (or borrowed) this book?

In closing this chapter, we must tell you (even though it may sound a bit hokey) that *our* success depends on *your* success. Full-time losers do not read books. But full-time winners usually do.

Please don't let us down.

THEORY

"They couldn't hit an

elephant at this dist—"

These were the last spoken words of (Union) General John B. Sedgwick, U.S. Army, Battle of Spotsylvania, Virginia, 1864. A man who grossly under-estimated the (Confederate) competition.

THE NO. 1 BEST SELLER

OR

HOW TO MAKE
$100,000
A YEAR
IN SALES

THE THEORIES OF SELLING

Every successful sales organization has a theory of selling. Whether the theory is implicit or explicit does not matter. What matters is that the theory is a workable one.

Macy's has one theory of selling and Wal-Mart another. And the theories are different for Neiman-Marcus and K-Mart. Management sets the tone, calls the tune, and the sales force does the rest. No organization can be successful without a theory of selling.

Each of your authors has a highly individualized theory. What works for one may not work for another. There is one point, however, on which the authors agree: we want *you* to develop a personal theory of selling. Your own theory. If the first theory fails, go to another. When you have developed a successful theory of selling, stick with it, refine it and use it with passion and persistence. Then, no matter who you are or what obstacles you face, you stand a fair chance at success.

We know of a salesman by the name of Harold Bettis. Mr. Bettis sells an inexpensive household item door-to-door. He has a theory about making 125 personal calls a day, six days a week, all year round. He claims to enjoy his work, considers himself successful and never discusses his problems with the clientele.

Mr. Bettis was born blind.

Another outstanding case of salesmen developing a highly successful theory of selling is that of identical twins John and Greg Rice. They are Florida real estate brokers who have developed a theory which Greg Rice states as follows: "People are always telling us we're lucky because we've been so successful. We tell them you spell luck *W-O-R-K*. We find the harder we work, the luckier we get."

In a good real estate year, the twins, in their young 40's, can sell close to 100 homes, with gross sales of nearly 10 million dollars. In addition, they are in demand on the lecture circuit and travel all over the country to give motivational speeches to salespeople.

None of this would be so unusual except that John and Greg Rice are each 33 inches tall. They believe they are the smallest identical twins in the country. To hear them speak, you just know they are enjoying life to the fullest. They speak with verve and enthusiasm. Do they worry about their size? Never. John says, "Most people spend a lifetime trying to create an identity. Ours is built in."

Their sense of humor always comes to the fore and they constantly joke about their size. John is fond of telling his audience, "Our motto is to think big. We always tell everybody our problem was we didn't start thinking big soon enough." Laughter is a big part of their sales appeal.

A favorite story of John's is of a night out with friends at a Chinese restaurant.

"We were seated at the table and a waiter came over to give us the menus. I asked him directions to the men's room and excused myself.

"The waiter stared at me as I walked off. Everybody always stares. Greg was still out parking the car. As I disappeared into the men's room, Greg walked in through the front door. The waiter did a double take and asked Greg:

"'How did you do that?'"

As for their sales ability, "When we're selling homes, our approach is a little different from the other salesmen," John says, "Instead of telling potential buyers to be sure to notice the gorgeous view, Greg and I tell them about the breathtaking baseboards and the knee-deep shag carpeting."

When they lecture, the Rice twins inform the audience that they are the sons of a poor Florida family and were handicapped by size from the time of birth. Then they challenge their listeners who complain or are unhappy or have not done well in the face of adversity:

"Look at all we've had to overcome and we've made it. What's your excuse?"

When Robert Louis Stevenson tells us: "Everyone lives by selling something," we believe him. We also believe those who tell us: "Nothing happens in this world until someone sells and someone buys." Another theorist tells us: "The art of salesmanship can be stated in five words: *believing something and convincing others.*" Yet another says: "The buyer is not looking for a product or service. The buyer is looking for a solution to a problem."

We could go on with the quotes. But at this point it is unnecessary. You see the point: there are countless sales theories. To succeed, you must somehow send a surge of power through your upstairs gray matter and *think up a theory.* Not ours. Not your spouse's. Not your company's. But your own.

In an effort to get you started on devising your very own personal theory, let us at least give you a hand down our own theoretical road and get you started. We believe:

1. The customer is the most important person in the world.
2. A No. 1 Best Seller makes himself (or herself) indispensable to the customer. (You must strive to make it better, faster, cheaper and smarter than the competition. And deliver on time. Or else.)

For us, these precepts work very well. If you disagree

with us, please do not simply throw our theory away. *Refine it*. Make the theory better. But make it work for you and the kind of person you are.

Now, if your brilliant and thoughtful theory ties in with the theory of your organization, so much the better. If all the pieces fit, you can and will be extremely productive. But if you are at odds with your boss, your product, your service or yourself, perhaps it would be better to look for employment where you can make all the pieces fit. Theories that work are, initially, comparable to miracles. We certainly cannot perform the magic for you. We need your help. *Together* we will find the way. If you are willing to put forth the physical and mental effort, we think you will find the results electrifying.

PERSONAL PSYCHOLOGY - PART 1

We have a theory or two of our own we would like to share with you.

First, *most* people cannot sell. Cannot and will not. Selling is so inimical to the psyches of most people that when the term *selling one's self* is mentioned, visions of prostitutes come to mind. When the average family has to dispose of a used car, there is generally a marital crisis. Garage sales are O.K. because otherwise the stuff would simply go in the trash. But when a big-ticket item goes on the block, panic sets in and the blood runs cold. In fact, if your spouse is running a high fever and the doctor will not make a 3 A.M. house call, you must not wring your hands in desperation. Take charge. Walk boldly into the sickroom and announce to your beloved: "Honey, we're going to sell the house!" Not only will the fever disappear, but the patient's flu symptoms will be replaced by hypothermia. Anguish will be replaced by a cold moaning and the sweats will be replaced by shivers and shakes. Simple suffering will give way to chilling fear. (Do not use this approach unless you have lots of extra blankets on hand.)

What most non-selling creatures of this world do not realize is that the surplus products of civilization are about six weeks ahead of the Apocalypse Horsemen. If there were a complete planetary crop failure for 12 weeks, the price of a loaf of bread would not matter. For most of the world inhabitants would be gone. The leaders of the nut-encrusted capitals of the world would be in terrible shape without a native population to push around and taxes to collect. But, fortunately, the surplus—small and fragile as it is—allows for a flourishing of the arts and sciences, of winning and losing, and of buying and selling. The non-sellers and handwringers view the world situation with despair and hopelessness. But *we* know better. *Any* surplus gives us hope and the opportunity to sell. Where there are no salespeople, there is tragedy.

In order to drive home our point on surplus, let us quote from L.M. Boyd's fine little book entitled *Boyd's Curiosity Shop*.

Q. "If all the farmers stopped producing food today, how long would the world's stockpile of food last?"

A. Two months maybe. When the ready supply exceeds more than two months' need, prices drop drastically.

The productivity and surplus of this country are the envy of the world. Therefore, good salespeople do not despair, for they know that in *surplus* there is prosperity, hope and opportunity for making some great sales.

Obviously, since you are reading this book, you have an interest in selling. But it takes more than mere interest to succeed. It takes *commitment*. Total commitment. You must work at it 24 hours a day, 365 days a year. You must work at it with all the strength of your heart, soul, mind and muscle combined. (If not, you will not be the great success we want you to be.) Then, in five years or so, you may slow down. To no less than 350 days per year. To do less is to commit yourself to failure.

One of the most commonly asked questions in a travel agent's office is: "Say, how do you get into this business? I'd sure like to be a travel agent. I just *love* to travel." Or, in a real estate agent's office, the refrain goes like this: "Hey, how can I get into real estate? I just *love* real estate."

There's nothing to it. All you have to do is sell yourself. Totally. Completely. Absolutely. And without complaint. Because if you don't, you will fail in selling. But don't put self-satisfaction at the top of your list. Put customer satisfaction on top and become TNOBS. Once you learn to become indispensable to your all-important customer, you cannot and will not fail.

Once you have taken our advice and made the commitment, there are still numerous pitfalls.

If you become the hottest salesperson in your organization and go to the head of the class, the board of directors will call you into a Special Executive Session Meeting and tell you that you have been promoted to the exalted position of Executive Vice-President of Marketing! But since you will be receiving a salary and will no longer be on commission, your income will be about half of what it was.

At this point in your life, Dear Reader, you must decide whether to take your lumps and stick around for the next indignity, or tell all those lovely gentlemen with the diamond stickpins and the button-down ears to go stuff it.

Again, we urge restraint.

Do not tell the directors to go stuff it.

Tell them you need a day or two to think about it.

Be gracious.

Smile.

Act humble. (English majors may, if they so desire, act *humbly*.)

Tell them it's the best offer you've ever had in your whole life and you're very grateful for the opportunity.

Then quit.

In almost every company, there are some managers who are absolute dolts. They rise to the top by politicking. Not by selling, but by politicking. They demean subordinates. They kiss the hands and feet of *their* bosses. Most company politicians would absolutely starve to death if they went out into the *real* world and had to earn their keep by running so much as a hot-dog stand. But within the labyrinthine cocoon of the corporate bureaucracy, they not only survive, they thrive! What's more, many of these ninnies are lawyers.

So quit.

If you have what it takes, you can and will do it elsewhere. Or better yet, you will do it on your own.

Write the corporate high priests a lovely letter of resignation and quit. The letter will go into the personnel file and never be looked at again. But you will be *eligible for rehire* and your next boss will be very happy about that.

In the meantime, back at the corporate funny farm, only the slickest of the slick will defy gravity, logic and human decency and slide to the top. The hard-working drones will be called in on their 40th birthdays and be given a Mickey Mouse watch and a set of walking papers.

It happens all the time.

It has happened to us.

It will happen to you.

But if you are as good a salesperson as we think you are, it won't matter.

In the end, your willingness to work harder and smarter for the customer's benefit will always prevail over the pitfalls and obstacles that others put in your way.

After all is said and done, selling, our kind of selling—very successful selling—is not simply an art, science or profession; it is a whole way of life.

Selling is believing in yourself and your ability to sell. For those who believe, an explanation is not necessary. For the disbelievers, an explanation won't help.

In countries where there are no salespeople, there are no surpluses. And where there are no surpluses, there is an abundance of misery. The Apocalypse Horsemen are about 60 seconds to the rear of the uncivilized tyrants, political murderers and other assorted desk-pounders. In those places where tyranny reigns supreme, bloodletting replaces marketing.

But where there are sales organizations selling good and decent products and services at fair market values, there is hope. And where there is hope, there is opportunity and the chance of success. Yours. Mine. His. Hers. Theirs. And ours.

Please come join us.

In the simple decency of our efforts, we not only serve humanity and civilization, we also help sustain them. For selling reigns supreme in the psychology of the marketplace.

PERSONAL PSYCHOLOGY - PART 2

Every one of us has down days. We also have up days. For reasons not clearly defined, we seem to go through cycles of euphoria and depression. If, on a down day, perhaps after a tiff with your beloved, you question not only life but why you are in sales, you must not despair. You could, on that very same Blue Monday, make the biggest sale of your life. It happens. And when it does, we assure you, the depression will disappear completely. Your mood swing will carry you from very low to very high. And without pills, liquids or potions. You may even cancel the appointment with your shrink. If the shrink balks and squawks, tell him, her or it that you just made a crazy sale and nothing else matters.

Go home that evening and forget all about the tiff. We assure you that if the sale was truly a big one, all will be forgiven.

On the very next down cycle, let us suggest the following: SIT DOWN AND WRITE AN AUTOBIOGRAPHY. *Writing* is one of the best therapies there is. You must, however, do this writing in an unusual way. (No. 1 Best Sellers are always a little unusual.) You must write of the past, present and future. And your aspirations for the future must be clearly defined. Even if you end up missing your goals by a large margin, you will still be better off than the drifters who will end up wherever the storms carry them. Pour your heart and soul into this magnificent tome and it will do wonders for your psyche. Not only will it prove to be highly cathartic, it will help you state clearly and for the record your values, goals, desires, needs and wants. Read it annually and make any corrections, deletions and/or additions that your little heart desires. We cannot stress the matter strongly enough: to be a success you must be goal-oriented.

In our travels we have talked to a lot of salespeople. We are astounded by the number of people who tell us they don't know exactly what it is they want out of life and how they hope to get it, much less where they would like to be in five years. We counsel these lost souls as follows: Why don't you sit down and *write* out the ten most important things in your life?

After item No. 3, most salespeople have a little difficulty. But we want you to be different. We want you to give us ten. The writing, in and of itself, can have a very beneficial effect on your psyche.

If you find our suggestion regarding the *writing cure* is more effective than the *talking cure* espoused by our Freudian friends, then simply smile every time you pick up this book. If not, then simply growl at your analyst.

PERSONAL PSYCHOLOGY - PART 3

Most people are not cut out to be salespeople. In a nation of about 260 million people, we have about seven million salespeople. Roughly 3% of the population. Of the seven million, perhaps 10%, or 700,000 salespeople, make a darned good living at it. Of that 700,000, perhaps 70,000 are doing what we all want to do. To wit: making a fortune.

Now, although these 70,000 salespeople represent a small *percentage* of all salespeople in America, 70,000 is still a very big number. And let us assure you that you can be one of this select group if you will simply work very, very hard every day of your life for the next ten years or so. And also follow our simple directions.

What we are getting at here is that the average Jane and John Doe know exactly what it takes to succeed but will not put forth the effort. John not only refuses to work hard and intelligently, but he also refuses to take the initiative when it comes to something as simple as selling his own car. When the moment of truth is upon him, he breaks out in hives and develops sweaty palms. Think of what he goes through when he has to sell his *house*! Paranoia sets in. Ask any real estate broker.

The simple truth of the matter is that, in the end, *all* salable properties get sold. *All* end-of-the-year cars get sold. *All* the manufacturing output of the world gets sold. In the end, everything gets sold. *Real* salespeople know this intuitively. *Non-salespeople* get the sweats. *Good salespeople* get the money. To put it bluntly, *you are the business.* Wherever you go, wherever you are and whatever you do, *you are the business The future is yours to create.* If you are looking to others to hand you the business, you probably do not belong in sales. For without your efforts, there is no business.

But making all the pieces fit so that your little cornerstone upholds the very underpinnings of Western civilization is not only difficult. On occasion it is downright brutal. If you have a good boss, he or she will recognize this and assist you over the rough spots. If you have a rotten boss, it may be time to move on. Whatever your decision, we urge you to give the job your very best efforts. If you are No. 1 in your own body, soul and psyche, you will, in the long run, prevail against terrible odds.

We know it's hard. And we sympathize. But in order to prevail, you must use a bit of psychology on yourself. You must know that you are not alone, that we genuinely wish to help.

How?

By giving you a continuous, never-ending boost. *We* know how good you are. *You* proved it by getting this far in the book. But do *they* know it, out there?

Probably not.

Therefore, we urge you to buy a full-length mirror and put it in your office so that you can see yourself talking on the phone. Then go to your local print shop and/or graphic designer and have them make a bold-faced sign that says:

THE
NUMBER
ONE
BEST
SELLER

Then paste the sign to your mirror. You will come in for a bit of ridicule from your office-mates, but pay no attention. Do as we suggest and you will close more sales in the future than you ever have in the past. Smile a lot while you're looking at No. 1 and your customers will love you for it. A smiling voice sounds and looks infinitely better than a grumpy voice.

Since you are your own best critic, take note of what you're doing wrong on the phone and correct it. *Always try to improve your presentation.* The mirror will help you. Look often at the sign and let that charming person in the mirror be your very best friend. Do it as your eager authors urge you to, and we promise you this: *that person in the mirror will not fail you!* In fact, you will notice an improvement. Your best friend will get you to dress more sharply. Your hair will be styled with more class. Your smile will take on a thousand wonderful nuances that you never knew existed before. You will speak more clearly. Your vocabulary will improve. Your sentences will not trail off. You will be more convincing. And you will stop picking your nose in public.

Bear in mind that although more than 90% of all new products fail and more than 90% of all new salespeople fail, failure will not apply to you. For we are about to embark on a journey that absolutely, totally, completely and truly does not and will not allow failure. By holding this book in your hands, you have become a No. 1 Best Seller. And like it or not, a No. 1 Best Seller is an ordinary person with extraordinary determination and an extraordinary will to succeed.

If you *do* need a bit of a boost on a down day, please consider the following:

1. If only 3% of the work force is in sales, then at least 97% of the people out there are prospective buyers. (Include your fellow salespeople and 100% are prospective buyers).
2. Approximately 70% of all sales pitches are made to the

wrong person.

3. If you make 1,000 sales calls next month to 1,000 decision makers, 453 of them will be gone from their jobs in one year.

4. You are always selling emotional satisfaction. Not just *theirs*, but also your own.

5. Who, pray tell, is that good-looker in the mirror?

6. Want to give your psyche a boost? Then look at that wonderful person in the mirror and SMILE! (We guarantee a smile back.)

HUMAN PSYCHOLOGY

Around the turn of the century, a bearded Austrian analyst by the name of Sigmund Freud shook the very foundations of western society with his theories. At first, nobody believed Dr. Freud was anything more than a sex-crazed old man snooping into the fantasies of his sexually disoriented patients. A certain segment of the public held him in contempt.

There were, of course, no absolute proofs for the good doctor's theories. Still, he did some miraculous things for his patients and, ultimately, for humanity. He was the founder of modern psychology.

Dr. Freud theorized that the human mind could be broken down into three basic components: (1) the id, (2) the ego and (3) the superego. The id he identified as the infantile part of the mind. It wants nothing more than to be constantly gratified. In an infant, the demand is for food, warmth, cuddling and as much sleep for the little id as it can get. The id is grasping and selfish. The id is concerned with avoiding pain and finding pleasure. In fact, Dr. Freud said the id is forever in pursuit of pleasure: the pleasure principle. The id is that part of the personality that buys playthings. If you know how to trigger the id, chances are you will make the sale.

As the infant grows into childhood, the ego develops, usually into larger-than-life proportions, and this is when the child starts to notice things outside of itself. Whereas the id tends to view itself as the center of the universe, the ego tends to see itself as just one part of the world, but an important part: the mighty ruler of a great toy kingdom. As the child grows and develops psychologically, parents, teachers, ministers, sweethearts and other distracting influences keep beating the poor kid down. And out of this constant nagging comes the superego—the human conscience. When the id, the ego and the superego are in mild conflict—that is, when people do things they know they shouldn't do and feel guilty about it—they become neurotic.

That's us.

On the other hand, when they do things they shouldn't do and don't give a hoot, they are known as psychotics. Such people generally become the bad guys who give every profession a bad name.

Children growing up in this nut-encrusted world have all sorts of psychological problems. For one thing, they love their mothers for all the comfort and tenderness only a mother can give, and their fathers for the money they can give. Now, contrary to what we hear from those who are absolute gender egalitarians, there really is a difference between mothers and fathers. The kids know this instinctively. In most families, the mother, who is the evolutionary victim of periodic glandular distress, comforts her children with food, hugs and kisses. Mother is deeply concerned with security for herself and her family. Mother frets and worries. Sometimes, if the phases of the moon are just right, she can get Father to blow his stack. When he does, she tells the children not to pay any attention and does her best to undermine his paternal authority. Father, on his side of the family structure, wants to be known as a nice guy. He has a psychological need to be well liked that makes Mom's quest for security fade to insignificance. Whereas Mom wants the money for the psychological security it offers, Dad would like to see their life savings blown on a testimonial dinner in his honor. As a result, there is tension in the family. Tension is probably the most outstanding characteristic in every family, since each of its members wants something different. When the tension erupts into a full-blown fight between parents, the child considers the whole trauma a bad dream, pulls the blanket over her head and goes to sleep. The following Sunday, when the in-laws come for dinner, Grandpa, who never was too bright to begin with, will ask the child whom she loves more. Mom or Dad? The child, nobody's fool, will reply in a voice dripping with maple sugar, "I love them both the same."

So the security-conscious kid lies, and the little fib is accepted and even praised by parents, relatives, friends and business associates. The child, bless her, has learned to play the game.

Although it troubles us, as humane and concerned authors, to reduce all this exquisite theory to blatantly commercial sales terms, we have our reason: the tensions created in childhood go on to create a great deal of indecision in adulthood. And indecision leads to sales resistance. Indecision also leads to other psychological problems. For example, when Johnny grows up to take his place in the world, he applies for work at the U.S. Government Post Office as a carrier. After passing his Civil Service exam, John begins to make his appointed rounds. He tries to please the great father figure (his employer) by going through sleet, snow, rain and smog. He tries to please all the little mother figures by smiling when they come to the door to get their daily allotment of junk mail.

So far, so good.

But someone *Upstairs* notices what a fine job John is doing and has him promoted to the *Sorting Room*. John works harder than ever in an effort to please everyone, but he has a brain-busting time figuring out where the little envelopes end and where the big envelopes begin. By virtue of his promotion, he is forced to *think*. Tension and indecision set in. John has a nervous breakdown. Which is a tragedy not only for him, but for you. Because, being incapacitated, he stops buying. He becomes for the duration of his siege the salesperson's mortal foe: a non-consumer.

The moral of the story is that we are all plagued by degrees of indecision. It is a built-in response to every act in our lives. Except for a few overriding pleasure principles, just about everything we do gets tangled up by indecision. Is it any wonder, when we are all conditioned from an early age to be indecisive? Few of us prepare our tax returns in January. None of us goes to the dentist at regular intervals. Writers *never* meet deadlines. Kids *always* say no.

It is at this point we must let you in on an extremely important trade secret: you must learn, *on your own*, how to overcome the indecision of others. Perhaps we can help you enormously by the examples in this book, but in the last analysis you are *on your own* when you decide on the best way to overcome a customer's indecision. This is one of the keys to great selling. We do not have a pat answer to every selling situation, but we do know that an answer exists for each and every situation. In most cases, you will have to dwell on the problems yourself and find the answer yourself. The results can be absolutely electrifying.

Therefore, Dear Salespeople, when a prospective customer says no, don't despair. Just keep looking and trying for someone who will say yes. Selling, after all, is a form of seduction. Before you can be a seductor, you've got to find a seductee. If you keep a client list of 100 and get a resounding no from every last one of them, go back to the top of the list and start over. Don't take no for a final answer. If you cannot get a yes right away, settle for a maybe. *Maybe people* are less screwed up, psychologically speaking, than *no people*. But for us, the most psychologically well-balanced people in the world are *yes people*.

Keep *them* on a very special list. Once the Yes List is established, you must do everything in your power to service the accounts. Even if you never sell all the people on the

Yes List again, if you prove to them repeatedly that you are a happy warrior who sends out flags on the Fourth of July and cards at Christmas and makes loving phone calls for the heck of it, the *yes people* will praise your virtues to other *yes people* and the sales will grow exponentially.

In the realm of human psychology, *yes people* are the ones who make the world hum.

APPLIED PSYCHOLOGY

Like it or not, selling is a form of seduction. Take the direct, head-on approach and you are liable to find yourself slapped in the face or worse. Very often, the best approach is a gentle, easy approach. Often there is a very definite desire on the part of the seductee to be romanced. And charm has a way of working its wiles. Romancing a person means making him or her (or it, for that matter) feel important.

For example, if you said to the object of your affections: "Hey, we're gonna @!;#$*!," you could conceivably end up in a dentist's chair being fitted for a whole new mouth. It is absolutely essential that you develop a charming style. (It must be genuine charm, for if it is not genuine, it becomes hypocrisy. We are very opposed to hypocrisy and deceit. In fact, when your authors have lunch together they *always* say please and thank you to the waitresses and busboys. Not because they want to sell something, but because little acts of kindness make everyone feel better. We even say thank you to the bartender. And pretty darn often, too. We help little old ladies across the street, assist damsels in distress when they have flat tires, and courteously answer each and every letter that comes in the mail. We do these things not because they are Holy Writ, but because they are right.) Charm and its handmaiden—human kindness—cannot be sold; they must be given and given freely. Once you have mastered the art of being a charming person by putting others completely at ease, you must learn to be a good listener. After all, those of us with an open mind and a good deal of charm have something to learn from others. One of the best ways to make another person feel important is to ask for an opinion.

In selling, as elsewhere, it is better to ask than tell. Remember: you cannot learn anything when you are talking. But you can learn a great deal by listening or reading. Furthermore, you have to close your mouth before your brain will work on the intake side of your cerebral manifold.

Now, since you have passed our course on basic psychology, we will take you by the hand and show you by example how to make this priceless knowledge pay off.

There are times and places when you should appeal to the id. Toymakers and food processors are absolute geniuses when it comes to triggering the id. We will not go into a lengthy recitation of their achievements here because they are so well known. For a thorough real-life explanation of what we mean, watch any kiddie show on television. Here we will give only a few brief, adult examples.

When the great writer, speaker and minister, Ralph Waldo Emerson, was having a time of it out in the barn trying to move a calf out of its stall, he called on his son for assistance. The elder Emerson pushed the calf from the rear while the younger Emerson pulled on the calf's neck with all his might. All to no avail. They shouted, pushed, pulled, and strained in every way possible. The calf would not budge. A servant girl was passing by and, when she saw what was happening, put her finger in the calf's mouth and led him willingly from the stall. (Which tells you something about those country girls.)

Now, if that calf had an id, this would be known as id-gratification.

Another case of id-gratification came to the fore when one day a father asked his little girl why she bought her gumdrops at the little candy store rather than at the drugstore.

The little girl replied that the old man at the candy store always gave her *more* gumdrops than the lady at the drugstore, who always gave her *less*.

The father's curiosity was aroused. Gumdrops were gumdrops. The prices were the same in both places. But whereas the lady at the drugstore put a larger quantity of gumdrops on the scale than required and had to *remove* a few to give honest measure, the old man at the candy store kept *adding* gumdrops from his ladle until honest measure was reached. So it *seemed* the old man gave more gumdrops for the money. Now, guess who sold more gumdrops. This is a minor case of id-gratification, but a technique that works when properly applied.

Our next topic is ego-gratification.

One day not too long ago (while we were listening) we heard an interesting story about a magazine salesman who went from being a catastrophic failure to remaining a catastrophic failure because of his attitude.

This salesman, who had an extremely defeatist philosophy, took a job selling magazine subscriptions. He considered this the last stop on a lifetime road of dishwashing and bussing in every greasy spoon on the Route 66 of life. He was so fed up with his station in life that he had come to the conclusion that selling would be his only salvation.

It wasn't.

Although he took the advice of his supervisor and dressed in a presentable manner, he did not make many sales. He tried hard enough, but he sold just a few magazine subscriptions to his chosen clientele: busy executives. (At least he had the dim beginnings of a theory.)

The salesman's clean-cut appearance got him into all the right offices, but the executives all complained that they did not have enough time to read magazines. At the low point of his despair, the salesman decided to commit suicide. He trudged home to his small apartment, put out the cat and pulled down the shades. Then he turned on the gas, and lay down on his bed. The hissing of the gas did not bother him, but the *smell* became more than he could bear. He rolled over and reached for his cigarettes on the nightstand. As he lit up, there was an explosion that shook the entire building to its foundation. Miraculously, there were no serious injuries, though the honeymoon couple upstairs certainly had a tale to tell their grandkids. (Psychologically speaking, this is what is known as a case of bruised egos.)

The hapless salesman, his socks blown off and his hair singed, was picked up and packed off to the County Jail Psychiatric Detention Unit for observation as a nut.

The Chief Resident Psychiatric Medical Officer at CJPDU told the salesman that since it was injurious to his health, he'd better give up smoking. Beyond that, CJPDU could do nothing for him. (Which tells you something about psychiatrists.)

Since the salesman's landlord, gleefully anticipating payment of the insurance money, refused to press charges, the salesman was released after three days of detention.

It seemed that *no one* wanted him.

Upon his release, the salesman returned to his shattered apartment, only to find the place boarded up and condemned as unfit for habitation. He pulled off a few of the boards and managed to get in despite the posted warnings. His cat followed him. He fed his cat, then sat down on his shattered bed to think of what he would do next. He looked up as he heard someone rambling around the hallway through the broken plaster and shattered glass. A moment later the intruder came into the room. It was a local real estate broker, reviewing the extent of the damage.

"Hi, there!" the real estate man said cheerfully. "How are you today?"

The hapless salesman, chin in his hands, three-day growth of beard on his face, and a hangdog look in his eye, said, "Terrible." Then he shook his head and added, "Absolutely terrible!"

"Now wait a minute, young man, have you lost a loved one or been stricken with an incurable illness?"

"No."

"Then why are you so down in the mouth?"

"Look," the younger man said, "I'm an unlucky guy who never gets the breaks, that's all."

"With *that* kind of an attitude, you're bound to have bad

luck. What do you do for a living?"

"I'm a salesman, I think."

"You are—or you *think* you are?"

"Hey, mister, I'm the guy who blew up the building. I was trying to kill myself and I almost killed all my neighbors. And my cat, too."

"Well," the real estate broker said, "that's not very nice. Why don't you let me take you out for a cup of coffee?"

"You—you want to take me out for a cup of coffee when I look like *this*? Why would you do a thing like that?"

"For no other reason than maybe it's the right thing to do. You look like you could use a little help."

"Tell you what," the younger man said, warming to his visitor, "let me make *you* a cup of coffee. Can I?"

"Sure," the real estate broker said.

"Oh, darn!" said the salesman, "they turned off the gas."

The two men struck up a conversation anyway, and after the salesman told his sad story, the broker said, "Look, you're going about this all wrong."

"You're telling me! But how can I do it right?"

"Well," the broker said, "let me tell you how I started. When I was about your age and got my first selling job, I sold adding machines. Those were the days before calculators and computers. But before I started, I went to all the adding machine companies and found out which machine could add the fastest. And when I found out—to my own satisfaction—that's the company I went to work for. Then I went into training and learned everything there was to know about my product. I wanted to get the psychological edge on the competition and the customers."

"That sounds like a good idea."

"Sure it was a good idea. Because I knew it was an uphill battle. Anyway, on my first day out, I was ordered by my supervisor to put a one hundred dollar bill in my wallet and an adding machine under my right arm and to start on the top floor of an office building and work my way down to the bottom floor. Now, when I asked to see the head of accounting in these various offices, I was told again and again that they didn't need any new adding machines and didn't have time to talk to me. So I started by saying, 'Look, I'm not just selling adding machines. I'm selling *time* and *speed*.' Usually the accountant would respond, 'What are you talking about?' So I would say, 'Look, if you'll give me a chance to prove it, I'll show you where *my* machine can add, subtract, multiply and divide a lot faster than *your* machine.' So we'd have a little competition and I'd beat these guys every time. They were dumbfounded. Here was this young kid salesman beating the pants off professional accountants with twenty years experience. After pointing out how much *time* they could save with my machines, I'd get the order. If they couldn't buy it, I'd get them to lease it. But I always punched the guy's *time* button. Something like that always appeals to a guy's ego."

"What's an ego?"

"You mean you don't know what an ego is?"

"Nope."

"Well, the first thing you better do is go the library and read a book on basic psychology," the real estate broker said.

"O.K., but what's an ego?"

"An ego is the *Real Me* or the *Real You*. It's like the main-spring or a battery in a watch. It's what makes people tick."

"So how am I going to use that to sell magazine subscriptions?"

"Well, first of all, put a one hundred dollar bill in your wallet."

"What will that do?"

"It will be a boost to *your* ego."

"Will it make my clock run faster?"

"Not faster. Smoother."

"Look, all of this sounds pretty good, but how is it going to help me sell magazine subscriptions?"

The real estate man smiled. "Let me ask you a question. When you go in to sell a subscription, what's the first thing they tell you?"

"That they don't have time to read *TIME*, that's what!"

"So what you have to do is tell them that you're going to sell them a *time-saver*. A magazine that puts it all together in one weekly summary. Why, if they would just spend one night a week with the magazine you're peddling, they could give up their subscription to the daily newspaper. And it's so well written they'll actually *enjoy* reading it."

"Hey, that sounds pretty good," the newly reborn salesman said.

"But let's take this one step further: what if you passed out a free sample of the magazine you're peddling?"

"I don't think my supervisor would like that."

"That's one of the troubles with most supervisors: they don't have any imagination."

"Well, I'm sure going to take your advice and see what I can do. Thanks."

They shook hands and went their separate ways.

The real estate broker, we know, went on to sell the half-demolished building for fifty cents on the dollar; we lost track of the magazine salesman.

Because of his self-destructive attitude, it is very likely the magazine salesman never made it in the field of selling.

But the real estate broker sure did. And still does. As a counterpoint to the above story, let us tell you of one of the most successful, admirable, and likable real estate brokers we know, a gentleman by the name of Jack J. Levand.

Jack was the first man in the United States who *truly* got a college scholarship by selling magazine subscriptions. From college he went on to selling specialty steel and thence to real estate. For our money, he was one of the best and most honest men in the business of selling. He had an enormous sense of commitment. When real estate sales were down, he sold specialty steel and vice versa.

When we last spoke to him, he was 85 years old. He told

us he planned to retire in four years.

Alas, he died at age 87. But he died happy and successful.

How did he do it? By ego-gratification. He spoke little and listened much. He was absolutely and uncompromisingly honest. When he sold the back lot for 20th Century Fox studios (two acres of land) to Goldrich Developers, the sums involved were rather substantial. The amazing part of the sale was that he was on a *specialty steel call* when the matter of real estate was broached. And why was Jack chosen? And why was the sale made? Because all the parties liked, trusted and believed in Jack J. Levand.

By satisfying the egos of others, he ended up with a bit of ego-gratification himself.

ID PSYCHOLOGY

Al and Lil Winnikoff are real estate agents in the Malibu area. They have been the agents for such luminaries as Bob Dylan, Carol Channing, Rob Lowe, Kristy McNichol, the Lennon Sisters and Kenny Rogers, to name a few. But the bulk of their business is done with lesser known lights in the human pantheon of flickering stardom.

The Winnikoffs have seen real estate agents come and go in the Malibu area. Unlike the real estate jungles of the San Fernando Valley, with a realty board of 10,000 members, Malibu has only about 400 realty board members. It is rumored, but not verifiable, that some of the agents in the San Fernando Valley practice voodoo and cannibalism. In Malibu, on the other hand, a small-town atmosphere prevails. Everybody seems to know everyone else, and if an agent resorts to wholesale blood-letting to make sales, he, she or it will not last too long. This is not to say that the agents in Malibu do not feel professional jealousy or suffer the occasional outburst of animosity. There are agents in Malibu who do not like one another. For example, Agent A hates, loathes and despises Agent B. But when a deal arises wherein Agent A has a seller for a six-million-dollar house and Agent B has the buyer, they work amicably together to make that deal and split the commission. Money has a way of smoothing over rough relationships. In our business, money (or just the prospect of money) sometimes makes smiling believers out of snarling pagans.

The agents who have consistently made a nice living from their sales are the ones who have had staying power. These are the brave men and women who have stuck it out through good times and bad and try every day to satisfy their customers' needs.

Contrary to popular misconception, Mr. Winnikoff is not the brains of the outfit. Mrs. Winnikoff is. If you don't believe it, just ask her. But unlike a lot of husband-wife and wife-husband teams, the Winnikoffs work very well together. The weakness of one is the strength of the other. They never play games with the clientele. However, situations arise where it would be best for either one or the other to handle a particular sale. For the most part, they cooperate perfectly and *they never compete with one another*.

Mrs. Winnikoff is an absolute wizard when it comes to analyzing the human nature side of a real estate situation. Her husband is a bit more of a technician. He is pretty good with numbers and analysis of documents. *He thoroughly reads each and every document relating to a transaction.* He can explain the fine print in a deed of trust, quitclaim deed or termite report. He knows how to translate geology reports and surveys into plain English. He has found survey markers in the Malibu hills that have lain dormant and hidden for 80 years.

One of their more interesting professional experiences was the sale of a small house for Archibald and Maria Cort.

Archibald was a warehouseman for a large firm in Santa Monica. The boys at work called him Archie. He had a pleasant personality, was very quiet and never, ever did anything to cross his wife or question her authority.

Maria, on the other hand, was a bit of a spoiled child. She had an id personality. She took large quantities of laxatives. She *enjoyed* fighting with people and winning. When she won, she gloated. She praised her winning to anyone who would listen. But she *hated* fighting with people and losing. Which was what happened most of the time. At these moments of loss, she sulked, abused Archie terribly, and took massive doses of Ex-Lax. She was petite, beautiful, and small-minded.

She fought with everyone.

Except Archibald.

For Archibald had been conditioned through the years not to tangle with the buzz-saw psyche of his pretty little thing.

One year for Christmas, Maria had Archibald buy her a gold necklace with attached gold letters that read: A-R-C-H-I-B-A-L-D'S P-I-E-C-E.

The boys at the warehouse never let him live it down.

Finally, one day, Maria's conflicts with her Malibu neighbors reached epic proportions and—in a fit of pique—Maria decided that she and Archie would rent the little house in Malibu and move to an apartment in Santa Monica, where they had *rent control.* At the drop of a penny she would discourse on the reasons why *rent control* was very good for Santa Monica but very bad for Malibu. Which is another story entirely.

The Cort house remained empty for seven months. In the following 12 months, the Corts went through four different tenants and 14 different real estate agents. Expenditures, mostly in the form of legal fees, exceeded income by a wide margin.

Two years after the fateful Cort decision to rent their little house, Lil Winnikoff said to Al Winnikoff, "You know, I think we should try to sell the Cort house. We would be helping them."

Al Winnikoff's blood ran cold. "The Cort house," he muttered, his voice cracking. "What makes you think we can sell the Cort house?"

"I just have a feeling that this would be a good time to sell it. The market is good and they're probably running at a deficit."

"Think you can handle this one alone?"

"No, but I think we can do it together."

And so it came to pass that the Winnikoffs took the Corts out to dinner at the world-famous, ocean-front Sea Lion Restaurant.

The then-owner of the Sea Lion, Chris Polos, was a 90-year old Greek of the epic mold. His wealth was on the order of Croesus. Naturally, he had read the classics. But he was a humble man. When Al showed up occasionally for lunch with his aging parents, Polos would always greet them with the same story. He would beat his 90-year old chest and say, "Look how healthy I am," thud-thud-thud. "I eat here three times a day." Polos and the Winnikoffs would then laugh together and break out in a babble of foreign languages. Polos spoke to the Winnikoffs in classic Greek and they, in their turn, spoke to him in pre-revolutionary Russian.

So it was a real problem when the Winnikoffs and the Corts were served their dinner at the Sea Lion, A-R-C-H-I-B-A-L-D'S P-I-E-C-E said to the waitress, "This is cold! Take it back and make sure it's hot when I get it!"

With that, Al Winnikoff, his sales antenna crackling furiously, got up and went into the kitchen with the waitress. They came across Mr. Polos, who was swatting flies.

"Al," he said, "what are you doing here?" He took Winnikoff by the arm and said, "You know what we *really* need for Malibu to grow? Sewers. We need sewers. Before you sell one more house, you should get us sewers. Everybody knows there are no sewers in Malibu."

Winnikoff took the waitress by one arm and Mr. Polos by another and said to them, "Look, we've got to make this food as hot as possible. I mean hot-hot-hot. Or else our guest won't be happy."

"Kathy," Mr. Polos said to his waitress, "Put the plate in the oven and make it hot-hot-hot. We don't want unhappy customers."

A-R-C-H-I-B-A-L-D'S P-I-E-C-E got a hot-hot-hot

meal and, by some miracle of restraint, the Corts and Winnikoffs made it through dinner without major incident.

But short-fused id personalities are always looking for a fight. The Winnikoffs kept the flaming torch of their ardor for a sale as far as possible from Maria's very short and highly volatile wick.

"Well," Mr. W. said at the end of the meal, "shall we discuss real estate?"

"No," Maria said.

"Yes," Archibald said, at exactly the same time.

Maria gave Archie a chilling stare that caused his fragile psychological defenses to break and shatter into millions of irreparable pieces.

In a feeble effort to repair the damage, Archie, in a nearly inaudible voice, said, "No."

"Well, maybe," Maria said, stepping on the shards of Archie's shattered psyche.

"Oh," Archie said.

"Archie!" his wife said. "Will you please stop interrupting me! I've got enough problems without you interrupting me. Now, where were we?"

"I'm not sure," Mr. W. replied. "But I think we were discussing the rental of your property."

"Oh. Well, I'm not sure. I hate the place. I absolutely hate it." Maria Cort then spent the next five minutes telling everyone within earshot why she hated Malibu in particular and real estate agents in general.

At the end of the diatribe, Mr. W. asked, "What do you want us to do?"

"What do I want you to do?" Maria Cort hummphed. "What do I want you to do?" she repeated. "I want you to help us!"

"Look, Maria," Mrs. Winnikoff said, "We can help you, but first you have to let Archie help us."

"What do you mean?" she demanded, eyes opening wide and eyebrows jumping upward.

"Well, first of all we have to get the place cleaned up."

Genius that she is, Mrs. W. turned to Maria and asked, "Can Archie do that?"

"Of course he can!" she said.

"Of course I can," he said.

"All right," Mrs. W. went on. "Once it's in good condition, we'll rent it for a year, manage it and take our commission monthly instead of in one lump sum. And if the market is good in a year, and you feel like selling, maybe we'll sell it."

"Sounds good to me," Archie said. "If we don't do something quick we'll lose the place."

Daggers of ice went from the eyes of A-R-C-H-I-B-A-L-D'S P-I-E-C-E right to the bull's-eye of Archibald's fragile heart.

"What's the next step?" Maria Cort asked.

"Well, first of all, we'll have to have you and Archibald sign a listing agreement for the rental," Mr. W. said.

"I'm not signing *anything*!" the id personality of Maria Cort said.

(Please allow your authors to digress for a moment. As a salesperson, you must know that under the statute of frauds in most states, it is absolutely essential that all real estate contracts, to be effective, *must be in writing*. If it is worth saying, it is worth putting in writing. To protect yourself, your company and your clientele, it is absolutely essential to reduce your agreements to writing. You will be far better off to lose the deal in the beginning than to lose your fee or commission at the end of the deal because there was no writing.)

The Winnikoffs got the signed rental listing.

They worked with Archie in getting the Cort house whipped into shape. Archie alone was a lot different than Archie-together-with-his-piece. He confided in the agents. In a moment of hushed secrecy he told them that Maria went to bed at night and sucked her thumb, and that they were desperate to sell. But first, they rented it for a year.

The agents made the sale approximately 14 months after

the dinner engagement at the Sea Lion Restaurant.

But closing the deal was not that simple. With id personalities, closings are never simple.

When final documents were to be signed, Mrs. Cort, with Archie in tow, met the Winnikoffs at the escrow company.

Mary Meadows, the escrow officer, was a pleasant, competent and slightly corpulent woman of middle age. The Winnikoffs had warned the lovely Ms. Meadows of Mrs. Cort's personality type.

Enter the sellers, (1) Archibald and (2) his piece.

The petite Mrs. Cort sat herself down daintily, turned to Archibald and said in a loud, meant-to-be-heard whisper, "I *hate* fat people."

En garde!

Forewarned, Mary Meadows placed the documents for signature in Mrs. Cort's hands and excused herself. When she returned five minutes later, Mrs. Cort said to the stout-hearted Mary Meadows, "I'm not signing that! And my husband isn't signing that ! Any of it!"

Mr. Archibald Cort gulped.

"And why not?" the plump Mary Meadows asked.

"Because it gives you the right to cheat me! Here, look at this! What's all this fine print on the back of—of—" she started turning the papers back and forth.

"Those are escrow instructions and the fine print on the back is standard boilerplate. All escrow instructions have it," Mary Meadows explained.

"I don't care who's got it! I'm not signing! Not unless you scratch out all the things I don't like."

"May I have those documents, please?" Mary Meadows asked.

"Here!"

Mary took the documents in hand, tore them up, threw them in the trash, and with a dignity only fat people can command, called to her secretary in the outer office, "Vicky, send in the next client, please."

Touché!

The Winnikoffs and Corts were dumbfounded. Archibald's complexion went from pale, waxy white to sickly ash-green. "Hey, what's going on here?" he asked in a crackling, dry voice that went four octaves above his normal tenor voice.

"Well!" Mrs. Cort hissed with indignation. "I *never! In my whole life! I never!*"

"Will you please leave?" Mary Meadows said, raising her eyebrows slightly.

Mrs. Cort jumped up and stormed out. Husband and agents followed.

Out in the parking lot, Mrs. Cort gave her canned Indignity Speech. We will not repeat it here because, like the Pledge Of Allegiance, we all know it by heart.

Archibald developed a twitch.

The agents, however, kept their cool.

At the end of the Indignity Speech, Maria Cort shouted, "What are we going to do *now*? I've already spent the money for a new car!"

Archibald twitched and hyperventilated.

Al Winnikoff took control of the situation. The deal was at the flashpoint. He knew he was dealing with an id. If he lost the deal now, 14 months of effort would go down the drain.

"Maria," he said, "we're going to do *exactly* what *you* want to do. I mean *exactly*. This deal is not going to be 50-50 or 90-10 or anything like that. It is going to be 100% your way. No deviations, no ups, downs or sideways. If we can't make it 100% the way you want it, we just won't do it." So saying, Mr. W. took the id-wind completely out of Maria Cort's sails.

Maria Cort looked at Winnikoff in a very strange, deflated way. "You mean you're not going to fight with me?" she asked.

"Absolutely not! Now tell me exactly what you want."

Maria Cort broke down and cried.

Archibald, his twitching and breathing gone out of control, was close to losing control of all other bodily functions when his piece shouted at him, "Hold me! You dolt! Can't you see I'm crying?"

He held her.

Then they all sat down in Winnikoff's car.

"What am I going to *do*?" she sobbed.

"Maria," the agent asked kindly, "where do you do your banking?"

"The Bank of America," she sobbed.

"Do you trust them?"

"Of course! Would I give them my checking account if I didn't trust them? But what does that have to do with selling my house?"

"Well," the agent said, a note of sympathy in his voice, "there's an escrow department at the Bank of America and they would. . ."

"You mean they'll do the deal?" she sobbed.

"They sure will. They'll be glad to get the business."

The true end of this little tale of dealing with the id personality was that the transaction was consummated at the Bank of America Escrow Department in Malibu, with near-identical documents and boilerplate, and a different but slightly more corpulent escrow officer.

And the moral of the story is:

Never argue with an id. Take the wind out of an id's sails by giving him or her everything *he or she* wants. And if the phases of the moon are right and luck is with you, in the end maybe the id will give you everything *you* want.

PROFESSIONAL PSYCHOLOGY

Now that we have brought you this far into the tangled web of psychological theory, we have an admission to make. We showed our description of Theory to a practicing psychiatrist (whom we shall refer to as Dr. X) for a professional evaluation. The psychiatrist (who was also a professor at a major university) was neither enlightened nor entertained. In fact, Dr. X was offended. He went into a professional diatribe, and when he finished castigating us for our insouciance, he made a profound professional and professorial attempt to explain the *true* meaning of psychotherapy. By the time Dr. X finished with us, we came away believing Sigmund Freud was a kosher pickle manufacturer and Carl G. Jung made toy trains. So we considered Dr. X a strange guy indeed. Very nice, but strange. But what *we* got out of the whole one-sided conversation was our own theory. Whether Freud, Jung or Dr. X were right or wrong is not relevant here. What is extremely relevant is how *you will apply your own theory* to the psychology of selling your product or service. If all those other guys can dream up a theory, so can you. If it works, stick with it. If not, modify it. But don't lose sight of the fact that your brains are every bit as good and capable and talented and beautiful as the next guy's. So use them. And how is it that we know you're so smart? Simple. *You are reading this book.* Is that smart? You bet. In fact, it's brilliant.

The Theory we came up with is this: whereas most therapists tend to be downers, most salespeople tend to be uppers.

Consider the following: (1) psychiatrists have a suicide rate 600% higher than the general population and (2) salespeople go in for analysis far less than the general population.

Why? They're too busy.

We have a little theory about the validity of therapy that goes something like this:

Suppose Joe or Jane Sales were on the psychiatrist's couch bewailing the loss of some sales. Then suppose Winnikoff and Prelutsky walked in and said: "We will give you $100,000 if you will get up off that couch and never come back." How many would stay and how many would go?

Our professional theory is quite simple: good profitable sales cure many ills.

The whole purpose of this chapter is to get you to think clearly, directly, positively and with great singularity of purpose. If they can do it negatively, then you can do it much better with a positive attitude. You don't believe it? Then consider the following:

"Adding sound to movies would be like putting lipstick on the Venus de Milo."

—Mary Pickford, 1925.

"Speaking movies are impossible. When a century has passed, all thought of our so-called `talking pictures' will have been abandoned. It will never be possible to synchronize the voice with the picture."

—D.W. Griffith, 1926.

"You ain't heard nothin' yet, folks."

—Al Jolson, 1927.

Had a bad day? Still not convinced? Then read on:

"I have found little that is good about human beings. In my experience most of them are trash."

—Sigmund Freud
1856-1939

"Show me a sane man and I will cure him for you."

—Carl G. Jung
1875-1961

"After 12 years of therapy my psychiatrist said something that brought tears to my eyes. He said, '*No hablo inglés*!'"

—(The Immortal) Ronnie Shakes

Still not convinced? Then put this book down and call the Psychiatric Hotline at 800-HELP ME. These are the answers *they* give to your problems:

"WELCOME TO THE PSYCHIATRIC HOTLINE......

"IF YOU ARE OBSESSIVE-COMPULSIVE, PLEASE PRESS 1 REPEATEDLY.

"IF YOU ARE CO-DEPENDENT, PLEASE ASK SOMEONE TO PRESS 2 FOR YOU.

"IF YOU HAVE MULTIPLE PERSONALITIES, PLEASE PRESS 3, 4, 5, AND 6.

"IF YOU ARE PARANOID-DELUSIONAL, YOU DON'T HAVE TO DO ANYTHING. WE KNOW WHO YOU ARE AND ARE WATCHING YOUR EVERY MOVE.

"IF YOU ARE SCHIZOPHRENIC, A LITTLE VOICE WILL EVENTUALLY TELL YOU WHICH NUMBER TO PRESS.

"IF YOU ARE DEPRESSIVE, DON'T BOTHER PRESSING A NUMBER. NO ONE WILL REPLY, AND YOU'RE JUST GOING TO DIE ANYWAY.

"THANK YOU FOR CALLING. HAVE A NICE DAY."

And don't say we didn't warn you.

EGO PSYCHOLOGY

As a general rule, men have big egos. True, there are exceptions, but our own observations tell us that, by and large, men are the ego freaks of this world. If you don't believe us, ask any housewife or secretary. Women are a bit more concerned with safety and security and men a bit more concerned with power and money. Women with love and men with lust. Women, with what they can give. Men, with what they can take. Women build cozy little love nests. Men build mighty monuments. Women become interior decorators. Men, architects. Note: In our business, be careful of the unknown and be careful how you handle the big-ego woman and the humble-pie man. Tread lightly. And let them do the talking.

What amazes us in the tangled web of human psychological relations is not that there is so much discord but that there is so little. For example, if the murder rate in Keokuk, Iowa, is two per 100,000 population, where is all the talk and gossip about the other 99,998 people? Murder makes headlines. But a man kissing his wife goodbye in the morning has *never* made headlines. Bad news travels fast. Good news hobbles in on a crutch.

As a salesperson, you will do better if you are optimistic rather than pessimistic. If you truly believe that more good things than bad things happen in this world, never tell the clientele anything bad or gossipy about friends, relatives or the competition. Try to be positive. That's what sells. And if you are dealing with men, it pays to have a cursory knowledge of the psychology of the male ego.

Confused?

Then read on.

Men like to be tough guys. They thrive on ego gratification.

To prove our point, we pass on to you one of the great sales stories of the decade.

Even in this era of electronic wizardry, the sales of products, parts and services between giant corporations are not made by the companies themselves, but by the salespeople. IBM does not sell to GM. But Harry Hufford at IBM can and does sell to his buddy, Joe Larson, at GM.

Knowing where and how to crack open the sales door of an obstinate buyer can yield big dividends.

Which brings us to the sales exploits of Harry Hufford.

Harry graduated from an obscure school in New Mexico known as Albuquerque U. He was at the bottom of his class, and as graduation approached, the Dean of Letters and Science called him in and said, "Harry, you haven't learned very much in your four years here, have you?"

"No, sir."

"But you sure have had a good time, haven't you?"

"Yes, sir!"

"And you majored in accounting?"

"Yes, sir."

"Did you learn much?"

"No, sir."

"Well, Harry, let me tell you something: we're going to let you graduate . . ."

"Oh, thank you, sir!"

". . . but on one condition."

"What's that, sir?"

"That you don't practice accounting."

Upon graduation, Harry got a job as a salesman for IBM.

They sent Harry to school and he was forced to learn a bit about computer technology and the company's products.

He was expected to pass a series of rigorous examinations.

He did.

And he survived as a salesman.

Five years, one wife and two kids later, his ego told him to move on.

He took a job with a small electronics component manufacturer. He had a knack for selling and sold the company right into the arms of a larger firm. His boss became a millionaire, and Harry got a kind word and a pat on the head.

He moved on.

He made a practice of becoming the vice-president of marketing for start-up, specialized electronics firms.

The humor and high-jinks of his youth gave way to the deadly serious study of his product line and the marketplace.

He took stock in these new companies at their inception, and after three wins and two losses found himself financially quite successful.

Twenty years after his graduation from Albuquerque U., he helped found a company that manufactured extremely high-quality, highly reliable magnetic read/record heads for magnetic tape systems in the computer field.

The college days of fun and games were pretty well over for our salesman hero, Harry Hufford. By this juncture of his life, his humor had disappeared, the youthful joys of the fraternity house had given way first to the gut-wrenching gallows of middle age, and finally to the eternal treachery of the marketplace. It was now a simple matter of *produce* or *die*. And being a producer can have its price. For Harry, the price was a duodenal ulcer and an irregular heartbeat.

According to Harry's new boss, the founder of H-Tronics, Dr. Montgomery Pfizer, H-Tronics could build a product superior to any in the world. With their ability and knowledge, Pfizer, Hufford and a few other ambitious men had started a company that did, in fact, manufacture mag heads that had a failure rate of less than one per 1,000. Their closest competitor, in Japan, produced a head with a failure rate of approximately three per 100.

Alas, the Japanese produced their product for $4 apiece while H-Tronics charged $10 per head.

In a business where a 3% failure rate absolutely cannot be tolerated for long, the H-Tronics product looked spectacular.

But *all* products must be sold. (For example: Lamborghini and Rolls-Royce automobiles are sold to some of the world's most discerning customers by some world-class salespeople at very class-conscious automobile agencies. Sorry, no cars sold at the factory. They don't have salespeople there.)

H-Tronics had a rough go of it for the first two years of its existence, which was the design phase. Next came the sales phase.

Magnetronics, Inc., a large manufacturer of magnetic tape systems, was the logical buyer for the H-Tronics mag heads. But for reasons Harry Hufford and his boss could never understand, they could not get a foot in the door at Magnetronics, Inc. They sent letters and brochures and made calls. All to no avail. They could only get as far as the secretaries.

The Magnetronics, Inc. vice-president in charge of purchasing was named Robert "Butch" Burke. He had a bloated ego, a negative reputation in the industry, and thoroughly enjoyed his tough-guy image.

And so it came to pass that Harry Hufford met his old IBM boss at a trade show and took him out for a drink.

Old Boss (to the bartender): I'll have a Shirley Temple, please.

Harry (to the bartender): Glass of milk, please.

Old Boss: Well, Harry, I hear you've done very well for yourself.

Harry: Not bad. How are things with you?

Old Boss: Not bad. But my IBM stock just keeps going up and down. These are very rough times.

Harry: Tell me about it. Think I should have stayed at IBM? Would I have been happier there?

Old Boss: Not you. You're not an organization man, Harry. You're a maverick.

Harry: Takes all kinds, I guess.

Old Boss: Sure does. Tell me, how is H-Tronics doing?

Harry: OK, but we're having a heck of a time getting in the door at Magnetronics. You wouldn't happen to know anyone there, would you?

Old Boss: As a matter of fact, I know Don Lufkin. He's some kind of V.P. there.

Harry: Do you know Butch Burke?

Old Boss: No, but I've sure heard a lot about him. Why?

Harry explained his problem and Old Boss replied, "Let me see what I can do. Maybe Don Lufkin can help."

They finished their drinks, shook hands and parted.

About a week later, Harry Hufford got a call from Old Boss.

Old Boss: Harry, you better write this down. You have an appointment with Butch Burke at his office next Friday, the 11th at 10 A.M. He's going to give you exactly five minutes of his time.

Harry (heart beating rapidly): I can't tell you how much I appreciate this. But can you hold just a minute while I put my boss on?

Harry, filled with excitement, got Monty Pfizer on the phone.

New Boss thanked Old Boss. They chatted for a few moments, then Monty asked, "Say, is there anything about this guy Burke we ought to know before we go in there?"

Old Boss: About the only thing I can tell you is that he's a dog nut. He raises Basenjis.

New Boss: Did you say Basenjis? The barkless, hairless African dogs?

Old Boss: That's right.

New Boss: Thank you. Thank you very much.

After they hung up, Harry ran into his boss's office. At the same time Monty Pfizer, coat in hand, ran out. "Harry," he said, "I'll be back in two days. Meanwhile, you're in charge."

"Hey, what's going on?" Harry shouted to his quickly fleeing boss.

"You're not the only salesman around here," the brilliant Monty Pfizer called back from a distant hallway.

"Yeah, but we've got to put a five-minute presentation together," Harry muttered to no one in particular.

Two days passed.

Harry worried. He had palpitations, cramps and a headache.

On the fated day, Friday the 11th, Monty Pfizer showed up for work at 8 A.M. He found Harry Hufford waiting for him.

"Hey, what's going on?" Harry asked.

"Be ready to leave at 9:15," Monty replied.

"OK, but where the heck have you been for the last two days?" Harry asked.

"At the library in L.A., reading everything I could find on Basenji dogs. And my wife and I have been running all over Southern California visiting kennel clubs and finding out everything we could about these wonderful Basenji dogs."

"Are you kidding?"

"Not at all," Pfizer replied. "I *really* did my homework this time." He sounded elated.

"So did I," Harry replied. "I've got a great five-minute presentation ready to go." He sounded dejected.

"Forget it," Pfizer said, "I'll do all the talking."

They left at 9:15 and arrived at the corporate offices of Magnetronics a few minutes before 10 A.M.

Monty Pfizer and Harry Hufford were ushered into Butch Burke's office at 10 sharp.

They shook hands and sat down.

Harry Hufford, remembering what he'd read once in a great sales book about talking and not talking, was determined that he would not be the first to speak. His heart was pounding out of control. He was sure his ulcer was leaking a lot of blood. With enormous difficulty, he maintained his silence. He was sure he was going to die. On his tombstone they would inscribe: HERE LIES HARRY HUFFORD. SUFFERED IN SILENCE. PUT HIS PRODUCT BEFORE HIS LIFE.

"OK, fellas," Butch Burke said, "pitch me."

It was more of a threat than a request for information.

Monty Pfizer leaned forward, squinted at a picture on Butch Burke's desk and asked, "Say, is that a Basenji?"

There were, in fact, dozens of pictures all over the office with Mr. and Mrs. Burke posing with their Basenjis. In the pictures the proud couple were showing off not only their dogs, but also their ribbons, trophies and dog-show clothing.

Harry peered at one of the pictures. He spoke not, but thought they were strange-looking but awfully cute creatures. The whole lot of them. Both dogs and owners. They all had pointy noses.

"That is a *prize* Basenji," Mr. Butch Burke replied.

"That's very coincidental," Monty Pfizer said. "My wife and I are thinking about getting a pair."

"You are?" the Egoist exclaimed, smiling for the first time.

"Yes, we are. We've talked to a number of AKC people and we've already decided on the bitch."

The talk about the barkless, odorless Basenjis went on for *one hour*, without interruption. Harry Hufford was impressed with his boss's knowledge of the dogs. And Butch Burke's knowledge, of course, was encyclopedic. They talked about how the dogs were revered in Ancient Egypt. How they were destroyed in North Africa and were believed to be extinct until the 20th century, when they were redis-covered in Central Africa used by pygmies as hunting dogs.

They were then re-introduced into the Royal Household of Egyptian King Farouk. But when the corpulent Royal Highness, the Illustrious Royal Leader of His Nation, heard one of his favorite Basenjis *bark*, he had the dog destroyed. Such is the generosity and love of an absolute monarch. (King Farouk was a lousy salesman and eventually lost his throne.)

Meanwhile, Harry's ulcers were killing him. His heart was about to burst. With enormous difficulty, he continued to maintain his silence. Like all good sales people, he would die without complaint.

At 11:00, Harry tugged meekly on Monty's sleeve and reminded him of their 11:30 appointment. He wanted to leave because he felt faint.

"That can wait," Monty replied.

Butch Burke was impressed with Monty's knowledge.

At noon, the H-Tronics men stood to take their leave of the Magnetronics man. Not one word had been spoken about either company or their product lines.

As Harry and Monty moved to the door, Mr. Burke called out, "Hey, why don't you send me a hundred heads?"

"I'll deliver them myself," Harry Hufford said. In the entire two hours, he had spoken only four words.

And he did not die.

Which brings us to the moral of this story. The first of two morals, actually: The moral of the story for Harry Hufford, Salesman, is a bit different than the moral for Dr. Monty Pfizer, Super Salesman.

For Harry, the moral can be reduced to one word:
LISTEN!
In two words:
LISTEN AGAIN!
In three words:
LISTEN SOME MORE!
In four words:
LISTEN TO THE CUSTOMER!
In five words:

SHUT YOUR MOUTH AND LISTEN!

Because if you do, chances are you will assuage the client's ego and make the sale.

After making the sale, Dr. Monty Pfizer and Harry Hufford, true salesmen that they were, did not go out and celebrate. They went back to the office, grabbed a sandwich, and returned to the business of selling magnetic heads.

In the following 12 months, Magnetronics bought 140,000 units from H-Tronics, for gross sales of $1,400,000.

But that isn't the story's only happy ending. For Monty Pfizer did buy a pair of Basenjis and came to love them. Each night when he came home from work, he spoke to the dogs before anyone else. They each got a hug, a pat on the head and a kind word of approval: "You *are* man's best friend and we sure do love you."

Which brings us to the second moral, a simple one: Know your client's ego.

Monty Pfizer was well educated, but, like all good businessmen, he tried to keep things simple. Alas, there are those who do not believe in simplicity. For example, the great German philosopher, Immanuel Kant, defined *ego* as "a transcendentally postulated unity either of appreciation or of the morally free person." Practitioners of psychoanalysis define the *ego* as "the largely conscious part of the personality that is derived from the id through contacts with reality and that mediates the demands of the id, of the superego, and of external everyday reality in the interest of preserving the organism." If you understand these concepts with perfect ease and clarity, maybe you should not go into sales. Maybe you should get a Ph.D. and go into teaching.

Monty Pfizer, who *did* have a Ph.D. (in electrical engineering), but at the same time understood simplicity, knew that *ego* was the Latin word for *I*. He also knew that Butch Burke had an *enormous ego*. He did not attack, abuse or insult the *enormous ego*.

How did he make the sale?

He took that *enormous male ego* and fed it to the dogs.

If you can learn to do that consistently in *your* business, you will undoubtedly become the No. 1 Best Seller in your field.

But there's more. Our little story of a sale made by ego-gratification not only has a happy ending, but also an interesting twist. For it came to pass that the illustrious Monty Pfizer, Ph.D. had indeed bought a pair of pet Basenjis and thenceforth he, and the Hard-As-Nails Butch Burke, V.P., became hard-boiled friends and were extremely competitive at all the AKC dog shows. They revelled in the combat for the first prizes and blue ribbons. Other kennel club members referred to their ferocious competition as The Basenji Wars.

Harry Hufford, great salesman that he was, refused to enter the friendly fray of the Basenji Wars. No matter how much his boss and number-one customer kidded, cajoled and ridiculed him, he would not do it.

He was certainly not a warrior.

He was a salesman.

He took the easy way out.

He kept his ego in check.

He raised Schnauzers.

Woof!

SUPEREGO PSYCHOLOGY (SACRED AND PROFANE)

We consider superego selling so important that we are going to hit you with it three times. We will discuss (1) the sacred, (2) the profane and (3) the immigrant aspects of superego sales.

Here beginneth the sacred portion of our text.

Our story takes us to Nashville, Tennessee, where the city's No. 1 industry is *not* country music. It is religious printing and publishing. The industry employs 12,000 people and has gross annual sales exceeding $600,000,000.

Nashville is home to Gideon's International, the world's largest Bible distributors. GI distributes 24 *million* Bibles annually, without charge. Gideon's International was started by a group of decent and devout salesmen who believed more in The Power of The Word than in the pleasure of the saloon.

Now, we do not profess to know the exact relationship between selling and believing, but we have come to the conclusion that many of the best salespeople are also very devout. (Heathens, take note!) The remarkable success of another Nashville company, Thomas Nelson Publishers, testifies to this fact. Most Bible salespeople believe devoutly that in their product lies the true salvation of the world; that superego = conscience; and that conscience = the will of God.

Samuel Moore, president of Thomas Nelson, was born in Beirut, Lebanon. His original surname was *Zaidy*, which means *more* in Arabic. He attended an American missionary school and believed, early on, that the selfless Americans were God's chosen people. The tyranny of events in his home town sent him quickly to America.

Although Sam Moore originally planned to become a doctor in Lebanon, he decided to come to the United States in 1950 to study economics at the University of South Carolina. On arrival, he had $600 in savings. Six months later, he was broke. Odd jobs could not sustain him. Desperation set in. How, he asked himself, would he survive his student years?

He saw a bulletin board notice that said: BIBLE SALES! EARN $100 A WEEK.

In our hero's own words: "The first week, I made $18. Oh, I was discouraged. I almost quit a hundred times. People slammed the door in your face. It's a very hard way to make a living."

But he did not *quit*.

He worked 75 hours a week, and at the end of the summer had saved $2,600. The following summer, Sam Moore began supervising other salesmen.

In 1957 he visited relatives in Nashville and, true to his own work ethic, recruited 23 students as Bible salesmen. At the end of the summer he was $27,000 richer. He was flabbergasted by his success.

In 1969 the prestigious British publisher, Thomas Nelson and Sons, offered Sam Moore a job. They wanted him to head up their American division. Great salesman that he was (and is), Sam Moore scraped up $2.5 million from his friends and *bought* the American division. Some time later, the British and American divisions merged and moved from tenth to first place in the religious publishing business.

Sam Moore, Salesman-President of the firm, takes a base salary of only $125,000 a year.

In his own words:

"I give credit for my success to God, only to God, because I am just a two-by-four businessman. I came from a minority background, from another country. Most would complain they didn't have the education . . . or resources, but I don't worry about this. I took God as my Partner . . . and God is with me. If I pray and seek *His* ways, He will bless me. And that is what He has done."

So much for the sacred theology of selling.

Here beginneth the profane portion of our text.

At the starting point of the Great Depression, there was a struggling young actor trying to break into the big time. His name was Spencer Tracy.

Actors, being abnormal cases of unbelievable enthusiasm, will do anything to break into what they regard as the big time. They will wait on tables, serve as stage hands, travel by thumb and live in the most abject misery to attain their goals. To succeed, they had best know something about (1) acting, (2) selling and (3) human psychology.

Spencer Tracy knew a great deal about all three. Long before the insidious psychological theories of subliminal perception and mental manipulation by hidden persuaders came to the fore, Spencer Tracy took a good hard look at his position. (1) He was broke. (2) He was an actor. (3) He was an unemployed actor. (4) He was hungry. (5) He had a wife and child to support.

Being a realist, he took a sales position with the Fuller Brush Company. The Fuller Brush Company people were delighted to have an additional able body on their sales team. Their delight derived from the fact that they did not pay their salespeople anything until a sale was made. In the parlance of the sales trade, this is known as straight commission selling. (In the parlance of the slave trade, this is known as you-know-what.)

But Spencer Tracy did something few other salespeople ever do.

To wit: *he developed a theory of selling.*

He did not go to work for the Fuller Brush Company on the same day he was hired. Instead, he told the sales manager he would return in three days.

And he did.

The bright Irish lad from Milwaukee shocked the sales manager by showing up for work looking like the lead in *Tobacco Road.* He was wearing an old shabby suit in which he had slept the preceding night, his hat was too small, his hair was terribly unkempt, and he had a three-day growth of beard.

The supervisor took one quick look, gulped and told Spencer Tracy, "You can't represent the Fuller Brush Company looking like that! Don't you understand that we've got a reputation to uphold?"

"I know," Spencer replied, "but let me tell you what I'm going to do for you."

The supervisor gulped. The bedraggled young actor *sounded* friendly and convincing, but he *looked* just terrible.

Spence went ahead with his sales pitch to the supervisor. "You've got to understand that I'm an unemployed actor and that I'm going to be your number one salesman."

"Not looking like that, you won't!"

"Do you think I'd lie to you? Now listen to me: I really need this job! And I'll stay 'til I'm Number One."

"I don't care if you stay ten years. You simply cannot represent the company looking like that!"

In his most ingratiating way, Spencer said, "Sir, I'm desperate. I need this job. I have a wife and child to support. And please don't look at my appearance as a disgrace. Look at it as my costume."

"*Costume!*" the supervisor bellowed. "What's wrong

with you people? Why do you always go around trying to convince people that the whole world's a stage?"

"Because it is. You've got to understand—"

"Now look here," the supervisor interrupted, "we're the ones who really understand this business. We know that for every seven calls you make, there will be one sale. We have a tried and true formula. You simply have to drop off the catalog, you have to give people a little gift and you have to look presentable. We have a theory that works."

"So do I," Spence replied. "But I'm going to sell 100% of my customers. What's your most expensive item?"

"The sweeper."

"And the next most expensive item?" Spence asked.

"Mops. But we don't sell very many mops. Every household in America already has a mop."

"Well, so does every house in Canada and Mexico, for that matter," Spencer said.

The polite argument between the future salesman and sales manager went back and forth. What bothered the sales manager most was the fact that, in spite of the young man's shoddy appearance, he was *likable* and *convincing*.

With some reluctance, the sales manager agreed to give Spence the usual bag of tricks, consisting of brushes, combs, soaps and snake oil samples. Spencer Tracy told him to forget it. He wanted mops. Mop-heads and mop-handles. All he could carry.

"Are you *crazy*?" the sales manager blurted out. "Don't you know 25% of the nation's work force is unemployed? People are broke! And mops are the toughest and slowest selling items we have!"

"Good. I'll take all I can carry."

"Oh, no you won't. No crackpot actor is going to ruin *my* reputation!"

"Not only will I not ruin your reputation, but when you see what I do for you, you'll be so proud of me you'll pop the buttons off your vest."

The sales manager was aghast. The company's reputation was based on brushes and sundries—not mop-heads and mop-handles. But Spence was not to be dissuaded. He got his left-side armload of mop-heads and his right-side armload of mop-handles, and, fully loaded, started off to the closest residential area he could find. As he stepped into the quiet residential district of Mulberry Street, he faltered and played the part of a mop peddler with a severe case of cerebral palsy.

Now, if you think playing the part of a salesman with cerebral palsy is hard for just one sale, try doing it for eight or ten hours a day.

Knocking on his first door, Spencer Tracy was greeted coolly by the lady of the house. But the great actor wasn't discouraged. He tipped his hat and introduced himself as a Fuller Brush Company mop salesman. Then he managed to drop all the mop-handles and mop-heads on the front stoop. In the clatter and confusion that followed, he managed, with great palsied difficulty, to retrieve one mop-head and one mop-handle from the mess at his feet. Before the door was slammed in his face, he said, with slurred speech, "Please, madam, please give me just ten seconds of your time. This is not an ordinary mop. This is a very special mop. It was designed by our company to be the easiest mop in the world to put together. Look how easily I can put it together!"

Whereupon the young actor put the mop-handle in his right hand, the mop-head in his left hand, and shaking uncontrollably, with no other props, gave his first prize-winning performance. It seemed minutes rather than seconds went by, while he did everything possible to that mop-head and mop-handle except put them together. To look at his twisting, fidgeting and grunting in feigned frustration, you would have thought he was trying to thread a needle with a rope.

Little did the poor housewife realize she was dealing with a future winner of Academy Awards. After several anguished moments of watching this desperate scene, the housewife, her superego aroused, reached out and said,

"Here, let me help you with that." Spencer Tracy, fully in control of the situation, happily let her wrest the mop from his palsied fingers. For he had theorized, quite correctly, that once she had the goods in her hands, once she touched it, she would buy it.

After assembling the mop, the dear woman of the house then patiently explained the simplicity of the operation to the inept salesman. In the little bit of banter that followed, the sale was made. And Spencer Tracy went on to use this technique again and again, making a pretty good living at it.

Now, not long ago, we had a conversation about ethics with a bunch of Bible salesmen. We related this story to them, and their attitude was that Mr. Tracy was dishonest and immoral in what he did. How could anybody make 100% of his sales unless he was a hopeless pagan?

We take a contrary viewpoint. We believe that this great genius of the American entertainment scene performed a worthy service for the housewives of Milwaukee: (1) He sold them a product they could use, (2) he charged fair market value, (3) he cheated no one, and (4) he worked hard at cultivating the superego of the American housewife.

So much for the profane theology of selling.

But the story doesn't end quite yet.

Interestingly enough, the Fuller Brush Company sales manager who was Spence's supervisor soon gained a reputation for selling more mops than any other sales manager in America. Of course he didn't really know what was going on, but he revelled in the unbelievable results. Unfortunately, when, a bit later, Spencer Tracy found a job in summer stock, his hapless supervisor had a terrible time justifying a warehouse full of mops to the regional manager.

Consciously or unconsciously, what our fine young actor had accomplished was (1) the arousal of the dear woman's superego through (2) a great theory of selling and his theory was that if she would touch it, she would buy it. There will be no testimonial dinners given in honor of Spencer Tracy, Salesman, nor will there be monuments erected to his sales expertise. But we cannot stress the importance of this little story strongly enough. Because Spencer Tracy, an impoverished and complete unknown during the deepest and most devastating depression of the century, *became the country's leading Fuller Brush Company salesman.* You can absolutely do it, too. You may not be Number One, but are Numbers Two, Three or Four so bad? But remember: to achieve this success you must use your head and your heart and develop your own theory of superego selling.

Hard?

Of course!

But it works.

After all, would Spencer Tracy lie to you?

(A side note: not only must salespeople learn to develop theories, but successful companies must do the same. The sales techniques of the 1930's must be adapted to the current marketplace. As a result of this learning process, the Fuller Brush Company has modified its sales techniques, and in certain cases pays its salespeople from 30% to 50% commission. They are also following the lead of competitors and giving home parties for neighbors who really can use their products. Like every other smart company on the move, they have made an honest attempt to satisfy their sales staff and their customers.)

But enough of Fuller's ancient history. Now let us bring you up-to-date on their No. 1 Best Seller in today's roistering, roiling marketplace.

This year's, last year's and probably next year's No. 1 Fuller Brush Salesman is a gentleman by the name of David Ofner.

Mr. Ofner did not begin his career as a salesman, but after being laid off as a supervising engineer for North American Rockwell, he knew he had to generate a good income for his wife and two sons. He was over 40 years old at the time. With Rockwell, he had had a prestigious position in which he supervised 35 engineers. Then, with chilling and devastating suddenness, *unemployment.*

He answered a Fuller Brush ad and invested $25 in a starter sales kit.

Rockwell's loss was Fuller's gain.

From that point on, Ofner went right to the head of the class. His annual gross sales for the past five years has exceeded $100,000.

How does he do it? For starters, he may pull a clump of grass out of your lawn and throw it on your porch. Then he cleans it with a Fuller carpet sweeper. Can't use a carpet sweeper? Then how about a broom?

Does this man have style? Does he have a theory? You bet he does. This man gets his cutomer involved in the sales process.

Mr. Ofner is No. 1 because (1) he has developed a following for about 20 years, (2) he cares and (3) he puts on a great show. To see him in action is to see a master at work.

"I've got wet mops, dry mops and dirty mops," he tells a steady customer with friendly enthusiasm.

"Dirty mops?" the customer asks.

"Just wanted to see if you're listening."

So successful are David Ofner's sales techniques that others have tried to invade his territory and steal his customers. From the outside, the invaders thought Ofner's territory was an easy mark beause he made so many sales. One nitwit, whom we will not grace with the word salesman, told customers he was Ofner's son. It didn't work. Ofner's loyal following called him and wanted to know the truth.

He gave it to them and sent the nitwit packing.

So much for the liars in our business.

On another occasion, another competitor tried to invade his territory. It didn't work.

In Our Hero's own words: "This particular gentleman is an asset to my business. He's obnoxious."

Ofner's success is not limited to door-to-door sales. He buys his company's products in bulk, at about a 50% discount, stores every single company product in his jam-packed garage, and sells to other Fuller sales people when they need a product *immediately*. When a regular customer calls, David Ofner delivers *immediately*. He is unusual in another way: Instead of giving the gift before getting an order, he gives the gift with the order.

What does this mean, exactly? Just read on to find out.

Whereas most successful door-to-door sales people have 150 to 200 steady customers, Ofner had 2,000. Every one of them on a 3-by-5 card. The card notes past purchases, probable hours a customer will be home, and personal notes such as:

1. Getting a divorce.
2. Pregnant.
3. Daughter in college.

On the next call, after learning these details, he asks something like the following:

1. "How are you enjoying living alone?"
2. "Did you have a boy or girl?"
3. "How's your daughter doing in college?"

In Our Hero's own words, "I want to inject some personal things. That's part of selling."

That's also part of a great history. Another part is humor. This Brooklyn-born salesman with the built-in accent pushes Fulla' brushes in his own inimitable style. All his female customers are young women. They may guffaw and chide him for his flattery but the enjoyment is mutual. "They keep me young."

He is friendly, but his time is precious. Therefore, he devotes a minimum of five and a maximum of ten minutes to each customer. (Unless it's a very large order or a complaint. Then he has all the time in the world.) He does not have to get his foot in the door because he never goes inside. And he never lies to the clientele. If he has an erratic product that works some of the time, he approaches the problem like this:

"I had a liquid bowl cleaner that was supposed to re-move rust from the driveway. In some cases it didn't work. So I stopped giving that demonstration. I would say 'Mrs. Jones, let's see if it removes your rust. If it doesn't, I don't want to sell it to you.'"

Another part of the Ofner Theory of Selling goes like this:

"Rule No. 1 is service."

And he means it! A customer once complained about the handle on her 15-year-old Fuller sweeper bending out of shape. David Ofner replaced the handle immediately and with a smile. No charge, of course.

We could write another complete book on David Ofner alone. But we don't have time and he doesn't have time. Suffice it to say we are proud of him. Had Spencer Tracy known him, he would have been proud of the man. After all, Best Sellers have a lot in common.

If you develop a sales theory of your own and follow it with passion, persistence, enthusiasm and a good vocabu-lary, you will beat every sales record in the office. Includ-ing your own.

Consider this chapter a research project that will make you a little wiser in the ways of direct selling. We culled the literature, for your benefit, and came up with some names and numbers on other No. 1 Best Sellers whose sales rec-ords were not meteoric, but darn good because they gave it all they've got.

How about Fred Wilmert? He is a 75-year-old Fuller Brush salesman with a prospect list of more than 1,000 regular customers in Baltimore, Maryland.

"Every since I was a boy, I wanted to be a salesman," he recalls.

Wimert makes about $20,000 per year. His workday starts around 2:00 P.M.

Many door-to-door salespeople work part-time. Kelly DiGrazia falls into this category. A charming, full-time, thirty-something mother of two pre-schoolers, she works exactly 2-hours per month selling housewares to her neighbors. In her own words: "The hardest part of going door-to-door is you have to do it cold turkey. I wouldn't say it is hard, but it takes a lot of guts."

Consider the following: In 1985, Elizabeth Brinton, age 13, was the world's No. 1 Best Seller for Girl Scout cookie sales. Her career began at age 6 in her home town of Falls Church, Virginia. How does she do it?

First, she gets their attention.

We quote the 104-pound heroine of the Best-Seller Gang: "My mom tole me, 'Look them in the eye, talk to them personally and speak up.'"

Mom sells real estate.

Elizabeth sells cookies.

Here is some of the best selling banter she uses.

"They're tax-deductible. We take checks." (Once when a customer pulled out a checkbook, she added, "Why not buy a whole case?")

Can't eat a whole box? "You can freeze them."

Can't decide on which of the 7 different varieties to buy? "Why not buy one of each so you can find out?"

Man with a lady: "Show you care! Buy Girl Scout cookies!"

Air Force personnel: "Fly with Girl Scout cookies!"

Navy, especially admirals: "Bring some back for your shipmates!"

A man from the USO bought four cases.

So famous did this darling of No. 1 Bestsellerdom become that she was once invited to a St. Patrick's Day celebration at the White House in Washington, D.C.

She found herself between George P. Shultz, Secretary of State of the United States of America, and Donald T. Regan, White House Chief of Staff of the United States of America. When they asked her about her many Girl Scout merit badges, she replied, "I sell cookies. You want to buy some?"

Although the direct selling industry suffered a decades-long decline, from 1976 to 1986, 1987 was a turnaround year. We believe the entry of women into the sales force had much to do with it.

Neil H. Offen, president of the Direct Selling Association, claims that not only are direct sales up, but records were lately broken for vacuum cleaner and encyclopedia sales.

And who is the country's No. 1 Best Encyclopedia Britannica Seller? Ki Yup Chang, a Korean immigrant.

And how does he do it?

One door at a time.

It is a certainty that not all of us can be great actors, athletes or politicians. But all of us who are committed to sales success, who have a theory and are customer-committed, can most assuredly become great salespeople. Some of the most successful salespeople we know told us they started as failures. It is an oft-told story. But when they got around to analyzing the keys to failure and success, they unlocked a theory from the dim recesses of their minds. They came to understand a bit about human psychology, made their appeals to the id, ego and superego (or in some cases all three), and from humble beginnings it was impossible to stop these great and knowlegeable superstars of the sales world.

We know that becoming a No. 1 Best Seller is difficult. But it's not impossible. If not a Tracy or an Ofner, how about a Prelutsky or a Winnikoff? Please bear in mind that your charming authors frequently say to one another, "If you can do it, anyone can do it!"

Therefore, ladies and gentlemen, we want you to go out there and do it! After all, you have an enormous edge over the competition. If you're smart enough to be reading this book, we know you're smarter by far than the poor misbegotten souls who are not reading this book.

Please don't let us down.

SUPEREGO GRATIFICATION

In the area of superego gratification, we turn first to charitable contributions. Armchair psychologists and other assorted head jockeys will tell you that people give because they feel guilt. Never argue with a psychological or psychiatric armchair expert. They know everything and concede nothing. They do not give to charity. They are lousy salespeople. But we know when *we* give to charity that *our* guilt is a lot better than *their* greed. We give. They grunt. We like our way better.

And then there are Bible salesmen. They are well-known for their appeals to the superego, and their approach is quite simple and direct.

But all of the above is obvious. In this chapter, we would like to enlighten you with a dissertation on a salesman, including his method for making a superego sale, a salesman who not only had a theory of selling, but extraordinary insight into the bedeviling problems that confront multiple sales in real estate.

Our hero, Ernest S. Crow, was a legendary real estate broker in Malibu, California. He knew the territory, the mechanics of the business and something about the players.

Ernest had some rather winning ways about him. He had sold houses to and for the superstars of stage, screen, TV, pop music and the slightly graying art form of rock `n' roll. For a full 6% commission, he would even sell to punkers or rappers. Or Attila the Hun, for that matter. But most of his sales were made to those who bought into the real estate market at a price slightly over their heads. Contrary to popular misconception, not everyone in Malibu is rich. Of the area's 19,000 inhabitants, approximately 6,000 are breadwinners. Exactly 16 of those make their mortgage payments on time. The other 5,984 are sweating it just like the rest of us. But for more money and larger monthly payments.

Malibu is a big area. It extends 27 miles along the Pacific Ocean. All the bad things that happen there make headlines. Good things are not even believed. But good things *do* happen in the area. People work, marry, live and die there. The major industry is real estate. The second largest industry is divorce.

When selling a home, Ernest never, never, ever lets the buyer and seller get together. (Unless they are both attorneys. In those rare cases, buyer and seller *deserve* each other, and Ernest lets them have at each other because they enjoy it so much.) This is because once, after Ernest S. Crow lost an $800,000 sale over *garbage cans*, he swore he'd never again allow the principals to meet.

Hard to believe, but what happened was that the buyer and seller got together in Ernie's office after a deposit receipt was signed and both parties had agreed on the price. The seller said, "I hate to tell you this, but I'm taking the garbage cans. They've got my name on them. All 20 of them."

To which the buyer replied, "You mean I'm paying you $800,000 for that barn and you're running off with the garbage cans?"

To which the seller responded, "They have a sentimental value. You see . . ."

(Please allow your authors to interrupt here and say that since you have all heard the canned speech on The Sentimental Value of Garbage Cans, we will spare you the misery and delete it from the text. Furthermore, it's not our intention to take sides on the issue of sentimental garbage cans.)

Suffice it to say, Mr. Crow's mouth went dry. His voice cracked. His heart palpitated to the danger point. In an effort to reconcile the tough-guy rhetoric of two egomaniacal men, he cleared his throat and said, "Gentlemen, if you'll just give me a chance I'll be glad to supply you both with new garbage cans."

Buyer: "Thanks, but I don't want *new* garbage cans. I want the old ones. They're not *personal* property. They're *real* property."

Seller: "Who says? You know as much about real and personal property law as my pet parakeet."

Believe it or not, the sale was lost. In spite of Ernest S. Crow's most valiant efforts, the sale was kaput. But he learned a very important lesson from all this: Never let the buyer and seller get together. No good can possibly come from such a meeting. Salesmen make a living from getting a buyer and seller to agree *separately and at a distance;* the parties will generally disagree when they are brought together in a threatening situation and have to prove their masculinity. No one wins in those situations.

But when you can transform that lesson of fighting egos into the triumph of a superego sale, then you go to the head of the class. Which is why we feel the following tale of Ernest S. Crow is so valuable a lesson for all of us.

He made deals that no one else could possibly make. He was absolutely brilliant in analyzing the extreme complexity in some sales.

For instance, there was the time Ernie was on the verge of selling not one, but *two* beachfront homes. One for $1,350,000 and the other for $2,750,000. Sales of this magnitude are not made every day.

The cheaper house was owned by one Dr. Maas Hideko, who agreed to purchase the more expensive home if he could remodel to his wife's satisfaction. Dr. Hideko sure was a swell guy and Ernie enjoyed working for him. However, the good doctor did have a few blind spots, and Ernie was one of them. To the eternal embarrassment of Mrs. Hideko and her son, he always called Ernie *Nick*. They notified Dr. Hideko repeatedly, and in beautifully hushed whispers, that the man's correct name was *Ernie*, not *Nick*.

But Ernie never let on. He simply smiled and got on with the business at hand.

Remodeling a beachfront home in California has become enormously complex in recent years, thanks to the California Coastal Commission. If you wish to build, remodel or even pitch a tent along the California coastline, you must first obtain a Coastal Commission permit. To proceed without one is to risk going to jail.

Since all permit processes are open to abuse, Ernie had his work cut out for him.

At this point in the discourse, dear reader, let us tell you that we—as salesmen—think the California Coastal Commission is the most corrupt, vicious, contemptible and underhanded bureaucracy in the state. We have never heard anyone who has appeared before this Grand Inquisitorial Body say a good word about them. To be fair about it, there is plenty of good to be said about the 12 commissioners. They are all honorable and upright pillars of the community. And if you doubt our word, just ask them. The commissioners, all of whom are political appointees, are well-versed in The Law, and some of them are downright brilliant. If and when they choose to destroy an individual, corporation, partnership or joint venture by denying the necessary permit, they always do it in a civilized, law-abiding way.

They destroy people with impunity, but it must be admitted that they do it in soft and gentle voices. They smile. And they whisper like guillotines.

The gentle and brilliant commissioners are aided by

staff members who are California state employees. The staff members are the ones who really recommend approval or denial for the permits.

At the time that Ernest Crow was doing business with Dr. Hideko, one of these powerful staff members was a charming young man by the name of Charles Foxworth III. Foxworth, or as his friends call him, Foxy, possessed a mentality completely devoid of psychological analysis. No id, ego or superego for this guy. Just greed. Pure greed. Only greed. If there was a qualifier to his greed, it was simply that his greed was smiling and whispering greed.

His fellow employees referred to him as Snake-Brain.

Our hero, Ernie, had seen his wonderful neighbor, Professor David Smith, hung out to dry *for seven years* before the Beautiful People at the Coastal Commission gave him a permit to build. Ernie had seen builders, developers, private individuals and real estate brokers go bankrupt because of the commission. He heard via the grapevine that Foxworth was open to bribes. That Foxy needed money for his own beachfront home in Malibu.

But our hero had never bribed anyone in his life. And he was not about to begin now.

And so it came to pass that Dr. Maas Hideko's sale and purchase, amounting to $4,100,000, the most important deal on Ernie's docket, became the most uncertain one as well.

He helped Dr. Hideko prepare all the documents. He agreed to be Dr. Hideko's agent and speak before the Coastal Commission. He was very nervous about the Coastal Commission hearing on Monday, November 15, at the Torrance City Council Chamber, the third time he would try to get Hideko's proposal okayed.

And then real disaster struck.

On the bright and sunny Sunday morning of November 14, Ernest S. Crow was in the shower when his hysterical wife, Betty, came into the bathroom screaming that the handle on the kitchen faucet had broken off and water was splashing onto the kitchen ceiling, walls, floor, appliances, cabinets, drawers, etc.

Even the paper towels had gotten wet.

Panic! Panic! Hysteria! Hysteria!

Our hero, dripping wet but undaunted, turned off the up-stairs shower and marched bravely downstairs to the kitchen.

Sure enough, there was water, water everywhere.

Even the family cat was aware of the problem, and had climbed into the cabinet under the sink to protect herself from the deluge. As she was licking her paws, a most peculiar thing happened. Her lord and master, stark naked and dripping wet, crouched down before her and started turning off the water shut-off valves beneath the sink.

So far, so good. Problem nearly solved.

But when Kitty-Kitty noticed Ernie's private parts flapping in the breeze, she stopped licking her dampened paws and bared her claws. Then she took careful aim and made a swipe at the poor man's most naked of naked nether parts. A successful swipe. When Kitty-Kitty connected, Ernie-Ernie let out a wounded howl and took off for the ceiling.

He never made it.

The poor man never made it.

On his anguished and howling way up, he smashed his forehead into the edge of the sink and gashed his wrinkled brow from end to end.

Where once there was only water, there was now blood and water.

Kitty-Kitty took off for the safety of her litter box. Ernie lay unconscious in a pool of watery blood. Betty-Betty stepped into the kitchen. She let out a bloodcurdling scream that didn't help her darling husband one iota.

But it gave her courage.

With the cool determination of a Florence Nightingale, she ran and got a towel to wrap around Ernie's bleeding head. That done, she ran and got a sanitary napkin to put on his bleeding you-know-what. That done, she called the ambulance.

When the ambulance arrived, there was the usual questioning about internal injuries and missing limbs.

No, Betty told them. Nothing like that. Nor was her dear husband allergic to aspirin. As Ernest S. Crow was placed, moaning, on the stretcher, his arms dangling to the sides, Betty followed the helpful and sympathetic young men outdoors and explained *exactly* what had happened. The ambulance attendants—both of whom had received their early training on a beer truck—laughed so hard that one of them dropped the slowly writhing Ernest S. Crow on the pavement, breaking his arm.

When our hero woke up in the hospital, he had a headache. His arm was in a cast. There was a pain in a place where he had never known pain before.

Never! At least not *this* kind of pain.

But, considering the unbroken string of bad luck, it was quite fortunate that Mr. Crow did not—we repeat, *did not*—get a skull fracture on that fateful, unforgettable Sunday morning.

His faithful wife Betty was at his side, stroking his cheeks and crying softly.

"Betty," he whispered, "is the water off?"

"Yes."

"Is Kitty-Kitty all right?"

"Yes."

"Are you all right?"

"Yes."

"Betty," he said weakly, "I want you to do me a favor."

"Yes," she replied, sniffling gently.

"I want you to go home and cancel all my appointments for today—Sunday."

"Oh, Ernie! And Sunday is your busiest day of the week."

"I know. But cancel everything for today. Understand?"

"Yes," she said, and was about to leave when her loving husband reached out and touched one of her two unbroken hands with his one unbroken hand. "But don't cancel *any* of my appointments for tomorrow. Understand?"

"Yes, but you only have one appointment for tomorrow and . . ."

"Betty," he said, weakly, "please do as I say. That's going to be one of the most important meetings of my life."

"But look at you!" she cried softly. "How can you go like that?"

"On a gurney," he replied. "And get Dr. Hideko in here. As soon as possible."

The ever-faithful Betty Crow did as she was told.

She returned in two hours with the horrified and sympathetic Dr. Hideko.

The patient was feeling no better. After the initial chit-chat, Dr. Hideko said, "Obviously, we'll have to cancel our appearance before the Coastal Commission tomorrow, Nick."

"No way," Ernie said weakly. "That's what I wanted to talk to you about."

"But you can't go like this!" the good doctor pleaded.

"Not only am *I* going, but *you're* going with me," Ernie said. "You're going to take me on a gurney, with an attendant giving me oxygen, and you and my wife at my side."

"But Nick," the doctor pleaded, "they've already turned us down twice."

"They won't turn us down this time."

And so it came to pass that on the following day, Monday, November 15, at 9:30 A.M., with its siren going full blast, an ambulance containing our hero rolled up to the Appointed Meeting Place of the California Coastal Commission. Then Ernest S. Crow was wheeled into the Torrance City Hall on a gurney. He had an attendant feeding him oxygen from a loudly hissing oxygen bottle and a nurse holding high a plasma bottle, and Betty Crow and Dr. Hideko by his side. The patient was breathing as loudly as he could.

The battle was enjoined.

To say the least, the commissioners were mildly upset.

But Foxworth was absolutely beside himself, with a panic that choked off his meager blood supply. The normally swarthy Foxy, the head of the Coastal Commission staff, went from his normal dark gray color to candlestick white. "My God!" he thought, "what if a reporter from the *Daily Breeze* or *The Evening Outlook* shows up and splashes this across the front page! I'll be ruined! Nothing is worse than bad press!" Then he ran up and down the line whispering into the ears of all 12 commissioners urging them to give this applicant an immediate *yes* vote.

The head commissioner's name was Yosemite Rockbottom. Although they were all theoretically equal, Yosemite sort of spoke for the pack. Yosemite was originally a chicken rancher from Petaluma. But now he speculated in beach houses and practiced usury on the side. He was a pleasant, smiling, whispering fellow who smelled ever so faintly of chicken you-know-what (rhymes with *sit*). He leaned forward and asked with deep and quiet concern, "What happened?"

"He was attacked by a wild animal," Betty Crow said in a loud, clear voice.

"And where did it happen?" the concerned commissioner asked meekly, sympathetically.

"In Malibu," Betty replied. "We're in the real estate business."

There was a nodding of heads.

"I understand," Commissioner Rockbottom said.

There was a hurried rustling of papers.

Then the vote.

12 to zero in Dr. Hideko's favor.

They were in and out of the commission meeting in less than five minutes. A substantial improvement over the applicant's last meeting, which had taken five hours and ended in an inconclusive result.

On their way back to Malibu in the Pruner Ambulance, Ernie whispered to Dr. Hideko, "Don't take me back to the hospital. Take me home."

"But your condition . . ."

"I feel better than I look," Ernie interrupted. "So I'm going home to take care of unfinished business."

"*What* unfinished business?" Betty asked.

"I have to give Kitty-Kitty a big bowl of cream."

Dear Reader, we could go on by the hour with an academic analysis of our preceding sales tale, but we prefer to conclude this story with Ernie's own words. And Dr. Hideko's, too.

After Ernie recovered, he attended a meeting of the Malibu Board of Realtors. He was surrounded by his peers, who wanted to know how he pulled it off.

"It was real easy," he replied with a twinkle. "I appealed to their superegos. But there was also some application of the greed theory." He took a sip of his Perrier and added, "Whatever you'd like to call it, Betty and I always try to make something good out of something bad."

"And furthermore," Betty Crow added, beaming, "he's healed up just beautifully. Do you think that's what he means when he talks about superego gratification?"

But Dr. Hideko had the very last word. He was as pleased as he could be with the salesmanship of Ernest S. Crow. So when all the dust settled, he called Ernie. He said a lot of nice things, but concluded the conversation with: ". . . and in case I forgot to say this before, let me say it now on behalf of my wife, my son and myself: Thanks, *Nick*."

THE SUPEREGO
IMMIGRANT

In the realm of superego psychology there are two major types.

1. Those who work on the superego tendencies of the customer and,
2. Those salespeople who supply the superego themselves because they are supersalespeople who have a well-honed desire to truly help others.

This chapter is designed to illustrate the latter.

Juvenile delinquents, like most other criminal losers and crybabies, respond to a challenge with: "Yeah but that's *hard*!" Like all seekers of instant gratification, these quick-fix artists find that achievement, work or effort of any kind is not to their liking. Excuses, for negativists, replace work. More time is spent *worrying* about homework than is spent actually *doing* it. People of the loser persuasion may make it once in sales and never have a repeat performance. Maybe *they* don't know why but *we* sure do, don't we?

With this in mind, we would like to introduce you to a No. 1 Best Seller who began his superego training around the age of 10 in a war-torn country.

Finn Skeisvoll.

Born 1930.

Place of birth: Avaldsnes Haugesund, Norway.

Livelihood: subsistence farming.

One of three brothers.

Father, Nils Skeisvoll, killed in 1944 along with 350 other passengers on an unarmed civilian ferry boat. Bombed by the pilot of a Stuka dive bomber. The innocent died. The guilty lived.

With scarcely enough food on the table to feed the three Skeisvoll brothers and their mother, all the boys worked while attending high school.

Finn took a postwar job at *Musik Huset* (Music House in plain English) and became a self-taught electronics technician. In addition to learning radio and TV repair, Finn *had* to help support his family, *had* to get good grades in school, *had* to please his boss and *had* to help keep the customers happy. He was the only 16-year-old in his home town who would undertake the tough job of installing an antenna in a mid-winter snowstorm on a wet and slippery gabled slate roof. If Finn was called to do the job, he never failed those who depended on him. And never complained about the fact that much of his work was dirty, dangerous and life-threatening.

Development of the superego came early to Finn Skeisvoll: he always tried his best to please others.

The word *failure* was stricken from his mind, tongue and lips. Serving others was his reason for being.

Madly, totally and happily, he fell in love with a Danish beauty from Copenhagen and became engaged in 1954. Her name: Bente Thestrup. They planned to marry in six months in America. But the best laid plans were not to be completed as hoped. Fate and a war intervened. Their marriage plans were delayed for 18 months.

He eventually made his way as a legal immigrant to the New World on borrowed money in 1955. Went to Seattle.

Took a back-breaking job as a gardener. Took enormous abuse from the boss. Smiled. Worked very hard. Never complained. How could he complain? He couldn't speak English. Eventually became a salmon fisherman in Alaska. Found the work hard, cold, exhilarating and profitable. Banked all his hard-earned money in Seattle.

When the Suez Crisis broke out in 1956, all U.S. entry visas were put on hold and Bente was officially barred from the country. But true love prevailed, and a year later she made it to the U.S. The happy couple married four days after her arrival in 1957 in that beautiful, sunshine-drenched city by the sea, Santa Monica, California.

Because they had no close family in Santa Monica, they invited Finn's ski club friends to share in their incredible happiness. In his own words: "...we invited all, approximately 75, to our wedding. We had the greatest wedding. It lasted three days. We have two great children, Tina and Erik."

Bente Thestrup Skeisvoll found an entry level job with Lawrence Welk, answering his fan mail. The beginning pay was very, very modest, but the job offered one great benefit: Bente had to learn English correctly and immediately. All the letters Bente sent out had a slight Danish slant and sounded as if they came directly from the lips of the maestro himself.

Finn took a series of jobs. Finally landed at Litton Industries, Guidance and Control Division in 1960, as an electronics technician. Because the aerospace industry has always been high-risk, Finn sought for ways to get into his own business. The opportunity struck in 1979. Finn joined up with SMC (Specialty Merchandise Corporation) in Chatsworth, California, and sold their products part-time while employed at nearby Litton full-time. In the parlance of the trade, Finn was not a salesman. He was a merchandiser. And an *independent merchandiser* to boot. In his own words: "...it's the best thing I ever did."

SMC is a large-scale import distributor. Their warehouse space is the size of seven football fields. That comes to 3,150,000 square feet of good stuff for sale. For a mere pittance of $24.95 they will send anyone a business kit that gets the whole merchandising thing started. The kit includes five catalogs which include a massive array of costume jewelry, toys, tools, leather goods and porcelain figurines.

The SMC purchasing team searches the world over for unique products that are primarily high-impulse, fast-selling gift items. Then the products are offered to their merchandisers for instant resale and profits. *The SMC price is always right.*

SMC takes great pride in the fact that their merchandisers can:

1. Begin with a very small investment in time and money.
2. Attain success without learning new skills.
3. Rely on SMC as a supplier.
4. Make immediate profits.
5. Work from the home.

The giant SMC showroom has stunning displays of over 3,500 items. When SMC's marketing director, Kerry Cox, told us "Our merchandiser costs are way below wholesale cost," we believed him. Why? Because your authors were so impressed with the product line they tried to buy some of the items. To no avail. "We can't sell you anything unless you're a *bona fide* SMC merchandiser." We were flabbergasted.

"But we're the authors of this book," we said.

"All the more reason," he said. "But why don't you talk to Finn? I think he can help."

He did.

And we continue with Finn's worthy story.

The SMC credo in this regard is quite simple: If the merchandiser profits, SMC profits. The company therefore goes to great lengths to assure the success of their merchandisers. In addition to the dazzling array of products, SMC

has an incredible variety of sales programs, training programs and excellent support services.

Since his former places of primary and secondary employment were quite close to each other, Finn spent his
morning and afternoon coffee-break times and lunch hours
running between Litton and SMC to place and pick up orders. The Skeisvolls then started their own company and
Bente became the Scan-Am Enterprises vice-president, secretary, order-taker, letter writer, shipper and customer service department rolled into one. She worked seven days a
week and, like her superego salesman husband, tried mightily to please everyone. Kids included.

To this day, adult daughter Tina helps out in the family
business when the occasion arises. So does son Erik. The
Skeisvoll family knows and practices that singular virtue
which has been known to humanity's best and most loving
practitioners since the beginning: success requires many
hands.

In 1980, they noticed that their biggest selling item was
a rose lamp. They couldn't buy and ship the individual items
fast enough. Trusting to his mercantile instincts, Finn Skeisvoll contacted a mail order house and landed a $20,000 or-
der. Terms and conditions: delivery in three days, payment
in 30. It was a piece of merchandising insanity. The time
constraints made a bank loan or factoring impossible. Full-
time employment at Litton didn't help matters either. But
the Skeisvolls made it. Memories of those Avaldsnes
Haugesund antenna installations propelled them madly forward. They took a $10,000 loan from their friend Kjell Ro-
land and paid him back handsomely in 60 days. With smiling gratitude, Finn gave his friend Kjell a bonus. It wasn't in
the contract, but Finn is notorious for giving the customer a
baker's dozen.

From that time on, Finn concentrated on U.S. and Canadian mail order houses. Although he has never met 98% of
the people to whom he sells and with whom he does business, his paperwork is perfect, all calls are thorough and

friendly and he never fails his customers in any respect.

But whatever we write about Finn is not nearly as compelling as his own heartfelt words of truth. Therefore, we give you the following words of a Norwegian high school grad:

> I have been in the mail order business for the last 28 years, and I think it's the greatest job anybody can have on this earth.
>
> There are 6,000 mail order houses in the U.S.A. and 3,500 in Canada.
>
> Money is not all of it. The fun and challenge you have every day, finding new products, travelling to gift shows all over the world (my wife loves these trips), and you combine them with vacations...As I said earlier, there is no job more perfect on this earth. I wish I had known about it when I was in my twenties.

As our interview rolled to a close, we were greatly impressed with Finn's well-honed superego conscience and desire to help anyone and everyone who approached him for advice. The best advice he can give to those who go into sales is: "DON'T GIVE UP! Sometimes people who are 90% there give up and never reach their goal. So keep going and don't give up."

He is thinking of writing a book or starting a school to help others. The book he will sell. The school will be for free. Not only is Finn a member in good standing of the Direct Marketing Association, but he is extremely open and honest about helping others break into the business. He opens up his books, shows copies of large-size checks, purchase orders, letters and whatever else the visitor wishes to see. His life and his business are open books. Honest books. Good books.

When we concluded our interview, the usual question popped up. "Finn, why do you do it?"

"Why do I do it?" he asked, incredulously. "Why do I

do it?"

We thought he was indulging in that great Scandinavian practice of answering a question with a question. So we re-phrased our own question.

"Finn, what gets you going? When you get up in the morning?"

"When I get up in the morning, all I have to do to get my start is to think about those antenna installations in Avaldsnes Haugesund for my old boss at *Musik Huset*."

THE GREED THEORY

Just as Sigmund Freud had a theory of the personality, there are those economic wizards among us who have theorized that the two motivating forces in all financial markets are (1) fear and (2) greed. We, as salesmen, have taken this matter one step further, and claim that *everyone* has a greed button. It amazes us that among the many thousands of books written on selling, we have not found one single chapter heading that mentions *greed*. Nor have we found *greed* in any of the indices. We came across a Von Stroheim movie entitled *Greed*, but nothing in any of the sales books.

Therefore, in our search for knowledge, we went to the troops in the field and asked about greed. It is an unpleasant topic in the sacrosanct halls and offices of many sales organizations, but among the troops on the firing line we got a few cynical belly laughs and a bushel basket full of stories. It seems everyone would like to get into print. Especially with stories about greed.

Whether the salesperson considered himself high-brow, low-brow or no-brow, he or she found that the greed factor always comes to the fore when there is money on the table.

So we know it exists. Just as we know the personality exists. And we are very willing to admit that our theory could possibly be ten bricks short of a load. *But like all theories, it is a starting point.* Perhaps all the high-caliber slicksters who have protected territories and easy-touch purchasing agents (who are glad to see each other over a three-martini, company-credit-card lunch) are right in telling us we're wrong. But our theory is very simple and straightforward.

It is our belief that there is a *greed button* in every human being. This greed button is positioned in the head just behind the eyes and right between the ears. The button is connected via greed ducts to the greed glands which pump greed enzymes into every cell in the body.

You don't believe it? You may disprove our theory as follows: advertise in your local paper for a four-day party during which all comers can have all the food and drink they want. If no one shows, we'll be glad to pay for all the food and drink. But make sure we get an announcement concerning your freebie shindig, because we want to be there to prove our side of the theory.

On a greed scale of 1 to 100, most people are around 50%. Avoid the 100-percenters. They are bad news and will get you into horrible trouble. The one-percenters end up feeding our less fortunate brethren and sistern in soup kitchens. Smile at them, be nice to them, but do not look to them for big ticket sales.

Our attention must be focused on the 50% gang. They not only have normal greed buttons, but they also have the money with which to buy. *Punch their greed buttons and you will make the sale nearly every time.*

In spite of all the great greed stories that have come our way, we have chosen just one to pass on because it is so supportive of our theory.

Not too long ago in the long, stringy township of Malibu, California, a struggling young real estate broker by the name of Ernest S. Crow was approached by a very young and enormously successful rock musician and composer with the highly original name of Buffalo Bill.

Buffalo Bill was ever so slightly besotted by fame, fortune and worldwide adulation. He tried to behave like a plain, decent aw-shucks kind of guy, but it wasn't easy. In a quiet and reflective moment, he would bare his soul and claim he wanted nothing more in the world than to be a very modest, down-to-earth human being just like Albert Einstein.

Buffalo Bill was referred to Ernie by other inhabitants of the entertainment world who had dealt with him and believed in his integrity. Ernie had enormous credibility.

The reputation was well earned. For Ernest S. Crow believed that he could outsell just about any other competitor with just a few basic rules.

1. Believe in your product.
2. Be *perfectly* honest with everyone and you will have an enormous advantage over the competition.
3. Be nice to everyone.
4. Know your product or service thoroughly.
5. Work very, very hard.
6. Answer all questions in a straightforward manner.
7. Listen.
8. Listen.
9. Don't talk. Listen.
10. Just listen.
11. Keep on listening.

After an extended period of listening to Buffalo Bill's modest achievements, four hours and 30 minutes, Ernest asked the Great Bearded Man, "Exactly what are you looking for?"

"A bargain, really. Y'know, a fixer-upper. Somethin' with a small, little house an' a great big spread to go with it." Whereupon Buffalo Bill spread his huge arms and hands wide. "But close enough t' the ocean so I can jus' walk down t' the beach."

"What you're looking for doesn't exist," Ernest replied. He had dealt with this type before. The Big (Modest) Man who had to have the biggest house on the block.

Buffalo Bill was thoroughly shocked. This was the first time in ten years anyone had said *no* to him.   "Now lookey heah, Ernie," Buffalo Bill said, exercising the utmost in modest restraint. "How come y'all got such a good deal fo' mah lead guitar boy, Ugly Fats Bogle? Why, he tole me he bought a fo' million dollah house fo' two mil. How'd he do that? Now y'all gotta do me a good one like that too. O.K.?"

"Not O.K." Ernest said.

Buffalo Bill undid his string tie, pushed his cowboy hat back on his head and took off his boots. The smell made all the flies in the office ecstatic. Ernest got up and opened all the windows.

The flies absolutely refused to go outdoors and play.

Buffalo Bill cleared his throat and leaned forward. Beads of sweat formed on his famous brow. He realized that he would have to unleash all his modest charm to get Ernie's attention.

"Now lookey heah, Ernie," he said, leaning forward and putting his stockinged left foot over his right knee, "they all tell me y'all got more smarts than a fox in college."

Ernie's intestines winced. But he gave no outward sign of discomfort.

The Great 20th Century Musical Man continued, with what he believed was his most persuasive diatribe, for 17 minutes straight. (Since all of you are familiar with the canned Persuasive Diatribe, we will not repeat it here.) At the beginning of the 18th minute, Buff stopped and asked, "Y'all listenin', boy?"

Ernie nodded his head yes. But not vigorously.

"Listening real good?" the Great Man asked.

Ernie nodded again. Same way. Same lack of enthusiasm.

Buffalo Bill took a deep breath. He was perplexed. His managers, accountants, handlers, grips, bass players, feeders and camp followers were ecstatic when he spoke. His fans went berserk. And the IRS, like the flies, had apoplectic fits over him, buzzing uncontrollably in his presence. But Ernie seemed to be unmoved. Buff was perplexed.

"Hey, Ernie Boy," Buffalo Bill said in a loud, friendly voice, smiling his most winning smile, "how come y'all ain't *enthused*?" He paused, proud of himself for using an uncommon verb. "Mad at me?" he asked impishly, removing a dead fly from his sock.

"No."

"Ain't got no houses fo' sale?"

"No."

"Ole lady cutcha off las' night?"

"No."

"Like t' have one o' my autographed albums? A twenny-two million best seller?"

"No."

"Hey, Ernie Boy, this is serious! Ain't nobody turned down one o' them afore! Whatchew thinkin'? Whatchew *really* thinkin'?"

"That you're crazy."

Buffalo Bill was caught completely off guard. There was a hushed silence in the office. For a brief instant, it even seemed B.B.'s friends the flies had stopped buzzing.

"Run that by me again," Buffalo Bill finally said.

"I said I think you're crazy."

Buffalo Bill jumped up, stamped his stockinged feet on the floor, scaring the flies half out of their buzzing wits, and laughed uproariously. He whooped, hollered and did a little war dance. Upon completion, B.B. went over to Ernie, put his hand on the Great Realtor's shoulder and said, "Well if that don't beat all! Ernie, you ole sonofagun, anybody ever tell ya you the Diogenes o' the realty business?"

"No."

"Ernie-Boy, we gotta get serious—we gotta get physical—man, we gotta get downright blowin' in the wind 'bout this here *project*!" He stopped briefly, proud of himself for using a two-syllable word straight out of a real estate dictionary. He sat down. Crossed his legs. Gave the flies a chance to settle down, then asked, "Ernie-Baby, whatchew gonna do fo' me?"

"Nothing."

"Well, if that don't beat all! Ya ain't got no house for me to buy?"

"I didn't say that."

"*What*? Didn't say *what*?" the Big Man asked.

"I didn't say I didn't have a house for you to buy."

"Ernie-Baby, ah'm just a plain ole country boy made good. Now, how come ya treat me this-a-way? Ain'tcha gonna' sell me no house?"

"Well," Ernest said, "now that I have your attention—"

"ATTENTION!" Buffalo Bill bellowed. "Ernie-Boy, ya really got mah *attention*! Hooeee an' wowee! For sure, certain and absolute true-blue, ya got mah *attention*. Now, Ernie-Buddy, whatchew got on yer mind? Ah'm all ears!" He let out a giggle and pulled on his oversize earlobes. "Lookey heah! See how big!" he tugged again. "Talk t' me, Ernie-Pal."

"All right. Let me begin by saying I'm not going to *sell you anything*!"

"Ain't gonna sell me *nothin'*?" Big Bill exploded.

"That's right," Ernie said. "I'm not going to *sell* you anything. If we find the right property, *you're going to buy*."

Buffalo Bill slapped his knee and whisked a hand across his socks. The flies took off. "Well ah'll be ham-dogged hung an' strung. Ya gotta explain all this t' me, Ernie-Friend. Sure *you* ain't the crazy one?"

"Not completely. What I'm getting at is this: I'm not going to sell you *anything*—you're going to *buy*. I don't care what you've heard about me—I'm not a hot-shot salesman. I'm just a hard-working guy doing his job. The very best I can do for you is show you what's available. If *you* find something *you* like, make an offer on it and I'll try to work out the details. Now does that make sense? And I don't need a copy of your latest album because I've already got it."

"Ernie-Chum, how come ya didn't tell me all that good news right from the start?"

"I was too busy listening."

"Well, Ernie-Comrade, ya seem like a nice, straightforward sorta cowpuncher, but I got sorta bad news fo' ya."

"What's that?"

"I awready seen every ten-million-dollar house from Malibu t' Holmby Hills. Don't like none of 'em."

"Have you thought about a lot?"

"How's that, Ernie, ya ole sodbuster?"

"If you buy a lot, you can build anything you want."

"Lots ain't no good. Too small. Man, ah tole ya, ah wanna big, big spread!" Whereupon he spread his arms wide. "A cattle-country spread. A place where ah can kick road apples!"

"Have you thought of moving back to—"

"No way!" Buffalo Bill cut in.

Ernest S. Crow scratched his head. "The only thing I can think of," he said, "is assemblage."

"Howzat?"

"That's where you buy five or ten parcels and assemble them."

"Now you're talkin' sense, boy. Now ya got it! Really got it!"

"But that's some of the toughest real estate around—assemblage."

"Ernie Buddy, ya got it! Now let's go do it."

"Now wait a minute. I can't just run out of here and go do it. It takes some planning. We have to make appointments, show you around, let you get the lay of the land."

"Ah'm all ears!" Buffalo Bill shouted, tugging firmly on his earlobes.

And so it came to pass that they worked hard and found the first parcel. It was a fixer-upper for $385,000. They opened the escrow on a Friday morning with a $50,000 deposit. That same Friday night, B.B. called Ernest S. Crow at home and said, "Ernie, Baby, ah decided ah don't want the house."

The peristaltic action of Ernest's intestines went into overdrive. But *unlike 99% of the world's salespeople, the mediocre salespeople, Ernest did not try to talk the Great Man out of his decision.* "Don't worry about a thing," Ernest said, controlling his voice with great difficulty. "I'll order the escrow people to return your $50,000 check Monday morning."

"Wanna know how come ah ain't takin' this deal?"

"That's not necessary, Buff. I'm only here to serve you, not question your judgment."

"Well ah'll be—Ernie, yer somethin' else! Thanks, ole buddy boy."

They hung up.

The following Saturday morning, Buffalo Bill called Ernest at the crack of dawn and said, "Ernie, y'ole hornswoggler, ah hope ah'm not callin' too early."

Ernest S. Crow cleared the sleep from his throat and replied, "You are, but that's O.K. What's on your mind?"

"Ah changed mah mind again. I want the house."

"All right, then we won't cancel the escrow."

"Good! Now tell me, Ernie ole buddy, whatchew doin' fo' breakfast?"

"Going back to sleep. My God, it's 5:15."

"No sireee ya don't! Ah'll pick ya up in five minutes in mah original, untouched 1947 Chevy pick-up!" Without waiting for a reply, B.B. slammed down the phone.

HERE BEGINNETH PART 2 OF THE
BUFFALO BILL HOUSE-BUYING SAGA.

Ernest S. Crow succeeded in assembling nine parcels for Buffalo Bill. It took about a year, and all parties were very discreet in their dealings.

Whispers in the Malibu Township rumor mill ran hot and heavy. We will not discuss these here because you have heard them all in your own community.

But for Buffalo Bill, the problem was very direct: he wanted a big, big beach spread and was willing to pay fair market value.

At the end of a year he had achieved 90% of his goal, but the last 10% was going to be the hardest. To finish assembling his lot, B.B. needed just one pice of property. Property that was owned by Dr. Hortense McGreedy.

If Buffalo Bill was crazy in an entertainer's sort of way, Dr. McGreedy was certifiably insane, to the point of cackling and laying eggs on a hot blistering sidewalk at high noon on the Fourth of July.

Dr. McGreedy had advanced degrees in chemistry, had buried five husbands, had a lot of money, a lot of property, and a greed button the size of a manhole cover. The mere mention of her name was enough to start tongues wagging with horror stories of deposits stolen, a vacant apartment rented to 16 different tenants, plumbing that was never fixed, neighbors driven to drink and courts clogged with her cases. The only near-normal aspect of this greed-driven woman was that she *detested* attorneys. But to deal with her was to know extremes of frustration and a host of other negative emotions.

Unfortunately, Buffalo Bill approached the lovely lady himself. He gave her a copy of his latest world-acclaimed album. She snatched it from his hands.

The battle was enjoined: The Righteous Knight-Entertainer *versus* The Wicked Witch of Malibu.

Whereas most greed buttons go *click-click*, Dr. McGreedy's was a mixture of hen cackle and large-sized gong.

"Howdy, ma'am," B.B. said, tipping his hat.

"Well, it's not for sale!" Dr. McGreedy screamed, slamming the door in his face.

"Ah shore hope ya like mah album," the Righteous Knight-Entertainer said to the closed door. He felt he had to say it because he had memorized the line. (On a more personal level, he would have been totally crushed if *anyone* disliked his music.)   Sadly, he went to the office of Ernest S. Crow.

"Look," Ernie told his star customer, "didn't I tell you to stay away from her?"

"Ah know, Ernie-Buddy, but ah was jes' tryin' t' do the right thing."

"No one can do the right thing with her."

"Think she'll play mah album?"

"I doubt it. She'll probably sell it at a discount to one of her tenants."

"How we gonna straighten out this here mess, Ernie-Chum?"

"We have two choices, Bill. One, we can *pay* Dr. McGreedy ten times the fair market value, or two, we can *trade* her a property with a little more value. In either case, we have to appeal to her greed."

(Please let us digress here for a moment and explain the need to think fast and clearly. In the few brief seconds it took to utter his words, Ernest gave Bill the benefit of 25 years of hard-fought, hard-earned and hard-won experience. We cannot stress strongly enough the importance of this type of experience. If you have it and can apply it quickly and without fanfare, you will succeed.) "Ernie, ah know ya ain't gonna believe me, but ah'm gonna bow out an' let y'all handle the whole rotten mess y'self."

"Thanks."

It was at this point Ernest S. Crow went to work to find a beach property for sale that was ever so slightly better than Dr. McGreedy's. Finding it, he sold the property to Buffalo Bill's *attorney* so that the Great Man's name did not appear anywhere on the title. Then he proceeded to make the trade with the bad doctor.

As a cautious and prudent real estater, Ernie did not go to see Dr. McGreedy alone. Instead, he went with his wife. They tried to make the meeting as sociable as possible, but the good doctor's greed-gong kept hammering away with great regularity.

"How would you like to buy this brand new record album CD by—by—what's his name? Oh, yes! *Buffalo Bill and the Chips*?" she asked. Cackle-cackle-gong-gong.

"How much?" Ernie asked.

"Well, it was $24.95. How about $15?"

"I just *love* his music," Betty said.

"In that case, make it $17.95."

Two visits later, the Crows struck a deal with the beautiful and charming Witch of Malibu. A greedy woman, she couldn't resist the idea of owning a more expensive piece of property than the one she already had.

But *opening* the deal was only one part of the saga. *Closing* it was quite another. For our illustrious hero had to deal with Dr. McGreedy on the selling side and with Buffalo Bill's attorney, business manager and accountant on the other. Sadly, the gang on the buying end did everything in their power to obstruct the deal. They also had oversized greed glands and drove Ernest bananas. But, and this is important, *he never discussed any of these problems with anyone but his wife*. You must learn to do the same. For if you blab about your problems to every flannel-mouth in the office, it will be all over town in ten seconds flat. Therefore, it is always best to suffer in silence. Or at least *appear* to suffer in silence. In the end, though, the deal closed.

When all the dust settled and the all-important *trade* was made, Ernest was mobbed by his fellow salesmen and saleswomen at the next realty board meeting, all of them asking *how he did it*. He remained composed, took a sip of his Perrier and said, "It was all very elemental. I first applied a little sales psychology. Then I simply pushed their greed buttons."

THE FOUR ELEMENTS OF A SALE

1. Attention
2. Interest
3. Desire
4. Close

ATTENTION

We chose to write about the four elements of a sale because they are so simple and easy to remember. Even your authors have no trouble with them.

There may be other, different elements. But we elected to use the preceding four because we can work with them in a neat and understandable way. With these elements in mind, *we make sales.* Follow our lead and *you will make sales.* You may use the elements as a flexible guideline and not as Holy Writ. On occasion, you may dispense with the first three elements and settle for the fourth.

For example, when a ready, willing and able buyer for a brand-new Ford F-250 pickup with all options on board cannot get it at Agency A, he may go to Agency B and close the deal quickly when he finds what he wants. If the saleslady at Agency B is merely on her toes, (1) paying attention, (2) aware of the pre-aroused interest in her product and (3) listening carefully to the customer's desires, she will (4) close. The world is full of stories concerning customers who are pre-sold.

We wish to digress here with a great sales story by Joe Girard. Joe is not only a No. 1 Best Seller but also a writer. His books, *How to Sell Anything to Anybody* and *How to Close Every Sale*, are well-written, useful, readable and intelligent and should be in your library of great sales books. Why? Because Joe claims, rightfully and truthfully, that when a prospective customer walks into the showroom, *he (or she) walks in to buy.* You don't believe it? Believe it. Joe for many years was the No. 1 Best Seller of Chevrolet automobiles in the good old U.S.A. His theory was and is that he could sell every customer a car. And he did. Our theory was and is that you simply can't make every single real estate sale. He's right and we're right. But the important point is that we each developed a theory of our own and stuck by it. The following story fully explains the reason for Joe Girard's success.

When a prospective customer walked into Joe's show-room, the woman was merely killing a little time. Why? Because it was her 55th birthday, she wanted to buy a new white Ford coupe, but the Ford salesman had told her to come back in an hour. Joe heard the lovely lady's story and said, "Happy birthday." Then he excused himself, went to his secretary's outer office and then returned to his own office, where he continued a pleasant conversation with a woman he now considered a prospective buyer. He said, "As long as you have some time on your hands, let me show you one of our coupes. It, too comes in white."

Fifteen minutes later, Joe's secretary returned with a dozen roses for the lady and made her day, and she almost burst into tears. Whether they sang *Happy Birthday*, we do not know. But one thing we can tell you with certainty: *the lovely lady ended up buying a Chevy from Joe Girard.* And how did he do it? Not by being tricky, sneaky or running his fingers through her hair. He did it by being honest and decent and compassionate. He did it by listening. And he did it out of kindness and common decency. His theory, like our theory, was suffused with the three basic elements of business: (1) honesty, (2) honesty and (3) honesty. And a dollop of kindness tied the whole thing together.

So read Joe's books. When he writes, the words are worth reading. When he speaks, it pays to listen. And when he acts, watch him, because the movements are pure sales poetry in motion. It happens daily.

If you spell sales success H-A-R-D W-O-R-K, you will close many deals. There will be a lot of buzzing in the front and back offices about your seemingly quick and easy sale, but you will have no illusions. You have spent a lifetime learning your trade and know very well that even the so-called *easy ones* are hard. They *almost* make up for all the miserable ones that never close. But not quite. In our business there are infinitely more downs than ups. It is one of the overriding facts of sales life. But if you can't go straight to number four on the list and close the deal immediately, you'll have to move to the earlier elements, of which ATTENTION is the first. To start a deal is often a matter of getting the buyer's attention. But we must tell you the matter of getting the prospect's attention isn't always applicable. For example, a gas station attendant need not try to get the attention of a motorist out of gas. Clerks and waitresses need not get the attention of anyone. (In fact, the trick as you all know if you've been in a restaurant or a department store lately, is to get theirs.) Salesmen and saleswomen, on the other hand, can no more afford to go unnoticed than actors, singers or baton twirlers.

ATTENTION
CONTINUED

The matter of getting attention—the right kind of attention—is so fundamental to selling that we will go into the matter in great detail.

The most common attention-getting device is to call someone by name. People love to hear their names, even when the names are something as outlandish-sounding as Prelutsky and Winnikoff.

Above all, though, people love to see their names in print. We know of a very successful real estate saleswoman who puts this ego-drive to good use. Her method is as follows: Once she has a buyer interested in coming to the office, she types up a label with the prospect's name on it and slaps the label on a manila folder. The folder is set to one side of the desk, where it will be in full view of the prospect when the interview begins.

Can you imagine how much squirming and glancing that prospect goes through, wondering what is inside the folder? The saleswoman, however, never opens it. She calls the prospect by name. (To digress momentarily: Many sales people are stumped as to whether to call Mr. and Mrs. Doe by their first or last names. Often you can tell just by looking. If you are in doubt, however, it is not impolite to ask how they wish to be addressed. For example, after openers you might say, "Mr. and Mrs. Doe, do you mind if I call you Jane and John?" Usually, assuming that their names are, in fact, Jane and John, and not Hilda and Irving, they will not object. You will now be on a first-name basis, and half-way home to a sale. In short, the right kind of name-calling may trigger a beautiful friendship and a beautiful sale.)

Once the saleswoman has the prospect's attention, SHE ASKS A QUESTION. This feature of the chit-chat cannot be stressed strongly enough. Our beautiful, charming and lovely saleswoman is a professional who knows THE PERSON WHO ASKS THE QUESTIONS CONTROLS THE INTERVIEW.

You must remember this because most salespeople let their tongues rattle uncontrollably without putting their brains in gear. If you really want to succeed in our field, you must learn to KEEP YOUR BIG MOUTH SHUT. Keep it shut and learn to breathe through your nose. Once you have the knack of it, you will discover that you are blowing away far fewer sales.

At this point we feel we must quote the great authorities on the matter of silence. We quote first from Publilius Syrus, who knocked around as a successful actor and writer 2,000 years ago. He said: "Let a fool hold his tongue and he will pass for a sage."

Which is not bad for an old-time one-liner.

Now, let us briefly review the attention-getting devices our sweet and kind young lady has employed thus far:

1. THE FOLDER
2. THE NAME
3. THE QUESTION
4. THE MOUTH PADLOCKED.

So far, so good. In fact, if you can follow these simple rules, you are well on the way to being a glorious success in the sales field. What? You want more proof? O.K. Then.

By virtue of certain evolutionary processes, the human animal ended up on the ragtag end of a family tree that gave him two ears and one mouth. Mother Nature did this with the clear and unmistakable intent that we should listen twice as much as we speak. Furthermore, you will learn absolutely nothing about anything if you use your mouth. But you will learn a great deal by using your eyes and ears. The entire educational process depends on it. Do you remember all those obnoxious people in school who asked the most pointless, stupid and disruptive questions in class? We give you our personal guarantees that none of those blabbermouths ever became great salespeople. Now to listen to some of the prattle by the losers at the water cooler, you would think some of those guys had two mouths and one ear.

To be a *professional* salesperson, you must learn to listen. In fact, the true professionals of this world do a lot more listening than talking. For example, when you are afflicted with a horrible illness such as foot fungus or a wart on your schnoz, and it becomes impossible for you to bear your cross any longer, you go to your doctor. Unless he's also your brother-in-law, he does not blab on about everything he ever learned about the subtleties of treating athlete's foot or the trick of removing a wart without removing the nose.

First of all, he has his receptionist make up a folder with your name on it. Then, after a four-hour wait in his reception room, you are ushered into the Great Man's office and the sales job begins. The doctor does not start off the interview with a diatribe on his own problems, such as his hook or slice, but starts by opening the folder and asking pertinent questions. On a prorated basis of $2,643.29 per hour, he takes his own sweet time and cleverly lets you do most of the talking. For a price, he appears to be interested in *your* problems. By listening and writing, he gets you to open up. You automatically assume that he knows what he is doing. He is in control. Seven years and a ton of money later, when your athlete's foot has crawled up to your groin, you may begin to have your doubts about the Great Man's dermatological expertise, but you can't fault his approach to selling.

The manila folder will have grown to the size of the Los Angeles and New York phone books combined, and you will run the risk of being arrested by the vice squad the next time you scratch your itch in public, but the good doctor, cool professional that he is, will remain undaunted. And as you shuffle into his inner sanctum for the 216th time, he will look at you as he did on visit number one and in his best professional manner say, "Now, what seems to be the problem?"

So remember:

The man (or woman) who asks the questions controls the interview, not to mention the purse strings.

If some of the louts down at the water cooler have offended Mother Nature by developing one ear and two mouths, attorneys have more than compensated in the other direction. Many attorneys have sprouted ears all over their bodies and ended up with a peep-hole for a mouth. They hear everything. But they sure don't say much. The business of listening has become so profitable that by now, even the ceiling, phones, martini olives and bedsprings of America have developed ears.

We do not recommend sprouting extra head handles as a good sales tool. Two ears are plenty, unless you're serving corn on the cob to four people. Just use the two little black, white, yellow, red or pink conch shells you have already to good advantage, and your authors will be proud of you. If you do it well enough, even your supervisor will be proud of you.

On the matter of listening, we must tell of a young salesman who decided to go into the soap business because there was no other work available to him at the time. After two frustrating months on the job and few sales to show for his efforts, he became a bit despondent and thought of going into another field. While calling on one of the grocers in his territory, the young man asked:

"Is there something wrong with me or my soap?"

"Why, no!" the grocer replied.

"Then why isn't anybody buying my soap?"

"Well," the grocer replied, wiping his hands on his apron, "if you ask me, it's because of this here Depression we got going. Now, if I had things my way, we'd start off first by getting us a new president and get rid of all them pinko politicians in Washington! Why, if they keep on like this they'll be putting all us small merchants out of business, and *then* who will you sell your soap to, eh?"

"You really think it's that bad?" the young man asked, eager to hear more about pinko soap bubbles.

"*Think*?" the grocer replied, wiping his hands again on his apron and warming up to his subject, "*Think*?" he repeated. "I *know* that's what's the cause of all our troubles. Been in this here store 40 years and ain't never seen it so bad. Why just the other day a fellow from Washington come in here and . . . ."

The political discourse went on for 17 minutes straight. The grocer paused briefly to take care of a customer, then lectured the salesman for another 13 minutes. But by this time, the grocer was no longer wiping his hands on his apron. He was pounding his fist on the counter.

The young salesman listened with awe. When he was about to leave, the grocer said, "And by the way, send me a half-case of Palmolive, small."

"Yes, sir!"

We do not know what happened to that grocer, but we know for a fact that the salesman went on to become the hottest soap salesman in America. He ultimately became the president of his company.

He asked for advice and when it was offered, he listened.

He listened...

He listened...

He listened...

To get this point across, we cannot point to any greater authority than Albert Einstein, the theoretical physicist who startled the world with his theory of relativity. When asked what he thought was the best formula for success in life, the Professor replied:

"If a is success in life, then the formula is a equals x plus y plus z. In this formula x is work and y is play."

"And what is z?" he was asked.

"That," he replied, "is learning to keep your mouth shut."

As we bring this chapter to a close, we must give a warning about *unlistening, non-listening, tin-ear* salespeople who have their mouthmotor running full throttle and their brains completely disengaged. The No. 1 Worst Sellers *never* listen. For example, one buyer, when asked on the phone by a salesman, "Hi ya, Jake, how are ya?" replied, "Fine. I just had my leg amputated!"

"Great!" spouted the salesman. "Now, how many cases you want me to send this week?"

To summarize, you may get a prospect's attention in any of the following ways:

1. Call people by name.
2. Ask a question.
3. Better yet, ask for an opinion.
4. Make up a folder.
5. Listen enthusiastically and pay attention.
6. Never talk while the client is writing a check.
7. Once you get the order, *get out*. Fast!

MORE ATTENTION-GETTING DEVICES

The attention-getting devices in this world are so numerous and varied that we cannot suggest that one approach is clearly superior to the others. The important thing is that you make the sale. Furthermore, there are so many things for sale in this world that each product or service will require a separate, creative approach. In other words, you have to keep your mouth shut, your ears open and, think. A few examples will prove our point.

In the hierarchy of the sales kingdom, car salesmen rank very close to the bottom. In addition to receiving a certain amount of verbal abuse, car salesmen have been assaulted, shot, and run over with cars they sold. It is, in short, a high-risk occupation. In an effort to overcome this negative image, one bright, cheerful and energetic car salesman decided to separate himself from the common herd. In his own individual way, he went to the supermarket, took a bunch of paper bags from the produce department and went to work on the parking lot. That is, he reasoned, where the cars are.

With the aplomb of a man who really knows what he is doing, our hero proceeded to write a note to each car owner on the lot. He wrote the notes on torn-off segments of the paper bags. Armed with a ball-point pen and his trusty Blue Book, the salesman wrote a personal note telling each driver what his car was worth on a trade, what the cost of a new car would be, and what the monthly payments would run. Then he slipped the note under the windshield wiper. Each note had a folksy, personal touch, and the salesman generated a great many leads from his activity. Since leads are essential for sales, the salesman also generated a great many sales. Many more than his co-workers, who spent hours at the water cooler complaining when they weren't standing around the floor all day waiting for prospects to walk in the door. Since most walk-in trade includes a high percentage of lookers, a bit of pre-selling with scraps of paper bags can work wonders for a man's commissions.

The paper bag program worked so successfully that many of the supervisors of competing dealerships pounced on the bright idea of printing up letters on stationery that were made to *look* as though they had been torn from paper bags. Then they hired little boys to put these printed notes under windshield wipers of every car in supermarket parking lots. It didn't work because it was totally bogus.

If you have ever noticed the tons of scrap paper that float around supermarket parking lots, you must bear in mind that most of that trash is not from cookie wrappers. That trash is the result of inept decisions made by unthinking salespeople who are not very ambitious or creative.

On a more positive note, let us tell you of smart little boys who take up selling papers or shining shoes. There is a clever story about a highly successful shoeshine boy who seemed to be much busier and far more successful than his peers. Like the other shoeshine boys, he had the appearance of a street urchin. Except for his shoes. While his eager but dullwitted competitors would ask, "Shine, Mister?" the ambitious, clever, smiling and enthusiastic shineboy *polished his own shoes to a very high gloss* before asking the customer, "Shine for Sunday, mister?" or "Shine to brighten your day?" or "How about a nice shine for your sweetheart?" In the life of a shoeshine boy, little things like that can make a big difference at the end of the afternoon. Having an eye-catcher the customer cannot miss, then saying the right thing in the right way can be a great attention-getting device and result in some fine sales.

The same successful shineboy went on to selling carnations in front of a night club. When confronting a middle-aged or elderly couple, the flower boy would say, "Carnation for your girlfriend?" But when he confronted a teenage couple, he asked, "Carnation for your wife?"

He smiled.

He kept his shoes polished.

He sold a lot of carnations.

And he also sold newspapers.

Speaking of newspapers...

Many years ago, newspapers sold for a nickel, and newsboys were charged three cents apiece for the papers sold, allowing them a profit of two cents per sale. Our enterprising young hawker, who sold newspapers every Saturday at the L.A. Coliseum during the football season, usually sold twice as many as his fellow street urchins. He did this by observing where and when his best sales were made. By a process of trial and error, he would find just the right spots. The young newsboy arrived on the scene at 9 A.M. Since game time was 2 P.M., he followed a sales program that started at the hot dog stands. By making the rounds to all the food vendors around the entire Coliseum, he managed to dispose of 20 to 25 newspapers. This took him up to 11 A.M. During the next two hours, he hit the parking lots to the north of the Coliseum, selling perhaps 40 to 50 newspapers. During this period he was constantly on the move, always smiling, always carrying a bag lunch his mother had prepared for him. By 1 P.M., he stationed himself quietly by the side of an extremely busy ticket booth, keeping a sharp eye out for an open wallet. No, our young hero wasn't moonlighting as the spotter for a gang of pickpockets, but very often, in the pre-game excitement, he would catch the name and address on a football fan's driver's license. As the ticket purchaser then proceeded to make his way to the turnstile, the young newsboy dashed around the other side of the ticket booth. Before the fellow disappeared through the Coliseum gate, he would be confronted by the out-of-breath newsboy, whose pitch went something like this:

"Mr. Alan Lurie?" the newsboy asked.

"How did you know my name?"

"Buy a paper and I'll even tell you your address."

Sometimes he even sold two. The attention-getting device was excellent. In the last sales hour between 1 and 2 P.M., he was usually good for another 25 papers. It was a rare Saturday when the ten-year-old newsboy did not clear $2.00. Which was about twice what the other newsboys made. When the supervisor asked him how he did it, the child modestly replied, "I work twice as hard."

Those were fairly good years for that particular newsboy. He not only averaged $2.00 per day in profits, but he also got free admission to all the football games, courtesy of the *Herald-Express*. He kept at it from age nine to age 14. From 1939 to 1944. (The people at the old *Herald-Express* were so impressed with him that they offered him a corner at a busy intersection. But the boy's mother refused.)

And the boy learned a great deal besides selling.

One bleak Saturday during the winter of 1942, the newsboy noticed a line-up of soldiers at one of the Coliseum gates. They never bought papers, so the boy ignored them. But one drunken soldier, in a fit of meanness, told the newsboy to shut up and attempted to hit him. Wise to the ways of a drunken soldier standing in line, the newsboy jumped away. The drunken soldier's buddies restrained their ill-tempered comrade, but the newsboy was terribly offended. He began to shout for an MP. Since the newsboy had a well-developed set of vocal cords and the lungs to match, there was an MP on the scene in a matter of seconds.

"All right, what's the trouble here?" the MP asked.

"He tried to hit me!" the newsboy said, pointing an accusing finger at the bully.

The MP spotted the outline of a bottle beneath the soldier's jacket. With one whack of his nightstick, the MP broke the bottle. There was a sudden smell of whiskey in the air. The MP muttered something about keeping it quiet and moved on. Of course, if looks could kill, our newsboy would not be here today to tell his story. It was the lad's first introduction to a form of negative selling. But what he really learned on his long climb to the top of the ladder was that you can't make every sale and that sometimes your attention-getting device can cause you some problems.

The story of this particular newsboy-shineboy-carnation seller has a somewhat happy ending.

He went into real estate and became quite successful. To this day he always shines his shoes, will buy a carnation from anyone, and gives a tip of 50 cents to every newsboy he meets at the Los Angeles Coliseum.

And now, salespeople, we are going to hit you, rapid-fire, with a whole lot of attention-getters that have improved the worldly lot of Our Gang. (Our Gang is that singular group of people who are the No. 1 Bestsellers in their own bailiwick.)

We know of a cosmetic salesman who services department stores. He always wears a raccoon overcoat. Summer and winter. It is his trademark and gets the conversation going when he sits down with a buyer. He is a great salesman because he knows how to get the buyer's attention *immediately*.

Next!

When a friend of ours complained about how slow things were going at his wife's coffee shop, we sat down to talk. The coffee shop was located in a medical building and the doctors were not buying. The food was great, the service was good, but biz was bad. We recommended the following: "Have your wife and all the waitresses wear nurses' uniforms with short-short skirts. White shoes, white pantyhose, white caps, white everything." They balked. They squawked. But finally they did it. Business skyrocketed. The tips became larger. Everybody got the attention they wanted.

Next!

When Carol Channing first starred in *Hello, Dolly*, her husband, Charles Lowe (a veritable genius at attention-getting), sent her into the cold, wintry streets of New York with a tea-cart to serve tea or coffee to all the wonderful people who were waiting in line to buy tickets for her performance. When the show's leading lady asked John and Martha Theatergoer if they wanted one or two lumps of sugar in their tea or coffee, it caught everyone's attention. It was not only a media event, it also became the talk of the town. When *Hello, Dolly* was made into a movie, without Carol Channing, it did not fare too well. But the musical-theater version was an incredible success.

And *we* know why, don't we?

Next!

Your authors are ever so slightly afflicted with mental imbalances. When they go to get xerox copies at the print shop, there is always a question (and usually an argument) about *who pays*. One day, before they could enjoin the battle, their friend Peter, an actor, showed up also.

"Peter!" they said. "How are you doing?"

"O.K."

"Peter!" they repeated. "*How* are you doing?"

Peter hemmed and hawed, muttered and mumbled, before informing Burt and Al that he had become a chimney sweep.

"*A chimney sweep*!" the authors exclaimed. "That's terrible!"

"Wanna hear what's *worse*?" Peter asked morosely.

"What could be worse than that?" asked the horrified authors.

"I own the company. Employees, payroll, taxes, sick leave. All that stuff."

The authors gulped. For one of the few times in their

entire lives, they were speechless. Nay, *dumbfounded*!

"I hate it," Peter said. "I just hate going out there knocking on doors and drumming up business. I hate being a salesman. Do you know how many people slam their doors in my face *every day*?"

Your charming authors felt their collective blood run cold.

"Now look, Pete, you've got to get a hold of yourself. After all, the whole world's a stage and you've got to play a leading part. You've got to get the prospect's *attention*."

"Anybody ever tell you guys you repeat yourselves and you're crazy?" Peter asked.

"All the time, all the time, all the time!"

Peter laughed. "So what's all this bifflewhack about getting the prospect's attention!"

"Look, Pete, why don't you do something dramatic and go knocking on doors wearing a tuxedo and top hat?"

"What will that do?"

"What will that do? What will that do? What will that do? Why, it will make a very special character out of you."

"Y'know," Peter said, "that really sounds like a pretty good idea. Think it'll work?"

"Of course!" the authors said, heaving a sigh of relief.

"And be sure to wear white gloves," Prelutsky added. "That's a great attention-getter."

"Gee, thanks, fellas," Peter said, a smile on his lips for the first time. "Let me know if there's anything I can do for you guys sometime."

"You can do it right now!" the authors said. "Loan us seven bucks so we can pay for our copies on a book about selling."

With great reluctance, Peter made the loan. On the way out he was heard muttering, "Gee, and I thought *actors* were bad. But it seems *writers* are worse. Those guys are all crazy."

Peter not only went on to become a world-renowned chimney sweep, but business boomed to the point where he could be more selective about the parts he was willing to accept from major and minor studios. He began to enjoy his work more. When the authors finally paid him back weeks later, they encountered a man transformed. Peter was enthusiastic. About everything.

The authors, pleased as punch, left Peter a different man than they found him.

". . . . and the best part of the whole show," Peter told them as a parting shot, "is that I can study my lines in between calls."

Next!

We know of a great real estate salesman who does his great patriotic duty on the night of July 3rd every year. For it is late on that night he goes planting nice-sized American flags on the lawns of all the people in his neighborhood. When the gang gets up, early or late, on the Fourth of July, voilà! Instant recognition. It is beautiful and they love it. He has had many favorable comments, but never a complaint.

During the gas crunch in Southern California, this same salesman ran an ad offering five free gallons to anyone who ran out of gas. He got more calls than the Auto Club. He also generated a following and has done very well for himself and his firm. For sure, our attention-getting No. 1 Best Seller did not sell real estate to or for everyone who nicked him for five free gallons, but with such a wide and deep reservoir of goodwill, who cares?

So please remember: You can't *buy* goodwill. *You have to give it away to earn it back.*

Next!

Did you know W.C. Fields was a professional drowner at Atlantic City beach before he became a famous actor?

Yes, a professional drowner.

His job was to swim out a way, then pretend he was drowning, flailing, splashing, yelling and spouting before they dragged him ashore and gave him artificial resuscitation.

The attention-getting scheme was always a winner. For

when the curious crowds gathered to see if the besotted actor-to-be would revive, the hot-dog vendors sold massive quantities of their food and drink to them.

Later, they paid Mr. Fields an agreed-upon split and thanked him for all the attention.

PAY ATTENTION: BUY THE COMPANY

We wish to refer you to one of the world's great salesmen. This guy is so good he sells his company's electric shavers in Japan. He is a national treasure. His name is Victor Kiam. His book, *Going For It!*, is a good book for No. 1 Best Sellers. We recommend it highly. Our primary interest in the book was in the chapter entitled *Closing the Deal: The Art of Selling*. We quote the author: "If business was indeed a game, I decided that selling was its grandest competition."

Mr. Kiam claims he always sold morally acceptable products that were top of the line. Years ago, when he sold bras and girdles for Playtex, he was literally swept out of a small clothing store in Tupelo, Mississippi. The store owner, broom in hand, said he never wanted to see Kiam or his samples ever again. Investigating the reason for this, Kiam found out the previous Playtex salesman had overstocked the store and left the owner holding the straps. We quote the author: "This sort of oversell is sinful . . . . You want your accounts to know that you have their best interests at heart as well as your own." With expert and humane sales savvy, Mr. K. arranged for a larger customer to purchase the small customer's excess stock, and then *serviced the small account*. He knew that once you have the customer's attention, you keep it by *servicing the account* and making yourself indispensable. (Do what other salespeople are too lazy or stupid to do). Thereafter, the store owner became a loyal Playtex customer.

The No. 1 Best Selling Mr. Kiam also informs us that he gets a lot of attention by asking an unhappy customer: "Is there anything about my product you find unappealing?"

Then he listens very carefully to the customer's words.

Then he tries very carefully to resolve the problem.

Then he writes the order.

Then he gets out.

Mr. K., Best Seller that he is, writes in clear, understandable language of such undesirable matters as: (a) deadbeat buyers, (b) bad sales techniques, (c) bad salespeople, (d) painting an *unrealistic* picture for the prospect and (e) overtalking. He tells us: *Business is where you are*. A territory must be built up. And working 12-hour days, six days a week will surely make *you* a No. 1 Best Seller.

When you go for it, please be sure your attention-getting techniques are the very best. That you serve all your customers, big and small, with genuine concern. And when you do, rest assured Mr. K. and your authors will be very proud of you for taking our advice.

Proud indeed!

INTEREST

Not too many people have heard of the obscure but great electrical engineering genius by the name of Nikola Tesla. He developed the basics for a-c power transmission, wireless communication and a host of other inventions too numerous to mention here. Our entire system of power generation, transmission and use was conceived in the great mind of Nikola Tesla.

He died impoverished in 1943.

Thomas Alva Edison, on the other hand, is extremely well known to a great many people. (Especially when they pay their monthly dues to the Edison Company.) Edison was certainly a great inventor, but not a genius in the Tesla class.

Tesla was a mystery man who held his cards close to his chest. He was very secretive about what he was doing and how he was doing it. He was an extremely poor salesman.

Edison, on the other hand, was a great salesman. He started out as a newsboy and ended up selling the world on electric lights, motion pictures and the phonograph. Although he patented over a thousand inventions, no one ever asked Edison to install electric lights when they were new and untried. The so-called experts of the day pooh-poohed electric lights as a fad doomed to failure. Undaunted, Edison went forth and installed his new electric lights *free of charge*. *Free* electric lights were absolutely sensational; when they were turned on for the first time, they created an enormous interest in the product. Even though Mr. Edison left the scene in 1931, he did such a great job that we are still paying for it today. Now *that* is really selling!

Your ability to generate interest will determine whether you succeed or fail in the business of selling. Surely a man as brilliant as Tesla knew he had to sell the world on his inventions, but he did not know how.

Edison did.

The need for attention-getting is known very well by the copywriters who put out all those award-winning ads. (And by anyone who read the two previous chapters.) But since the copywriters never follow up on those ads, they are among the world's most exploited and abused wage slaves. Copywriters may get all the glory, but salesmen get most of the money. How? By arousing interest.

Once you have gained the prospect's attention, either by ads, doorbell-ringing, letters, folders or pulling them in off the street, you must arouse their interest. The best way to arouse interest is to tell the prospect what you are going to do for him or her.

We know of a talented author who wrote a book about the land business. In an effort to generate sales, he decided to visit every bookstore in California. After finding out how many bookstores there were in California, he cut his project down to *most* bookstores in California. Since he did not want to walk into the bookstores empty-handed, he decided to enter each store with a small gift for the proprietor or manager. His choice of gift was a small box of chocolate-covered mints.

So he did the most logical thing and called various candy wholesalers to get information on their prices. The wholesale candy manufacturers would not sell him their products because he did not have a retail resale license. In the parlance of the literary-minded, this is what is known as stupidity. But our author-hero was not to be dissuaded from his noble purpose: namely, to arouse the interest of the bookdealers in his book.

So he trotted off to the local discount department store and asked at the candy counter for their cheapest box of mints. The product was marked at 98¢ retail, but wholesaled at 60¢.

"What if I buy a gross?" the author asked.

"A who?" the clerk asked.

"A gross. Twelve times twelve. One hundred and forty-four."

"Is that a special kind of candy?" the clerk asked.

Undaunted, our hero replied, "No. You see, I would like to buy 144 boxes of mints."

"Oh."

"Maybe even more."

"Well, I can't sell them to you," the clerk said.

"Why not?"

"Because I don't have that many in stock."

"Well, is there any way I can order them?" he asked.

"I don't know," she replied. "You'll have to talk to my supervisor. Wait here and I'll go get her."

Our author-hero blanched, but maintained his composure. A few moments later, he noticed a group of women at the far end of the candy department, whispering and pointing his way. He assumed, correctly, that they were talking about him. When the clerk and her supervisor approached, he girded his loins.

"Hello, I'm Ms. Simpkins and I understand you would like to buy 144 boxes of mints. Is that correct?"

"Well, not really. You see, I'd like to buy five gross if the price is right."

"Five gross?" the supervisor said, her eyes widening slightly. "Why that's five times 144 which is—"

"That's 720 boxes of mints," the bright young author said.

"What are you going to do with them?" Ms. Simpkins

asked.

"I'm going to make a big mint pie," he replied.

The clerk and her supervisor looked a bit incredulous. "You're sure, now?" the supervisor asked.

"Of course I'm sure! Now, what do I have to do to get a price on 720 boxes of mints?" the author wanted to know.

"Well, first of all, we'll have to talk to the store manager."

The young author blanched again.

When the store manager arrived on the scene, he was all smiles.

"You like mints?" he asked.

"I'm crazy about mints."

"Fine. If you'll give us a deposit for five gross of Poopsie's Famous Mints, we'll be glad to order them for you at 60¢ per box. Now, just a minute while I get a piece of paper and figure this out."

"Don't bother," the author said, "It comes to $432 cash. Will a 10 percent deposit be all right?"

"Oh yes, that will be just fine." Turning to his second-in-command, the store manager said, "Ms. Simpkins, will you write up the order and take this man's money?"

"Yes, sir."

As soon as the store manager was gone, Ms. Simpkins turned to the clerk and said, "Suzie, write this up and take the man's money. O.K., honey?"

Suzie was left alone with the author. In her shy and retiring way, she took his order.

"Your name, please."

"Leo Tolstoy."

"How do you spell that?"

What this proves is that there is a deep, wide and jagged line that separates good salespeople from clerks and order-takers.

Back to the point: the author had a theory. The author wanted to catch the bookdealers' *attention*. He wanted to generate *interest* in his book. And he wanted very much to *sell* his product.

The author went on to see his noble work go through two editions in hardback and far more than two editions in paperback. Not only did the book sell well, but the author is very well remembered by all those lovely, exploited people in the bookstores. The author was genuinely interested in them, else he would not have made such a glorious mint pie in their honor. The bookdealers, in their turn, took a great interest in him. In almost every bookstore, the author was asked how the book was doing. The matter of interest was mutual and reciprocal. But the author did not stop there. When he appeared on TV or radio, he passed out boxes of mints and followed each appearance with a letter thanking the commentators for their fine interviews. It is the kind of groundwork that might make his next book sell even better.

But let us continue with our discussion of arousing interest. *The key feature in arousing interest is to tell the prospect of benefits to be derived from buying the product or service.*

For example, we know of a real estate salesman who works exclusively on listing properties for sale. He never sells these properties. He leaves that to other, more heroic members of the sales crew in his office.

Since a listing commission represents about 40 percent of the total commission, this salesman makes a practice of knocking on doors (to get *attention*), handing the lady or man of the house a check for $1,000 (to create *interest*), and saying, "How would you like to sell your house with this check as a deposit?" (to generate *desire*). If he is not thrown out on his ear or knocked down the stairs, he gets them signed up for a sale right then and there (to get the *close* he wants).

Since the salesman is looking for a listing only, he tries to get the prospective sellers to list their property at a salable, fair market price. He then explains to the sellers that there are many prospective buyers who will buy at that price and that a *real* $1,000 deposit check will be forthcoming soon. As far as the salesman is concerned, he closes his deal when the homeowners sign the listing. He achieves his purpose by telling the prospect what he is going to do for her. He does this in question form. He gives facts and certain corresponding benefits. He studies the neighborhood, has an up-to-date computer print-out of neighborhood house prices, and knows what he is talking about. He makes the homeowner the hero (or heroine) of the situation. We know for a fact that this particular salesman makes more than any other salesperson in his office.

Going back for a moment to that highly successful car salesman: he also arouses interest by asking people if they would like to get a fixed number of dollars for their used car. If they respond and show up in the showroom, he helps the situation along by telling them what he is going to do for them. Above all, he does not talk too much. Furthermore, he remembers that he is dealing with people who have responded to his paper bag notes. All of these prospects are pre-sold. The odds are weighted heavily in favor of selling these people, whereas the odds are very much against selling casual lookers.

Once the *attention* has been gained, let us say, by sending out letters, it is absolutely essential for a good salesman to follow up all the letters with a phone call to start generating interest. To be sure, most prospects will not buy. But those who do can make the day very profitable.

On the matter of writing letters and following up with a phone call, it is advisable to write to the president of a given company (or other such top-dog, like the homeowner). A week later, when you call to talk to Mr. President, his secretary will reply, "What is this in reference to?"

You will say, "This is in reference to my letter last week concerning the purchase of Grand Coulee Dam." (Or whatever else you may have for sale.)

"Oh, yes. I remember," the secretary replies. And she *should* remember, because *she* is probably the one who is running the company. But *he* is making all the big sales.

"Oh, yes, I remember now. We referred your letter to our company treasurer, Mr. Prinkle. Hold the line a moment, please, and I'll transfer the call."

Now when Mr. Prinkle gets on the horn, you must greet him with, "Hello, Mr. Prinkle, my name is Jack Doe and I'm calling in reference to that letter Mr. President sent you concerning the purchase of Grand Coulee Dam."

At this point, you may be sure that Mr. Prinkle is all ears. He has heard the name of his boss, Mr. President. His interest will certainly be aroused. But you must be brief. If you make your point clearly, quickly and honestly, you may even get rid of the dam. (Unlike marriage, great deals are not made in heaven. They are sometimes made when prospects least expect it. You will pass your exams in salesmanship when you pull off just such a coup.)

We hope you have found this chapter on interest stimulating and thought-provoking. Since we started out with a commentary on Edison's sales ability, we would like to conclude with a look at what an interesting man he was.

Long before he could *sell* the electric light bulb, he had to invent it. On approximately the thousandth try, he was successful. When a reporter asked him if he ever got discouraged, or found the failures depressing, or ever thought of giving up, or lost interest, Edison replied, "Not at all. What I discovered was 999 ways *not* to build an electric light bulb."

DESIRE

On the technical side of creating desire, you must try to paint a word-picture of the prospect using and benefiting from the purchase of your product or service. Put the customer in the picture and make him or her the hero or heroine. Try to do this with verbs in the present tense. And if you feel you can do two things simultaneously, smile.

Inasmuch as you have come this far with us, we are going to grace you with an example of this very concept.

Once upon a time, there was a young man who worked for a newspaper in a big city. He was a big, strong, healthy young man with a young wife and baby to support. He loved his wife and baby, but he sure had a lot of mixed feelings about his supervisor. His supervisor had bushy eyebrows, no neck, and teeth that looked like stale puffed rice. On mornings-after, the supervisor's teeth looked like stale puffed wheat. And on top of that, he had the kind of breath that could peel paint off walls.

The young man was happy with his wife and child and he loved to be home with them. But when he thought of his work, he was very unhappy. Unlike the more fortunate people on the staff who did interesting work, the young man pushed around huge rolls of paper all day long. He envied the other paper-pushers—the people upstairs—who had nothing to complain about because they were closer to Heaven on the fourth floor than he was in the basement. One day when his supervisor arrived at work after a particularly rough night in the bars—with his teeth looking like deep-fried soot—the young man became particularly miserable. His misery reached the point of desperation. In keeping with that world-wide yearning for improving one's station in life, the young man decided to talk to his Uncle Charley, who was in real estate. In fact, he had bought his home through Uncle Charley. And he got a good deal. And Uncle Charley got the commission.

So that night the young man and his wife invited Uncle Charley to dinner and discussed their problems with him.

"Well, it's like this," Uncle Charley said expansively "I'm just a salesman down at Day Realty, and I know Mr. Day doesn't like to hire part-time salesmen, but let me see what I can do. Now, you realize that you'll have to go to school and study to get a license. Are you willing to do that?"

"Yes, sir!" the nephew said emphatically.

"And since Day Realty is the busiest office in the city, you won't have much training or much help, but you sure will learn the business there."

Before he could go on, his niece-in-law asked meekly, "How much money can Richard make?"

"If he works hard, maybe $25,000 this year. And much more next year. Probably $100,000. If the market is right. But the market fluctuates and you always have to prepare yourself for the bad times. BELIEVE me, the bad times always come."

The niece-in-law said a silent prayer for the good times and gave Uncle Charley an extra-large helping of dessert.

Richard accepted the challenge. He studied assiduously for six months and passed his salesman's examination. With the bloom of youth on his cheeks and a great love for his family in his heart, he went to Day Realty every Saturday and Sunday to try his hand at selling real estate. He did this for six months, and did not make a sale.

His wife, meanwhile, did not realize what a tough time of it her husband was having. She still had happy visions of an extra $25,000 that first year. But she had a problem with her husband's job, too. She didn't appreciate the fact that he was away from home so much. In a meek and timid voice, she mentioned this to him.

"Not you, too." he said.

"What do you mean?" she asked.

"Well, I'm failing at real estate. Down at the office they call me Poor Richard. And now you're unsatisfied, too."

"Oh, no!" Poor Richard's wife cried. She put her head in her hands and sobbed uncontrollably. The baby cried too. Richard only barely managed to choke back his own sob. He put his big, strong arms around wife and child and tried to comfort them. Between sniffles, his wife looked up at him and said, "Well, at least you still have your job on the news-paper."

At which point all thought of crying vanished. Instead, Poor Richard thought of his supervisor with no neck and the chameleon-like teeth. He girded his loins.

"He's the only man in the world whose teeth change color every day!" he said.

"What are you *talking* about?"

"Some days his teeth are yellow, some days brown and some days they're even black. They're hardly ever white! I can't stand it!"

"Richard, what *are* you talking about?"

"My supervisor's teeth!"

Whereupon Poor Richard's wife, not knowing what to make of her husband's strange behavior, cried even more uncontrollably.

"I can't stand it!" he said again. "I've got to get out of there!"

"But how?"

"I don't know, but I'll do it! I'll talk to Uncle Charley."

And he did.

Their conversation went something like this:

"Now look," Uncle Charley said, "you've got to be doing something wrong. You *seem* to be doing everything right, but something's wrong. You come in every weekend bright-eyed and bushy-tailed, you're clean-shaven and your suit is pressed—"

"And my teeth are white," Richard added.

"What has that got to do with it?"

"Plenty."

"Well, I think we better talk this over with Old Man Day. He's been around a long time and he's one of the best salesmen in the business."

"Do you really think he can help me, Uncle Charley? I'm getting sort of desperate."

"*You're* getting desperate! *Mr. Day* is getting desperate! He's been giving you a phone and a desk for six months and you haven't brought a dime into the office. You must be doing something wrong. If you don't make a sale pretty soon, he's going to throw you out on your keester."

"Really?"

"Really."

The next Saturday morning Poor Richard, true to form, arrived at Day Realty to put in his time. Before he could sit down to collect his thoughts, though, Mr. Day was upon him.

"Don't get too comfortable, Richard. I had a long talk with your Uncle Charley, and I'm going to try to help you out. If he wasn't such a good friend, I never would have consented to this arrangement."

Poor Richard had a sinking sensation in the pit of his stomach.

"I want to see what you're doing wrong," Mr. Day said. "I'd like to have you take me to the Prinkle house—you know which one, don't you? I want you to take me there and try to sell me the house."

"Yes, sir, that's the FHA repossession. It's been fixed up very nicely."

"That's right. Now let's go."

"Your car or mine?" Poor Richard asked.

"You're doing the selling, so let's take your car. Are you sure you've got everything? Have you got the key to the Prinkle house?"

"Oh, no, I forgot."

"Well, get it. It's number 72 hanging up on the key-board."

Poor Richard got the key and they were off. On the way to the Prinkle house, he jabbered incessantly about what a nice day it was, the desirability of the area, the number of schools, the name, rank and serial numbers of all the churches, the shops and their owners, the trouble with the local phone company, and the problems he was having on the job at the newspaper. He went on without interruption for ten minutes straight.

When they arrived at the Prinkle house, Richard started to get out of the car. Mr. Day put a restraining hand on him. "Just a minute," Mr. Day said. "I think I'm beginning to see a pattern here."

"A pattern?" Poor Richard said.

"Yes, a pattern. A losing pattern."

"A losing pattern? What do you mean?"

"I mean just that. For one thing, you talk too much. You've got to learn to keep your mouth shut. You're talking when you should be listening."

"Listening? But if I don't say anything, nobody in the car will talk."

"That's where you're wrong. You break the ice by asking questions. People like you more when you ask them questions. They think you're interested in them."

"But what kind of questions?"

"Intelligent questions like why did you pick this area or how many bedrooms do you need, or what kind of house are you looking for. In that way you qualify the buyer."

"Qualify? Richard asked. "What does that mean?"

"If they qualify, if they have the money, motivation and

desire, they're buyers. If they don't qualify, they're look-ers."

"Oh."

"And one other thing, don't ever let me hear you com-plain again. Nobody is interested in your problems. If you give the impression of being a crybaby and a loser, nobody will ever buy anything from you. I don't care what kind of heathen nitwit your supervisor is. I already *know*. I sold him a house. He lines the walls with beer cans and he's a terrible guy, but I sold him a house. I promised him five cases of Johnny Walker Black Label and he bought the house. So don't ever complain.

"Everybody hates a loser. Sometimes they hate a winner too. But they *always* hate a loser. When the boys in the of-fice are standing around the water cooler or the coffee pot complaining about the deals they missed, get away from those people as fast as you can. The *losers* in this or any other business would rather talk about a million-dollar deal they lost than a hundred-dollar deal they made. Among the losers, blabbing is a substitute for thinking and gossip takes the place of truth.

"So remember, *nobody* in this business cares about *your* problems. But since you're the salesman, you're supposed to care about other people's problems. Just like a psychiatrist, you get *paid* for listening. If you miss one deal, go on to the next one right away." Mr. Day let go of Richard's shoulder. "O.K., let's go inside and you give me the sales pitch."

They entered the house and Poor Richard made a com-plete tour of the premises, pointing out, "This is the living room, and this is the master bedroom, and this is the bath-room, and this is the den, and this is the closet," and on and on. When he was through, Mr. Day said, "Does it have an attic?"

"I don't know," Richard said. "I'm not sure."

"Richard, I don't know what we're going to do with you, but you sure go about this thing bass-ackwards. For one thing, *you don't know your product and that's terrible!*"

"But I know where all the rooms are."

"So does the kid next door. But that's not what sells houses. Now, if you don't know if there's an attic, you tell the customer, 'I don't know, but I'll find out and let you know.' *And be sure to let them know.* And just for your information, this house does have an attic. You get into it by a crawl hole in the upstairs bedroom closet. All these tract houses have that feature. Now let's go outside and I'll sell *you* the house."

They went out, turned around and started over. On their way in Mr. Day said, "Boy, what a beautiful day!" He opened the door and let Poor Richard in. They walked right up to the fireplace in the living room.

"Have you ever lived in a house with a fireplace?" Mr. Day asked.

"No, sir."

"A fireplace is a nice thing. Of all the nice things about a house, a comfortable house, a fireplace is somewhere near the top of the list."

"Why?" Richard asked.

"Well," Mr. Day said, smiling, "you've got to imagine yourself in front of this fireplace on Christmas morning. when it's cold and raining or snowing outside. Do you have any kids?"

"One. Just one. But we're going to have another one. At least that's what my wife tells me."

"Do you have a boy or a girl?"

"A little girl. Eighteen months."

"Well, when she's four or five and she's got a little sister or a little brother who's two or three, and they come running downstairs on Christmas morning and start tearing at their presents under the Christmas tree and you're standing here with your arm around your wife and there's a fire going in this fireplace—well, Richard, let me tell you, that is one of life's finest moments. Tell me, do you ever write poetry?"

"No, sir."

"Well, at a moment like that, you'll *think* poetry. Believe me, I lived through it with my own kids and now I'm living through it with my grandchildren. Every year I buy each of the kids a cord of wood. It sure is a great feeling. What's more, if you ever have a rough winter day at work and you come home with the weight of the world on your shoulders, it's nice to forget everything just by playing with the fire. You can waste hours poking it and messing with it—or just looking at it. It's a very pleasurable way to waste time. I love it. Other people love it. You'll love it, too. Do you think you'd enjoy a home with a fireplace?"

"Oh yes, sir!"

"Richard, let me tell you one other thing. If it's raining one winter night—a Saturday night—and you don't really have anyplace to go or anything to do, and the kids have had their baths and are in bed and you're alone with your wife in front of the fireplace, that's another one of life's great pleasures. If you have any kind of a fertile imagination, you'll enjoy that fire in more ways than one. I'll wager that you and your wife will fall asleep in front of the fireplace. And when you wake up you'll laugh about it and drag yourselves off to bed. I know, because I lived through it—having a house with a fireplace can be one of life's great pleasures." There was a long pause, then Mr. Day started walking away, saying, "O.K., let's go."

"But you didn't show me the house!"

"Richard, you ninny, I don't *have* to show you the house. You can *see* it for yourself. *Selling* is my job. My job is to find out what you like about the house—or what you *might* like about the house—and sell you on that. If you like knotty pine, we'll go into a knotty pine den and count the knots. If you like a large work area, we'll go in the garage and figure out how to arrange your workbench. Once I sold a house to a writer who wanted a quiet place to work. I got him up into the attic, and that attic is so small both of us couldn't get into it—but that's what sold him the house: an attic with a light in it."

"Was he a good writer?" Richard asked.

"Good? I don't know if he was good, but I do know he was crazy. All writers are crazy. Does any normal person enjoy working in a cramped attic? Richard, listen to me. Because I don't have much time to train people. Your job is to find out what people want and try like the dickens to help them get it.

"Let me tell you a story. When I first started selling, I sold insurance. I went straight to the office of the richest, meanest, toughest old coot in town. Old Man Grundy. He was a straight-laced Calvinist. I cooled my heels in his outer office for hours before he would see me. When I finally got in to see him, I could barely talk, I was so scared. Somehow, though, I managed. But I didn't walk in and say: *How would you like to buy some insurance*? Instead, I said to the old man: *Mr. Grundy, I know you don't need any insurance, but I have a program to help you with your missionary work.* That was the only time I ever saw him smile.

"Then I laid out my program to him. And before the week was out we had set up The Grundy Foundation and I was quite a celebrity in Wilksville. Now *that's* selling! But I sure didn't tell him about my problems. The surest path to failure is to tell everybody your troubles.

"O.K., now let's go. By the way, did you bring your deposit receipt book?"

"Oh, no. I forgot."

"Well, don't ever forget again. Carry it with you at all times. Carry two pens and a deposit receipt book. They're the tools of your trade. And don't be afraid to ask people to sign on the dotted line. All right, let's go."

When they got back to the office, Mr. Day turned to Richard and said, "Do you think you learned anything?"

"Oh, yes *sir*. That fireplace speech was just great!"

"Well, let me tell you, Richard, you've gotten the benefit of 30 years of selling experience in just one hour. Now if you don't make a sale in the next two weeks, I'LL FIRE YOUR ASS!"

For a brief instant Poor Richard's vision blurred. He thought he saw Mr. Day's teeth change color.

Time marched on.

With the fading bloom of youth on his cheeks and a great love for his family in his heart, Poor Richard girded his loins, determined to sell that house just as Mr. Day had told him to do it.

Two weeks later he came dancing into the office. He was elated. He jumped up and clicked his heels. He had just sold his first house. In one hand he had a check, and in the other hand, a signed deposit receipt. He charged into Mr. Day's office and told him the good news.

Mr. Day smiled and shook his hand.

Then Richard dashed off to tell Uncle Charley.

It was truly a great moment in Richard's life. And no one ever called him Poor Richard again.

Richard went on to become the pride and joy of both his family and employer. He not only became a member of The Chamber of Commerce, Lions, Optimists, Rotarians, P.T.A. and Y.M.C.A., he also became a TOP PRODUCER in his local area. Furthermore, he quit his job and said goodbye to his supervisor and his supervisor's bad teeth forever.

His story, however, has a somewhat sad ending. For no matter how hard Mr. Day and Uncle Charley tried, Richard would never, ever sell a house without a fireplace.

In sum: remember, to create desire you must (1) try to paint a word-picture of the prospect using and benefiting from the purchase of your product or service, (2) put the customer in the picture and make him or her the hero or heroine, (3) speak with verbs in the present tense and (4) if you feel like it, smile.

CLOSE

The action we are all looking for is the closing action. As salespeople, we all want to close the deal. And the best way to get the action you want is to ask for it.

Every sales manager and every sales book has something to say about closing. The stories and truisms are legion. "Nothing happens until you close" is one of them. Another is "Nothing happens in this world until somebody sells and somebody buys." But to get that kind of action, you must ask for it. To illustrate our point, we must relate a brief but true story about one of the world's great industrialists. His name was Henry Ford.

One time, it seems, the Great Mr. Ford was in the market for a very large insurance policy for himself. And when he bought it, the news was blazoned across the headlines of every newspaper, not only in Dearborn, Michigan, but in Detroit as well. One of Mr. Ford's closest friends, an insurance agent, read the news with stunned incredulity. The insurance agent's friend, Henry Ford, had purchased that huge insurance policy from a competitor, a completely unknown salesman. With a terrible feeling of anguish, the insurance agent burst in on his industrialist friend and demanded: "Why, Henry? Why didn't you buy that policy from me?"

Henry looked up and said, "You never asked."

In this case, simply asking would have produced the right kind of action. The insurance agent could have easily closed his deal.

Do not be afraid to start with a trial close by asking a question. For example, find out what people *don't* like about your product. If they say the color is wrong or the doors do not hang right, you can be sure the prospect is *thinking* about your product. Then you should take the next logical step and find out what people *do* like about your product. Once you have started this kind of dialogue, your chances of closing are infinitely better than for sales people who *argue* with the customer. The color can be changed and the doors can be made to hang right, but nothing will get an offended prospect to return to the scene of an insult.

There are many ways to close a deal, and although you may instinctively know when to ask, you must also know *how*.

To illustrate: we know of a great salesman who learned his selling lessons in the Army. As an incorrigible cut-up, the young man found himself pulling K.P. quite often. Rather than waste his time bemoaning his fate, he decided to make an in-depth study of the eating habits of recruits in boot camp. He decided to take a three-pronged approach. When dispensing apricots in the chow line, he asked the following:

1. You don't want apricots, do you?
2. Result: 90 percent of the GIs said no.
3. You *do* want apricots, don't you?
4. Result: 50 percent of the GIs said yes.
5. What'll it be, one dish of apricots or two? Result: 90 percent of the GIs took apricots. (50 percent took one dish and 40 percent took two dishes.)

That same salesman sells a lot of computer equipment for his company today, and whenever he has the chance, *he gives his customer a choice of buying decisions.* Then he tries to close.

But he does not stop with that approach alone. He has a flair for creative selling. He once got wind of the fact that an airframe manufacturer was in need of a complete computer system similar to the type his company sold. With no previous contact and no appointment, the salesman loaded one of the company's 3,000-pound computer systems on a truck and drove to the airframe firm to make a cold call on the company president. When the salesman finally got into the president's office, he asked where he might install the computer for a demonstration and made a $100,000 sale in less than two hours.

He made an assumptive close.

Of course, going directly to the president of a company is not always the right move. To illustrate, there is a story told of James H. Rand, Jr., who started out as a salesman of bank equipment and rose to the position of Board Chairman of Remington Rand, Inc. As a young salesman, Rand called on Frank Munsey, who was preparing to open Munsey Banks in Baltimore, Maryland, and Washington, D.C. The eager salesman spent quite a bit of time with Munsey, who wanted to know a great deal about the bank equipment Rand was selling. When the interview was over, Munsey said, "I'll give you a letter to my manager in Washington and you can go after him for the order."

With high hopes, Rand caught the next train to Washington, told the story to Munsey's manager and got a $25,000 order for bank equipment. At that time in history, when $25,000 was big, big money, the sale was so large it made headlines in many of the financial newspapers of the day. But in his eager haste to close the sale, Rand forgot all about the letter from Munsey. He found the letter in his pocket some time later, opened it and read, "*Learn all you can from this man, but do not buy anything from him if you can help it.*"

That's what a little enthusiasm can do for you. If you are

hot enough, you can even close by mistake.

There are an infinite number of approaches to getting the action you want, and every close will be different. But you must be aware of the possibilities of a close. Even if people say *no*, they still might mean *maybe*. And if they mean *maybe*, you can very likely get them to say *yes*. For example, when Mrs. Home Buyer complains about the hideous color of the living room, you can be sure she is thinking about a remodeling job. And if she's thinking about *that*, she's already thinking about buying the house.

One of the most successful real estate saleswomen we know makes a point of *never* showing more than two houses to a prospect. Then she asks, "Which house do you like best?" If the client shows a preference, she will continue to work with him or her. If not, she will go to the next prospect. She always gives her prospect a choice of buying decisions.

When asked where she learned this she said, "I started out as a leasing agent in New York. We would show a man two offices and then ask, 'Which view do you like best?' If he was undecided, we considered him a deadbeat. Then we would go on to the next prospect."

Now, the fact that the preceding approach works well for our friend does not necessarily mean it will work well for you or for us. In fact, Winnikoff, who is ever so slightly deranged, has sometimes worked *for years* with prospects who have a lot of wrinkles to iron out of their deals. And the amazing part of it is that most of his deals close. On more than one occasion he has had a client say, "You know, Winnikoff, you're *different*."

At which point he smiles and says nothing. It is his firm conviction that a closed deal merits a closed mouth.

SOME CLOSING TECHNIQUES

The closing technique for a computer saleslady is far different from that of a carny barker. And they both differ from the technique of a gandy dancer. (Grab the dictionary, kids.)

We, therefore, feel compelled to give some advice and some examples.

First, the advice.

Once you have made the sale, GET OUT. If you prattle uncontrollably in the customer's presence, he may cancel the order. Just as we are sometimes sorry for things said in anger, we can be just as sorry for crazy things said in moments of extreme joy. When you are overcome with extreme emotion, chances are you will not be thinking clearly. But that does not mean you should cut off the client in any way. It means you should not make a pest of yourself.

After the sale is made, SERVICE THE ACCOUNT! Whether you sell used cars, microchips, homes, insurance or wholesale books, SERVICE THE ACCOUNT!

Service the account by phone, mail, or in person. But do it. Do it in a sensitive, intelligent, and honestly helpful way, and we promise you results. To be sure, there will be problems. Some of the accounts will complain. You are advised most strongly to service those complaints with the same honest, good feelings you felt at the moment of sale. That is the key to great sales. Make yourself indispensable to the customer. You must service the account. It may be unpleasant, but it must be done if we are to succeed.

For sure, you are going to run into some bad people in our business, make the sale and then wish you had not. These bad people drive everyone crazy. The bad guys probably cause over 90% of the problems and provide only 5% of the business. All lending institutions spend more time trying to collect from a small percentage of deadbeats than from all their good accounts combined. Therefore, avoid bad sales. Do not close a sale just because *you* like the deal but *only* if it is good for the customer as well. Your failure to follow this simple advice will absolutely come back to haunt you.

Don't believe it?

Then believe this: irate customers have murdered salespeople. Car salesmen have been run down by their lemons. Gun salesmen have been known to be on the receiving end of a bullet they sold to a subsequently unhappy customer.

Ours is a high-risk business. Therefore, when you close your deals, avoid bad people and bad situations. But no matter what the pain and agony, try to close the deals you believe in.

Not too long ago, we went to a sales seminar and had a great time listening. The girls and boys put on a great dog-and-pony show. We were amused and we were impressed. The seminar was mainly hype, but sometimes that's what it takes to reaffirm our own sales standards.

One of the highlights of the evening was *closing techniques*. The speaker discussed 30 ways to close the sale. There were rapid-fire examples of the quote-sheet close, the silent close, yes-yes no-no close, we're-far-apart close, what's-your-best-deal close, sold-sign close, sorry close, proposal close, hesitation close, private-loan close (be sure to watch out for this one—it could cost you dearly), high-pressure close, low-pressure close, ten-dollar-bill close, have-to-talk-to-wife (or husband) close, buy-the-lunch close and on and on.

Not once were customer needs or desires mentioned.

One of the stories they fired at us went like this.

Big Ben Bettenberg, a veritable giant of a salesman, started out selling pots and pans. He was so "good" at it— "Cook in my pots and pans and you'll save all the vitamins and your family will be so rich and healthy you're sure to go to Heaven"—the Number One Pot made him a sales manager.

Big Ben went around banging his pots and pans and scraping the bottom of the barrel for salespeople. On one occasion he came up with a bankrupt farmer by the name of Bleak Zeke.

Bleak (or Zeke, as his friends called him) came in with very few sales. Big Ben went to Zeke's farmhouse to find out why.

When he walked into the dark and dilapidated kitchen, he took one look at the ancient wood-burning stove and had his answer. Zeke was cooking with a set of Sears, Roebuck and Co. pots and pans! Well! If you are going to sell Fitalife pots and pans, should you not be cooking with Fitalife? Should not a Chevy salesman drive a Chevy and a Ford saleslady a Ford? Of course!

Big Ben, his sacred belief in the purity of his product somewhat compromised and his innate sense of closing techniques nearly shattered, picked up a skilletful of cold, greasy pork-and-beans and flung the whole mess of pottage against the wall. As the skillet clanged to the floor and the beans slid slowly down the wall, Big Ben convinced Zeke, for his own good and for the health and prosperity of his family, that he should cook only in Fitalife vessels.

The deal closed.

Zeke died and went to Fitalife Heaven.

Big Ben went into the insurance business, wears a Rolex, lives in a big house and bought a Chevy truck for his college-age daughter. At least that's what he told us at the end of his diatribe on closing.

We do not want you to make those kinds of sales. Those are Big Ben Bully sales. They offend us on religious grounds. For instance, what if Zeke came back to haunt the Bully? Then what? The whole episode gives our profession a bad name, that's what.

So remember: clean deals, clean closing.

Do it our way and we will tell you about some genuinely important closing techniques, and how to employ them.

THE PUPPY DOG CLOSE

It is written in an ancient text that the Puppy Dog Technique is a great way to close a sale. And we've got more stories to tell you about puppy dogs than a pet food salesman. Those stories, however, will have to wait for our next book. The close is what is important here. The puppy dog close goes as follows:

When a man walks into a pet shop with his seven-year-old child and asks to see that puppy dog in the window, the shop owner, all smiles, takes the puppy from his kennel and—ignoring the father completely—hands the puppy to the child. Can you imagine that sweet, lovely child giving up that cuddly puppy? Can you imagine the father's reluctance to turn off the joy his child feels while holding that puppy? Hence, the puppy dog close.

How does this apply to the sale of other goods and services? In the case of selling computer programming, it is simply a case of: try it, and if it doesn't work, we'll discontinue the service. Two years and 14 billion dollars later, it does not matter whether the customer likes or dislikes his puppy dog, since it is now a full-grown animal. At this point the customer is fully committed. Hence, the puppy dog close.

How does this apply to the sale of television sets? We know of an appliance dealer in Des Moines, Iowa, who so dreaded the thought of going back to cornhusking that he read a book on selling. When color television burst upon the world, this particular appliance dealer set up a small viewing section in his store, where his friends and neighbors could come and view the modern miracle. He passed out free coffee and doughnuts to the viewers. At the first indication of interest on the part of the viewer, he would say, "Now don't worry about the price. Just let us come out and install it. You think about it for two weeks and if you don't like it, we'll come and take it back. Absolutely no charge, no gimmick, no obligation. Just try it. No harm in trying."

After installation and the subsequent two-week period, the dealer would call—during prime time, of course—and ask Mrs. Farmer how she liked the set.

"We haven't decided yet, but I'm busy right now. Can I call you back?"

"Don't bother, Mrs. Farmer. Just keep the set another two weeks. That's right, no cost or obligation."

After one month, you can be certain that all of Mrs. Farmer's neighbors knew she had a color television. And what would the neighbors and their children say if a color set was removed from the Farmer's house in the clear light of day? It's almost enough to make a man want to become an appliance salesman. In this case, the puppy dog close worked and worked very well. (Which is probably more than you could say for the set.)

The appliance dealer saw the handwriting on the wall. He knew that, when Des Moines was saturated with color television sets, he had to introduce new products into his store or go the way of the harness makers and blacksmiths. He, therefore, introduced computers, fax machines, answering machines, car phones, cellular phones, VCR's and CD players to the buying public and sold them all by using the puppy dog close. His theory proved good because more than 99% of the customers ended up buying the products.

The application of the puppy dog close to the sale of homes is quite interesting. Had we not experienced this technique as applied to homebuyers, we would not believe it. At first we thought the technique applied to mobile homes only, but this was not the case. The system applies to new homes as follows:

Mr. and Mrs. Brown are shown the glories of owning a new fireplace in the Woodlake Garden tract of East Covina. They fall in love with the fireplace, but they're not too sure about buying the house.

"Well," the salesman says, "why don't you move in this weekend and try it?"

"But how can we move in?" Mrs. Brown asks. "There's no furniture or anything!"

"Look," the salesman says, "have you ever camped out?"

"Well, of course!" Mr. Brown says.

"Then why not camp in?" the salesman asks.

"*Camp in*? What do you mean *camp in*?"

"Well, if you've got a couple of sleeping bags, just come on in and set up camp here in the house for the weekend. Try it and see how you like it. I'll even bring some wood so you can have a fire in the fireplace. I think you'll have a fine time."

After a bit of banter and some hemming and hawing, the Browns consent to try the house for a weekend.

In most cases, it works. The weekend takes on the air of a vacation, instead of a deep concern over principal, interest, taxes, insurance and crabgrass.

THE BEN FRANKLIN CLOSE

Neither of us ever met Ben Franklin. But judging from his autobiography, he was quite a guy. Anyone who goes on record as preferring the turkey to the eagle as our national bird has a certain gut appeal to your authors.

The wit, wisdom, charm and grace of this homespun hero have even provided us with material for this book.

Without digressing into an essay on how to use the Ben Franklin close, we'll give it to you short and sweet, because we think that's how not-so-gentle-Ben would have wanted it.

If ever you are confronted with a difficult buyer, and she can't make up her mind as to the merits of what you are selling, take a blank sheet of paper and draw a line down the middle, like so:

The next step is to put a plus (+) on one side and a minus (-) on the other, like so:

Then you give the sheet to the young lady in question and ask her to list all the good things about your product on the plus (+) side and all the bad things on the minus (-) side.

If you can't get ten pluses (++++++++++) or at least five pluses (+++++) for every minus (-), we have failed in our mission and you are showing the prospect the wrong product. Be certain you let the lovely lady do all the writing. Chances are she will make the sale for you. And when she does, rest assured that Winnikoff, Prelutsky and Franklin will be very proud of you.

THE MARCIA TYSSELING CLOSE

This closing technique is so unique we didn't know exactly what to call it. So we ascribed it to the lovely young lady whose theory is so unique she deserves her own chapter.

Marcia hails from St. Paul, Minnesota, and although she made it through high school, she never quite made it through St. Cloud University and UCLA to get that bachelor's in special ed. The reason: she became a nanny for Melissa, daughter of Joan Rivers. The pay, the perks, progress, and promotions on this job were so good, the full time employment went on from 1982 to 1990. She was promoted from Melissa's personal nanny to Joan's personal assistant.

Now, contrary to all the gossip at the glue works and tabloids, there are some very nice people among the rich and famous. The personal and professional relationship between Marcia and her employer has always been and remains excellent. So, when employee Marcia told employer Joan she wanted to go into her own business, the boss helped.

Really helped.

And in November, 1989, Star Wares on Main was born

in Santa Monica, California.

This very exclusive shop deals in genuine Hollywood collectibles. The store contains an abundance of movie and stage costumes, icon pieces, props, personal items, relics and autographs. Through the years, Star Wares has sold the ax that Jack Nicholson wielded in *The Shining*, the (Hollywood) gold bars from the film *Goldfinger*, Christopher Reeves' *Superman* costume, the motorcycle used by Sean Connery and Harrison Ford in *Indiana Jones and the Last Crusade*, Judy Garland's gingham dress from *The Wizard of Oz*, and James Dean's jacket from *Giant*. There are literally hundreds—nay thousands—of such memorabilia (items worthy of our memory) sold by this No. 1 Best Seller.

Although her sales theory has carried her far in life, there are also the down times. What to do? Pack up $130,000 of *unordered* merchandise and send it to a Mississippi river boat gambling casino whose floating theme is Hollywood memorabilia under glass. She has done this repeatedly and rarely has a single item been returned. Through her efforts, the boats are made not only beautiful, but interesting.

It is a given that Marcia Tysseling is smart, pretty, charming, kind, and devoted to customer satisfaction. She helps some of the biggest name stars in the world thin out their wardrobes and closets. They love her and so do we. After all, when this book was published, Marcia bought the first 100 copies.

No. 1 Best Seller indeed!

P.S. If you seek free entertainment and wish to hear Joan on the answering tape, call (310) 399-0224 after hours.

MORE TALES TOO GOOD NOT TO TELL

The following, all of them real estate closes, illustrate many points made in earlier chapters, but are too good not to tell. First: Around the turn of the century, the U.S. government opened up certain lands in Southern California to settlers who would improve the property. An average parcel was 160 acres. The Leon Brent clan, consisting of a father and three sons, picked up four of these parcels and made the improvements required by law.

Seventy-five years later, the old-timers had passed on, but their heirs still held title to the property. All the heirs were extremely old and had never seen much profit from the land. But, being a hardy and hard-headed bunch of pioneer stock, they held on. One day a broker approached the Leon B. clan heirs with an offer of $2,000 per acre, or $1,280,000 for the whole package. The broker asked for a ten percent commission.

To put it mildly, the Leon B. clan heirs were living in genteel poverty. They *needed* the money. But they were plagued with indecision.

The real estate broker, a wise old man who did *not* need the money, told the sellers, after a week of waiting, that the deal was off. And it was. Because the offer was only good for seven days. At that point, there was pure panic on the part of the sellers. They offered the broker a larger commission and offered to drop the price.

He waited a few days and then put the deal through on the same price and terms as originally submitted. He never said anything derogatory to *anyone* about either the buyer or the seller.

The deal was closed.

Next deal.

Indecision is a problem that plagues rich and poor alike. One of the classic tales told by salesmen is that of Samuel Horowitz and F.W. Woolworth. Mr. Horowitz was in the real estate business, and Mr. Woolworth was a merchandiser of repute. It seems that Mr. Woolworth wanted to build the Woolworth Building in New York, but had a terrible time making up his mind about the best approach to his problem. He talked to many but would take advice from none. Most developers and salesmen were driven to distraction by Mr. Woolworth, but Mr. Horowitz persisted in making his calls and presenting his ideas to Mr. Woolworth.

On one occasion, after what seemed a fruitless session between Messrs. Horowitz and Woolworth—a session during which Mr. W. continued to show the same evasion and indecision he had shown from the beginning—Mr. H. got up, extended his hand and, with a flash of anger said to Mr. W., "I want to tell you something, Mr. W. You are going to build the largest building in the world, and I am going to build it for you. Good morning!"

Mr. H. snapped his briefcase shut, turned on his heel and walked out on Mr. W.

When construction of the Woolworth Building was underway some months later, Mr. W. met Mr. H. at the construction site and said to him: "Do you remember the morning you told me I was going to build the largest building in the world and that you were going to build it for me?"

"Yes," Mr. H. replied.

"Well, I was never able to get that out of my mind."

This is another case of indecision conquered. Of course, Mr. W. did not know why he was indecisive. But *we* know, don't we? We are very proud of ourselves, readers and writers alike, for having the knowledge of why *everyone* is indecisive. All humanity is programmed to be indecisive by the barriers set up by all the browbeating authority figures. Break down the barriers and there's a good chance you will make the sale. It is this type of knowledge that pays dividends, because knowledge is power! Use it wisely and use it well.

A further analysis of the problem between Mr. H. and Mr. W. shows that there are numerous factors involved in such a sale. We could say that this sale: (1) appealed to Mr. W's vanity, (2) sparked his desire by making him the hero of this little drama, (3) generated interest by use of the words "the largest building in the world," and on and on. But the essential feature of this sale, the reason *why* Mr. Horowitz closed, was that *he found out what his customer wanted and went to great lengths to help him get it*. This is one of the keys of all great selling. If you can apply this key to *your* selling situation, we guarantee you the orders will pile in. And faster than you ever imagined.

Now that we are about to end the chapter on the real estate close, we must tell you again that once you have closed, *get away from the buyer as fast as you can*. Do not stick around after the close, because the customer may change his mind if you do. It is for this very reason waitresses and waiters *take away* the menus once they have taken the order. If they *leave* menus, the customers will invariably change their minds. And *we* know why, don't we? Because people are naturally indecisive.

To summarize the matter of closing a real estate deal:

1. Do not be afraid to ask for the sale.
2. Ask for an opinion and ask a closing question.
3. If it doesn't work, ask again.

4. Give your customer a choice of buying decisions.
5. Assume that your customer will buy. Make an assumptive close and make more than five calls.
6. Close with enthusiasm.
7. Study various closing techniques and apply them to your situation (e.g. *how will I apply the puppy dog close to the sale of beds?*).
8. Write letters (but only if they're *good* letters).
9. Study the indecision of your buyer and figure out a way to overcome it.
10. Find out what your customer wants and go to great lengths to help him (or her) get it.
11. Once you have closed the sale, snap your briefcase shut and GET OUT!

THE PROSPECT LIST
PART 1

If you can (1) get a prospect's attention, (2) arouse interest, (3) create desire and (4) follow through with a close, you will make the sale. But once you have plugged these four elements of a sale into your gray-matter computer, we encourage you to begin with another fundamental in the practice of selling: *start a prospect list*. There are many ways of generating prospect calls: (1) direct mail, (2) ads, (3) cold calls, (4) television—which is, incidentally, the greatest sales medium in the world, (5) radio, (6) schools, (7) women's clubs, (8) men's clubs, (9) churches, (10) door-to-door, (11) personal acquaintances and (12) friends.

Once you have started a *prospect list*, you must follow up with a *client list*. This is the list of the world's most important people: the ones who have already purchased your product or service.

Prospect lists are generated in many ways. Some by design and some quite by accident. Some for the rich and some for the poor. Some for the young and some for the old. GM has one list and GE has another. *Playboy* has one and *The Reader's Digest* has another. Some people buy prospect lists and others sell prospect lists. Fortunes are made both ways. But without a prospect list, no sales organization can exist. For our purposes, we insist that you start your own prospect list. This is part of the creative selling process. It is a must. And make sure it ties in with your theory of selling.

Among the more interesting stories told about the creation of prospect lists is the one about a list generated *by accident*.

Some twenty years ago, three partners went into the stamp business. They made their appeal to young stamp collectors and sold most of their packets for 25 cents. After ten years in business, they sold most of their packets for 50 cents. And in the twentieth year, their most popular packets sold for one to five dollars.

They not only kept up with inflation, but took enormous pride in having raised an entire generation of collectors on stamps anyone could afford. They developed an active mail order list of over 300,000 satisfied customers. About 100,000 of these customers had been with them over ten years.

The ads for these packets always started off: *SEND NO MONEY!* They never dunned anyone for money and their bad debts amounted to just a few percent of sales. The fact that they had so few deadbeats to deal with made their business hum. They did approximately $900,000 per year gross business.

Then.

An old friend from high school looked them up and was surprised to see the size of the operation. By this time the stamp company rented a large facility and employed many people to make up the packets.

"Say, this is quite an operation," the old-time friend said. "What's your profit margin?"

"About ten percent of gross sales," they replied.

"You mean to tell me you make $90,000 a year on gross sales of $900,000?" the old-time friend asked.

"That's right," they replied. "We can each take a salary of $30,000 a year."

"That's insane! Why, if I make a $900,000 sale, I get a minimum commission of $225,000," the old-time friend said.

"Good Lord! What are you selling?" they asked.

"Desert land," the old-time friend replied, "and my commission is 25 percent of the sales price. Sometimes it is 50 percent. It looks like you guys are in the wrong business. Or maybe you like to work hard for your money."

"But if we can keep on this way, we'll be making $60,000 a year in another 20 years," the three partners said.

"Look, friends," the old-time buddy said, "do you know what you *really* have here?"

"A stamp business," they replied.

"A STAMP BUSINESS!" the old-time friend shouted. "You're crazy! You've got a PROSPECT LIST with 300,000 paying customers! Do you know how much that's worth?"

"About a penny a name," they replied.

"A penny a name! Why, if you can get ten bucks a month out of 100,000 of those people, that means a cool cash flow of one million dollars a *month*."

"But hardly any of our customers will buy ten dollars worth of stamps a month."

"Stamps! Who said anything about stamps! We can sell LAND! For ten bucks down and ten bucks a month for thirteen years. That's a million bucks a *month* for thirteen years. We can split the million bucks a month with a landowner and that will give us $500,000 a *month*. Split that four ways and we'll each have an income of $125,000 a *month*!"

The stamp dealers went into a huddle: 18 seconds later they said, "We'll do it."

Not only did they do it, but they did it quite well from a financial viewpoint.

After a year of struggling with the project and investing large sums of time and money, each of the four partners did realize a return of approximately $125,000 per month. Shortly after the first year, they gave up the stamp business and devoted their efforts to real estate, yachting, golf, and psychoanalysis. The friendships deteriorated and none of these men ever again did business with one another. Only their respective analysts know why.

But that's neither here nor there. What's important is that the major events noted above are basically true.

Where and how you generate a prospect list will depend on your creative talents. But if you are willing to seize the opportunity when it arises, the rewards can be staggering.

It's important to note that prospect lists never remain static. The universe is undergoing constant changes, and your prospect list had better be in step with what is going on *out there*. Prospects may move, go out of business, retire or switch from selling stamps to selling land.

Whatever the reason for the change, old prospects must be eliminated from the list and replaced with new prospects. The most successful *small* advertising firm we know makes eight new calls each week: four calls on Tuesdays and four calls on Thursdays. Mondays, Wednesdays and Fridays are used to service existing accounts.

The man responsible for this program makes well over $100,000 a year. He sends out approximately 20 *personal* letters each week and follows up with 20 *personal* phone calls. He keeps a data bank in his computer for each prospect, and would never think of talking to the prospect without the data bank in front of him on the screen. He asks the prospect about his wife, kids and dogs.

Bear in mind that because a prospect says no today does not mean that he will not buy at some time in the future. A long-term study of industrial buying habits proved conclusively that 75 percent of all business produced by salesmen was sold after the *fifth* interview. The study also showed that 83 percent of salesmen quit calling on prospects who did not buy *before* the fifth interview. In short, if you are steady (without being obnoxious), you will most likely make most of your sales after your fifth call.

We believe there are four types of prospects:

1. New prospects. (Keep a list of 200 new prospects going all the time and we will take you out for a beer.)
2. Lost prospects. (If they're not dead or bankrupt, go after them again and again.)
3. Prospects who are fence-sitters. (These guys can drive you crazy. They always say maybe. Be sure to see them *at least six times* before giving up.)
4. Customer prospects. (These are the good guys. Keep them happy and keep in touch.)

When considering how to handle these prospects, we remember the following conversation, between a professional and a novice.

Novice: I asked for the order but didn't get it. How come?

Pro: I'd have asked for it again.

Novice: You mean you would ask him *again*?

Pro: Sure. I would ask for the order three or four times.

Novice: But when do you stop asking for the order?

Pro: When I get it.

That said...

In our travels on prospecting we came across an interesting, little-known company called Inquiry Handling Service. IHS answers mail and telephone inquiries generated by phone calls, newspaper and magazine ads, and then passes the leads on to *their* clients. They have a very impressive client list, which includes many of the world's leading corporations.

IHS also holds seminars to teach *other* companies how to establish their *own* inquiry handling service. Is IHS worried about cutting its own throat? Of course not. According to IHS President Michael Simon, there's plenty of business out there for everyone. The biggest problem in his business is not the competition, but *indifference* on the part of his clients' salespeople.

"Our main competition is apathy," Mr. Simon said, adding that many companies do not follow up on their leads with persistence.

A No. 1 Best Seller cannot afford to be apathetic or lazy.

In closing this chapter on prospecting, we think you will do well to spend at least 30 minutes a day thinking about new prospects. Not only will this improve your sales record, it will rattle your brain cage and get you started in the right direction each day. You can also use it as a ploy when your wife asks you what you are doing. Then you can say, "Shhh, can't you see I'm working on my prospect list?"

THE PROSPECT LIST
PART 2

In the good old days, prospecting was a relatively simple matter. For example, the office manager (or owner) of a real estate firm allocated a *farm* to each of his salespeople. The *farm* consisted of a given territory ranging from four blocks square to 40 miles square, depending on the population density. The salesperson went out armed with giveaway calendars, notepads, pens or pencils. The salesperson gave each property owner on the farm a free gift and met as many owners as possible.

The giveaway gift always had the office name and number on it. The salesperson did this *farming* (or prospecting) every working day for four hours a day. At the end of a year, the *successful* salesperson would be down to two hours of *farming* each working day, and at the end of two years the salesperson's phone would be jangling off the hook in such a way that further *farming* was unnecessary.

Those who played by the rules and tilled their plots diligently are still busy after 38 years in the business. They see the newcomers fail after 30 days of frantic effort and shake their heads in disbelief. In California alone, where the competition is fierce and one person in 75 holds a real estate license, over 90% of all people who study hard to obtain that license *never make a sale.* Maybe *they* don't know why, but *we* sure know, don't we?

We know of sales organizations that sell items such as cutlery, cookware, vitamins, cosmetics, vacuum cleaners and toilet-paper oil filters. They hit a town, map out the territory and send out teams of salespeople to make the sales. They always show a profit because they know exactly how to get the job done. We are not passing judgment on their *modus operandi* or the value of their products or services. All we know is that *organized* people get the job done. One of the old-timers told us that if you are organized, the sale is already half-made. In fact, when a rag-tag gang of marauders becomes successful, it is then called, in hushed, reverential tones, *The Organization.*

But life in these times has become vastly more complex than it was in the days of yore. High-tech is not only here to stay, it will become more complex with the passage of time. Approach the sales manager of any high technology company and he or she will tell you their greatest need is for *qualified* salespeople. By definition, a qualified salesperson is one who is: (a) highly organized, (b) extremely knowledgeable about the product or service and (c) extremely hard working. To paraphrase Charles Kettering of General Motors fame: a problem well stated is already half solved and a job well organized is already half done.

Qualified salespeople know this instinctively. What generally happens in many cases is that after High-Tech Company A has trained and nurtured a *qualified*, brilliant and highly motivated salesperson, Higher-Tech Company B lures the salesperson away with promises of greater glory and more money.

But wherever the salesperson finds himself (or herself), he or she must produce sales to justify the salary, commissions, stock options and company pension plan he or she gets, as well as the health, dental, life and company car insurance. To guarantee continued employment (high tech, low tech or no tech) the salesperson *must* have a good prospect list and the ability to expand it.

We have seen low-caliber salespeople break out with zits when the matter of the prospect list arises. Many of these no-tech people end up working for bucket shops that advertise as follows: *LEADS—LEADS—LEADS. We supply you with sales leads. All you have to do is sell us your soul*!

Or words to that effect.

If you enjoy that kind of selling, then by all means go to it. But if you enjoy *our* kind of selling, read on.

The marketplace has become so sophisticated you can *hire* sales organizations to do your prospecting for you. It takes a little time and money to ferret out these people, but there is not a sales-oriented publication in the country that does not advertise prospecting services. They may call it something else, such as *market penetration* or *account executive referrals*, but it all boils down to *leads* and the establishment of a *prospect list*.

In the speeding world of high technology, research and development careens around marketing corners so fast it leaves the team players breathless. Entire books are written about the need to define and find the *economic buyers* in big companies. In good times the economic buyers can usually be found in the purchasing departments with discretion in the hands of purchasing agents. In bad times, though, very often the president or CEO will make the buying decision.

The matter of selling to a big-time buyer and keeping track of who signs the checks has become high art in our business. The matter of finding the *exact* person with whom you should deal in your sales exploits has created a whole new offshoot in the computer industry. It is a database industry which will direct you with uncanny precision to those who will buy your product or service. A prospect list of this type is pure gold. If you seek out the software wizards who can help you the most with your selling, if you work very, very hard, and if you are willing to pay the price, you are sure to succeed.

If you find the cost of such services too high, seek out companies that will sell or lease you an automatic phone-calling machine that also takes messages. Now, when your charming authors get a call from one of these nitwit machines, they automatically hang up. But, because *some* people talk back to the machine, your sales organization can be amply rewarded with an ever-expanding prospect list. If 99% of the calls your hired-call-machine makes result in hang-ups, think of the 1% that succeed. Your autodialer can reach 1,000 people a day. If 1% of them talks back, you have reached ten new prospects *each day*.

We spoke to the owner of an insurance agency who increased his volume threefold in one year with the help of automatic dialers. Like it or not, the world will always need insurance. If the agent fills that need, the sale will be made. The automatic dialer that our insurance agent friend uses, which helps him fill client's needs, is indeed a clever device. For it not only *calls*, but if the charming prospect on the other end is interested and answers at the proper interval with a name, address and phone number, the machine, which is voice-activated, will record this information and proceed with other questions, like so:

Machine: Thank you for your name, address and phone number. Now that we have that information, will you please give us the make and model of your car?

Prospect: 1996 Chevrolet four-door station wagon with a 350 V-8 engine, air, overdrive, cassette player and a great two-tone paint job in blue and white. I just wish my mileage was a little better. And my wife was a little more careful. It's already sort of a wreck. But a *dependable* wreck.

Machine: Thank you. Will you please tell me if you use it for business, pleasure, or both.

Prospect: Business, pleasure and a whole bunch of hauling. You see, we take our kids to St.

John's Parochial School and we have to haul
the kids there every day when it's our turn.
That's like five days a week every other
week. On the other weeks, Jane McGrade
does the hauling. I don't know how these
women can stand it!

Machine: Thank you. Now, will you please tell me how
many miles you drive per year?

Prospect: About ten thousand, I guess. Wait a minute—
make that twelve thousand. We burn a quart
of oil every 2,500 miles.

Machine: Thank you. Now that we have that information, will you please tell me if you have had
any major accidents or moving violations in
the past 12 months?

Prospect: None! Not a one! Except my wife got a parking ticket five years ago. That was really
dumb. She should be more careful, y'know.

Machine: Thank you. One of our salespeople will call
for a personal appointment in the next 24
hours. Good-bye.

Prospect: Goodbye.

Click!

In this particular case, the prospect is somewhat pre-sold
and the chances of the salesperson closing are pretty darn
good.

We were told by the owner of the insurance agency that
his lowest-paid employee makes about $60,000 a year, and
he himself about $250,000. These sums represent a three-
fold increase in sales over the preceding year, when the firm
did not use autodialers.

Here is another slant on telemarketing. Allow us a short
quote from the finest publication of its kind—THE
KIPLINGER WASHINGTON LETTER:

Telemarketing, calling folks who bought cars or

had them serviced at dealerships in years past. "A way to keep us fresh and in their minds." One dealer has each sales person call for two hours a day. "Pays off."

The prospect list is as much a tool of selling for us as medical knowledge is to a doctor and legal expertise is to an attorney. If you don't get it and use it, you will never get the job done. You will not become the No. 1 Best Seller in your league. And you will become a disappointment to your charming authors. We cannot allow that!

As we close this chapter, we feel compelled to inform you of a few dangers concerning the improper use of auto-dialers. Those beautiful, charming and lovely creatures we will refer to as the Fairest Sex complain bitterly about getting machine calls while they are in the shower. Under such dampening circumstances, the lovely ladies end up *hating* the machine, prospects lists, the company, the salespeople and anyone who happens to walk into the house at that Moment of Naked Truth.

The situation has become so serious that our writer friends at the *Reader's Digest* have come out *against* the machines and squarely on the side of The Naked Ladies! The veiled threat and well-armored complaint is that such calling machines violate the *Constitutional Right of Privacy*! O.K.? O.K. In response, we have heard it rumored from one of the members of the *Playboy gang* that *Reader's Digest* is all wet. We will not go into the reasoning process here, but the situation has become so serious that even Dear Abby has been brought into the fray. She has informed us that if you do not wish to be solicited by phone, register your complaint at:

> Telephone Preference Service
> Direct Marketing Association
> 6 East 43rd Street
> New York, New York 10017

Frankly, we don't care what any of the above have to

say or how they say it. The fact is that everyone can listen or hang up as they choose. But *you* must prospect. All we ask of you is that you do it with good taste, a gentle touch and a toleration of those who condemn you. After all, we would never, never, ever dissuade anyone from reading *Playboy, The Reader's Digest* or even Dear Abby, because they have to make a living, too.

And as dedicated salesmen, we sure have a lot of respect for the size of *their* prospect lists.

Therefore, go out into the wide world and prospect. And prosper. And we will be very proud of you.

Very proud, indeed!

INSURANCE SALES

(Barton B. Barton, Ph.D., University of H.K.)

We close this matter of insurance sales with an interesting and fictionalized story about Betty and Bart Barton, Insurance Brokers Extraordinaire. Betty is absolutely the brains of the outfit. Bart pulls a wagon of his own making. But without Betty, Bart would be pulling a wagon of an entirely different sort. Most likely one with three squeaky wheels.

Betty, all her scholarly life, was a straight A student. Always lived by a set of well-defined moral rules and down-to-earth, practical values. She will work 20 hours a day when the job requires. Never complains. Never failed or betrayed anyone in her entire life. Well-groomed when the occasion requires it. But wears blue jeans and running shoes to the office whenever she feels like it. Is a wonderful mom to two adolescent kids and one infant. Loves Bart and treats him like an equal. What's more, she's absolutely beautiful.

Bart, born Barton B. Barton III, was a hard-core, full-blown heroin addict in his late teens. At that time in his life, the wagon broke down completely. No wheels at all. Just junk.

Bart's father, Barton B. Barton, Jr., was a well-educated man with a Masters of Science Degree in mathematics and a

J.D. from the University of Michigan. The old man was big on brains and achievement, became a federal judge, but had a fluid defect: he drank.

Sylvia Turner Barton, Bart's mother, who holds a Bachelor of Arts Degree in English and a Master's in Education, knew she had to get away, with her two daughters, from a drinking husband and a snorting son.

The Barton family broke up in 1968. And Bart, tall, blond, handsome and foot lose at age 17, ended up alone in the house. With no parental guidance and an omniscient adolescent attitude, he knew with certainty he could not become addicted by *snorting* the stuff. Addiction was only for those poor misbegotten souls who *injected*.

It took a while but he eventually found out how wrong he was.

But by then, his entire world was about to collapse. He and one of his snorting buddies had amassed a small drug-tainted fortune and Bart found himself addicted to the tune of $1,000 per day. But Bart is a very nice guy and charming. Therefore, gave freely of his time, money and charm to his friends and went down the tubes completely in January, 1971. He was then 20 years old, and by this time the wagon was not only without wheels but minus the handle.

Since this early foray into sales was without estimable social value, the authorities nailed him. But under the auspices of a very fine attorney who had once been his father's law partner, he was not sentenced to do hard time. Instead, he was released to the Team House Street Foundation in Chicago. The attorney also got Bart's record expunged. So if you want to get the dirt on Bart, you'll have to rely on this book rather than the public records. The Foundation was not Bart's idea of fun, but he toughed it out anyway. After a Foundation year, he came to the adult realization that life offered him three options.

1. Go to jail.
2. Die of an overdose.
3. Stay clean and stay alive.

He chose option No. 3.

He also realized that he needed discipline and went into the army. Upon discharge, he was not only clean and straight, but also broke.

What to do?

Look up his old buddy, Barney Bennet, and get a job in telemarketing insurance sales. This type of work did not require an insurance broker's license. Just the gift of gab. To make a decent living, all he had to do was set up six appointments daily for the *professional* insurance salesmen in the office and they would hopefully follow up with the real sales.

After he got the hang of it, Bart got on the phone and set up 22 appointments in a row. All 22 appointments were set up in just two hours of calls. They had to send Bart home that day because the 10 *closers* couldn't keep up. He was told he was creating too much business.

But what *really* upset Bart was that the boss was cheating him on his commission checks.

He studied for his insurance broker's exam and succeeded on the first pass. Quit the cheating boss forthwith and called the local insurance brokers in the phone book, starting with the A's. Needed a job. Found one with an All-state Insurance Group. The office policy was simple, clear-cut and highly understandable. It was a nice live-or-die ultimatum the boss gave his salespeople. The policy gave employees two choices:

1. Succeed and stay.
2. Fail and go.

Bart stayed for two years and won every award the company had to offer.

He moved on and worked for two independent insurance agencies. He specialized in condominium and apartment house insurance. He considered it a great learning experience. When selling to apartment owners, he *knew* who was boss. But confronted with a five-party board of directors for a condominium project, Bart had to make an on-the-spot decision: who was the *real* decisionmaker among the five members? Take your pick and home in on that person, give the best price, terms and service and then go to the next appointment.

Bart sold a lot of insurance.

Bart continued his education.

But he didn't have a lot of money.

Just enough to get by. Full-time school and near full-time work were beginning to get him down.

Enter Betty Hanover from Oak Park, IL.

First meeting: Christmas day, 1981, Chicago, IL at U.I. It was a case of Summa Cum Laude meets struggling insurance salesman-student.

Conflict.

As in all great love stories, Betty found herself torn by opposites.

On the one hand, if she could correct her biology professor in front of the whole class regarding the proper proprioceptive function of kinesthesis as it relates to the ganglia of cephalopods, and also get an A+ on a term paper that made a brilliant argument against the anti-Hegelian, pessimist philosophy of Arthur Schopenhauer vis-à-vis the theological tracts of Friedrich Ernst Schleiermacher, how much trouble could she possibly have in getting Bart straightened out? Compared to those other complicated people, Bart was a piece of cake.

So, Betty did a sales job on herself. She considered the positives and negatives of the situation.

On the plus side, the guy wasn't bad looking at all. He was gentle, kind, and soft spoken. And he had a real cute smile that got to her every time. And he had dimples too.

On the minus side: (1) He was broke, (2) He did not yet have a degree and, (3) The sound of that squeaky wagon drove her to distraction. After all, Bart was physically, morally, and legally an adult and he *had* to do something about his private little four-wheeler. So what's a young, beautiful, brilliant, and dazzling Summa Cum Laude to do in a situation like this?

Intellectualize.

Her college goal was a Ph.D. But her life goal was a guy.

School was hard. But Bart was easy.

Schopenhauer and Schleiermacher were dead and gone, and nothing could be done about them. But Bart was here and now, and his biggest problem could be solved with a can of WD-40 lubricant.

When her psychology professor referred to *stroking* as *kinesthetically tactile stimulation*, she knew she was ready for a career change.

OK. So Bart wasn't much of a prize.

But she married him anyway.

He showed SO MUCH *promise*.

What more could she ask?

And the beauty of it all was that the promise was fulfilled.

Back to Oak Park.

Broke.

Moved in with Betty's parents.

Talked things over.

Decided on insurance.

Harry Hanover, Betty's dad, loaned them $750 to start their business. They offered him:

1. Twenty-five percent of the business in the form of a dandy looking stock certificate or,
2. Return of the $750 in six months.

Mr. Hanover opted for No. 2

In today's market a one-fourth interest in Barton Insurance Enterprises, Inc. is worth $1,700,000.00 U.S money cash. If Harry feels like crying, he doesn't show it. He says he did it all for his unborn grandchildren.

But to return to the beginning. Bart and Betty put $400 of the $750 towards rent for an empty office in Oak Park, IL. They used the other $350 for supplies, furniture and junk food snacks.

The Hanovers supplied real food and lodging.

The kids worked side by side, 16 hours a per day for four years. When the business poured in, 20-hour days were not uncommon.

They concentrated on commercial real estate insurance. Apartments, shopping centers, condominiums and commercial office buildings.

They are now down to 11-hour days. With only six - seven - or eight - hour days on the weekends.

Unlike his brilliant, beautiful, and talented wife, Bart never quite made it through college. He is three units shy of a bachelor's in business administration but claims to have a Ph.D. from the School of Hard Knocks.

It wasn't easy in the beginning and it's not easy now. For Bart and Betty work hard at their business. Their two adolescent children help out. Their infant son is too young to stuff envelopes. But his time will soon come.

Barton B. Barton has made an intense and thorough study of all the commercial and multiple dwelling property owners within a 50-mile radius of his office in Oak Park, IL. His circle of expertise covers Boone County in the north to Kankakee in the south. For good clients he goes as far west as La Salle.

When Bart calls a prospect, he often knows as much or more about the property than the owner. When a prospect calls *him*, Bart can rattle off the stats re: current loans, approximate value, year built, type of construction, number of stories, number of units, purchase date, the county tax assessor book, page and parcel number, land and improvements tax data, local code violations (if any exist), the owner's name, address and phone number plus the names and addresses of the best nearby restaurants. For Bart loves good food. The days of cheap snacks are over.   It has been rumored among the cognoscenti that if an owner paints a building within that 50 mile radius of Bart's office, he will know the color before the paint is dry.

When asked, "How do you know all this?" Bart replies, with modesty and kindness in his voice and a twinkle in his eye, "It's my *business* to know."

In truth, he gets his info out of a local real estate directory. That costs $3,000 a year.

Now that Bart's wagon is fully operational, we asked if he would care to give a word of advice to the new initiates on smooth wagon-pulling.

His advice: "You need only two things to succeed:

1. W-O-R-K and
2. FOCUS."

We are proud of Bart for following our advice and developing a theory of his own. We suspect (but do not know for sure) the theory that drives Barton Insurance Enterprises, Inc. is more financially profitable than the brainstrain couch potato analysis practiced by most unhappy analysts.

True to our further advice re: avoiding the bad apples, Bart maintains he loses about 5% of his clientele annually. And what does he say about this attrition? "Good riddance."

To which we add: "Amen."

"Bart," we asked "are you making $100,000 a year?"

"More like $100,000 *a month*," he whispered.

"And what are your favorite charities?" we asked.

"The Team House Street Foundation."

"Any others?" we asked.

"Anything that helps kids. We support and give generously to organizations that help kids."

Therefore, ladies and gentlemen, if you see a clean-cut businessman pulling a smoothly operating wagon down

Wall Street, in New York, and want to invest $750 in his enterprise, let us inform you that it's too late. He even turned us down. But if you are looking for commercial insurance within 50 miles of Chicago, climb in that wagon and sit back for the smoothest, nicest and most comfortable insurance ride of your life. The price is right. The service is great. The people are real.

Barton Insurance Enterprises, Inc. is an ongoing success because they *care*. Or, as the brains of the outfit put it to us: "It's our *business* to care."

KNOW THY PRODUCT!
PART 1

We begin this portion of the discourse with a warning and a threat: KNOW THY PRODUCT! Because if you don't, you will fail. It is true that there are salespeople with limited product or service knowledge who succeed for a while. But in the long run they are doomed. There are millions upon millions of salespeople who score *once*—by luck or accident—and never make it again. They wonder why. They twist and toss at night, fearing the worst: that they will have to go back to the old supervisor and ask for the old job. Again. And they will be lucky to get it. Why? Most likely because they did not know—really, truly, honestly and genuinely know—their product. The failures, like bad kids in school, failed to inquire, study and learn. In simple terms, they did not do their homework.

Let us illustrate.

Way, way back during the middle of this century, a bright and eager young business student at the University of California got a job selling shoes at Leeds Shoe Store in Berkeley. The young man's name was Francis John Johnson. The shoe store boss, Howard Stein, had worked his way up in the ranks and *knew* something about selling shoes.

Howard Stein boasted to his regional manager that from now on, he was going to break in his salesmen *right*. Either they learn something about shoes and the Leeds system, or they don't get hired. Before he hired the student, he forced Frank to memorize the shoe-numbering system.

The student, who had been raised and schooled on the merits of memorization, learned the system rapidly. In 13 minutes flat, over a cup of coffee. He returned to Howard Stein, Manager, 13 minutes after the memory assignment and took the exam. Stein was impressed. He told young Francis John Johnson to come back for one hour per day each day, Monday through Friday, to familiarize himself with the actual numbering system and with the stock on the shelves.

If Frank could live up to the boss's expectations and learn what was expected of him, he could start work the following Saturday. He was promised 7% of regular shoe sales, 15% of P.M.'s (*post-mortem* or dead shoe stock that had to be moved out immediately) and 20% on findings (shoe polish, snap-on buttons and bows and rhinestone clips).

As a bright, articulate, but slightly shy young man of 19, Frank accepted the challenge eagerly. He made a handsome appearance in his suit and tie and had a very bright, kind, boyish smile. He was a good, serious student who wanted nothing more in life than to be a great football center (which he was), graduate from the university, get a swell job, marry his beautiful, blonde, fun-loving childhood sweetheart, Joan Jonnie Truelove, and succeed in life. He was ambitious and enthusiastic.

After the Monday study and learning period of one hour, the young student said, "Mr. Stein, do you realize that there are some errors in the company's numbering system? For instance—"

"Nobody's perfect! Even the university's not perfect!" Howard Stein snapped back. "You expect this system to be perfect?"

"No sir, but—"

"Listen to me, kid," Howard Stein said, seizing the shy, young, student football player by the arm, "I know it's not perfect. Everybody in the company knows it's not perfect."

There was something very gruff and firm and yet very likeable about Howard Stein. He had a twinkle in his eye and an infectious smile on his lips. "Now before you start, let me tell you something important: you're in for a lot of frustration in this or any other business. Not only is the numbering system a little off, but we're always a little short on sizes. We never get enough 7B's. Even so, we still sell more shoes to more women than just about any company in America. Know why?"

Francis John Johnson was about to answer, but Howard Stein went on with machine-gun rapidity. "Because *most* of the time we can and do satisfy the customer. Otherwise we'd be out of business in a week. So how does that grab you?"

"Well," Frank started to say.

"Great!" Howard interrupted. "You're going to make a *great* shoe salesman!"

And he was.

Why? Because in addition to learning the frustrations of the numbering system and size shortages, Frank Johnson did something very few salespeople ever do. He did his home-work. And he knew his product. He went to the University of California Library in Berkeley, where he did most of his studying, and looked up the word *shoes* in the Encyclopedia Britannica. He knew that the Britannica was a primary source of information for everything. His speech professor, a truly great man by the name of William Shepard, had taught Frank in his freshman year that if you wanted to know about *anything in the world*, the Encyclopedia Britannica was the place to start.

And what a start.

Within a month, and with a minimum of effort, Frank knew more about shoes, shoe history and shoe construction than anyone in the store. Including Howard Stein.

Everyone knows where the arch is and the same goes for the toe, heel and sole. But who knew about the throat, vamp, collar, foxing, breasting and mudguard? Frank knew.

He read about the history of shoes and was impressed by the story of a 4,000-year-old pair of sandals unearthed in Egypt, that were as serviceable today as the first day they were worn. And the sandals had been built on what was probably the world's first assembly line.

Whenever Frank sold slippers, he told the customer that the Cinderella *glass* slipper was probably a mistranslation of the French word *vair*, a kind of fur, for the French word *verre*, meaning glass.

When he sold galoshes or overshoes, he told his customers that the Romans named the product from a Gaulish wooden shoe, which had a rawhide upper and was used in the rain, mud, sleet and snow by ancient soldiers and postal workers.

And the *louis* heel was named after the no-good, rotten skunk-lecher King Louis XIV of France. Louis had an affinity for sweet, young blue-eyed blondes. But the minute they became pregnant, he threw them out of a side door of the castle, barefoot and penniless. Because the betrothed of Francis John Johnson, Joan Jonnie Truelove, was a blue-eyed blonde, the very thought of King Louis XIV doing all those terrible things to young girls made his blood boil. (Of course, he never let his customers know that.) In addition to being a lecherous pervert, King Louis XIV was only 3 feet 6 inches tall in his dainty little flat feet. But he wore his louis heel shoes, *mais non*!

Then, by God, all the other 3-foot 6-inchers in the court had to look up to him. (Tall people at that time and place were definitely *out*. Midgets and cretins were *in*. And the court jester was a dwarf hunchback who always looked up to the king.) At that time in history, French commoners were forbidden by royal decree from wearing a louis heel. The fashion-conscious king had special foot-crushers built in his torture chambers for people who tried to copy-cat a commodity as precious and important as the royal heel. Obviously, the Sun King did not care about or believe in shoes for the swinish multitude. It took American ingenuity to do *that*.

And as for style, during the Middle Ages, laws, both secular and religious, were passed down telling the worthless peasants what styles they could and could not wear. Speaking loudly for God and the divine right of kings, royalty and clergy would not allow the chambermaid or the footman to wear shoes that were reserved for superior types of human beings who were very, very high up in social, political or religious strata. And if you did wear forbidden shoes, you were liable to get your legs broken. Or worse. Men, women and children were beaten, branded, hung, drawn, quartered and burned alive for wearing the wrong shoes. Saint Crispin, the patron saint of cobblers, practiced what became known as "the gentle craft" (shoemaking) by selling cheap shoes to the poor and peddling a little Christianity on the side. For his efforts, the Roman Emperor Maximian had Crispin beheaded. But not before he had his hands and feet, arms and legs broken to prove that no piddling Christian was going to mess with the All Powerful Roman Empire. S.P.Q.R.!

It always grieved Frank to think that at one time in human history people died because of their shoes.

But the Edison brothers, the founders of Leeds Shoe Stores, had put an end to that nonsense forever.

And they hired nice young men like Francis John Johnson to prove their point.

That Frank became one of the best part-time salesmen Howard Stein ever hired surprised no one. Not only was he smart, quick to smile, and enthusiastic, he was also very kind. He did what every famous and successful actor, actress, rock star and politician has done from the beginning of time: he did his home-work and HE DEVELOPED A FOLLOWING! It was not easy, but he did it.

How?

By being perfectly honest with his customers and serving their interests first. While other shoe salesmen were experts with innersoles and shoe stretchers and were constantly wasting a good deal of their time trying to turn a 6½B into a 7AA or an 8B into a 6½C, Frank simply told the customer the right size was out of stock. But he could order a pair if they wanted him to.

Many of them did.

But Frank's crowning glory was selling white bucks and saddle shoes. To girls with cerebral palsy.

It happened like this.

One rainy Saturday, a mother brought her teenage daughter to Leeds for a pair of saddle shoes. The girl had foot problems and she also had cerebral palsy.

Frank seated the young lady and her mother and took off the shoe from the girl's right foot.

"I've had a terrible time getting the right fit," the mother complained.

"O.K.," Frank said, "let's see what we can do." Then he looked at the girl and said, "Will you please stand up?"

He put the foot-measuring Brannock device under her right foot. Because of the palsy, her foot was unsteady and her toes curled up. Then down.

The girl almost fell over.

Frank looked up at her with a smile and said, "Hey, put your hands on my head and hang on." The palsied girl was embarrassed almost to the point of tears, but grab she did.

It was just as she feared. The good-looking shoe salesman was wearing greasy kid stuff. But she held on anyway. At least he didn't have dandruff.

With both hands, Frank pressed the young lady's foot down *flat* on the measuring device. A perfect 7B. They did the left foot the same way. The left foot was a mite smaller, but not a 6½B. Then he looked at the size she was wearing, which turned out to be a 6C. Too short and too wide.

He was appalled.

Without sounding harsh or angry, he explained, as best he knew how, that whenever girl and mother buy shoes, they should stand up for the foot measurement and make sure the foot is flat on the measuring-stick. Contrary to all the misinformation peddled by millions of lazy shoe clerks, you cannot get a good shoe measurement by sitting down.

"You have to do it like this," he said, pushing down again on the young lady's foot with both hands.

Then he went and got her a pair of shoes. Size 7B.

Perfect fit.

He broke down the heel, bent the sole repeatedly, and softened up the shoe as only a football player knows how. He then told the young lady that if the left shoe felt just a little bit large, she should wear two socks on her left foot to take up the slack.

The girl, her mother, and all their friends became customers of Francis John Johnson for the entire four years he was in college.

They called him Frankie.

They loved him.

Howard Stein loved him.

The Edison brothers loved him.

And in his own special way, Frank loved his job. True, there were frustrations, disappointments, rejections and abusive customers. Howard had warned him about these things in the beginning. Nevertheless, our young hero stuck it out. Unlike other shoe-clerks who came and went in a month, Frank stayed on for years.

He developed a following.

He knew his product.

He succeeded.

He invited his co-workers to his wedding.

Joan Jonnie Truelove did not like the name *Joan,* so she asked her friends to call her Jonnie.

After finishing school and marrying his beloved Jonnie, Frank left his job as a shoe salesman and got a job as a stockbroker.

Selling was his thing. And now, love.

After three months of marital bliss, Frank's old football buddy, Buzz Ivan Ivanovich, breezed into town from Dayton, Ohio. Buzz went directly to his friend's stockbrokerage office, where he found Frank sitting in his own small, cramped and private cubicle.

The football buddies embraced, shook hands, laughed and carried on.

"Hey," Frank asked, "what brings you here from Dayton?"

"The company sent me," Buzz replied. "I'm setting up the company computer display for the West Coast Computer Show. But I don't have to start until tomorrow." Changing the subject, Buzz asked, "How's your beautiful wife?"

"Great!" Frank replied. "Here, let me call her at work and tell her you're in town. She's got a great job as a legal secretary."

"You sure are a lucky guy," Buzz said. "Tell Jonnie I'm taking you both out to dinner tonight."

Frank put the phone down. "No way, man, you're coming to *our* place. We lucked out with this great little apartment right down here on Van Ness, and *you're* coming to *our* place for dinner!"

"Hey, man, no way!" Buzz said. "I gotta get a hotel room and clean up. I've been six hours on a plane. I feel like an old jock strap."

"O.K." Frank said to his friend, "let's do this: you go to our place and get cleaned up—"

"You're sure it's O.K.?" Buzz asked.

"Of course! We'll surprise Jonnie, have dinner at our place and then take in a show afterward," Frank said. "How about it?"

"O.K.," Buzz replied, "but the show's on me. O.K.?"

"O.K.," Frank replied. "Here's the key."

Buzz Ivanovich sauntered off to his buddy's apartment, locating it with no difficulty. He let himself in and was impressed with the impeccable good taste and cleanliness of the place. "Lucky dog," he muttered, thinking of his bachelor-pad stench back in Dayton.

He located the shower, upstairs, and proceeded to clean up.

Just as Buzz Ivanovich was upstairs stepping into the shower, Jonnie Truelove Johnson was downstairs entering the back door of her little love nest.

She heard the shower going and began humming a tune as she took two TV dinners from the freezer and put them in the microwave. Then she washed her hands, set the table and lit two candles. After that she put a bottle of Poland water on the table for herself and a cold bottle of beer on the table for her darling husband. She knew how he loved beer.

Then she went upstairs into the bathroom, reached behind the shower curtain, grabbed him you-know-where and said in a sweet, lilting voice, "Ding-dong, dinner's ready." She then dried her hand and arm on a towel and went downstairs humming a tune from *Naughty Marietta*.

As she entered the kitchen, her darling husband entered the back door.

"Hi, Jonnie!" he said to his wife. He stepped forward to kiss her.

She stepped backward very quickly. "Frank," she said in a strange, horror-laden whisper, "what are you doing here?"

"I live here!" he said happily. "Remember me? I'm your husband."

"Oh, no!" she said, breathlessly. "I'm afraid something terrible has just happened. I think I've been used!"

"Used?" he asked, getting more concerned by the split second. "Who used you?"

"You did!" she uttered in a strange whisper.

"I did? Jonnie! What are you talking about?"

His mind began playing funny tricks on him. He remembered somewhere in the distant past his father had muttered dark, inexplicable warnings, and the boys in the locker room had warned him about women in general, but this! How could *this* happen to *him*?

He noticed she had gone pale.

He was mortified. He had never seen her like this before. "Are you sick or something?" he asked, his voice cracked and filled with anguish. He stepped forward to take her in his arms and tell her how much he loved her.

"Don't touch me!" she warned, holding up her hand. "Don't you *dare* touch me!"

"Jonnie," he asked, incredulously, "what's wrong?"

"Who," she asked slowly, methodically, dramatically, painfully, "is upstairs?"

"Buzz—"

"Buzz Ivanovich?" she asked slowly, methodically, dramatically, painfully.

He nodded his head and said, "Yeah, he just flew in and—"

"You mean—I mean—" she stuttered. "Do you mean to tell me that Buzz Ivanovich is *up there* using *our* shower?"

"Yeah, what's wrong with that?" Frank asked.

"Oh my God!" she blurted out, scaring Frank completely out of his wits (for he had never heard her swear before), "Oh my God! I've been raped!"

He seized her arm.

She pulled away.

He pointed his index finger heavenward, to the running shower. "You mean to tell me—did Buzz—if he laid a hand on you—I'll *kill* him! Did Buzz do something bad?"

"No!" she blurted, "*you did!*" Whereupon her face turned beet red.

It was the first time in his life he had seen her like this. His heart palpitated out of control. His sensory perceptions came to a screeching halt. His nerve endings freaked out. "Yeah, but you're my wife."

"My mother warned me about things like this," she hissed. Her skin color subsided from enraged red to inflamed pink.

"Do you have a skin rash or something? he asked.

"Oh my God!" she swore again. "How *stupid* can you

get?"

And so saying, she seized her purse and—forgetting the
TV dinners, burning candles, Poland water and cold beer—
stormed out of the apartment.

Frank ran after her.

She walked straight down the street, westward, eyes
forward, nostrils flaring and breathing the young-bride
equivalent of dragonfire. She did not give her confused husband so much as a sideways glance as he ran alongside,
waving his hands and arms, begging for an explanation.

And so, fellow salespeople, thus ends our story. As our
young Frankie and Jonnie fade slowly in the sunset, we are
not going to tell you what the marriage counselors will tell
you about little acorn mistakes growing into mighty oaks of
misunderstanding. Oh, no! We wouldn't even *consider* a
thing like that in a book like *this*. From our viewpoint, your
success and livelihood are far too important for glib analysis. We know and now you know the extreme importance of
our very important story.

The moral is:

KNOW THY PRODUCT!

Because if you don't, you will fail.

P.S. Our Frankie and Jonnie story has a somewhat bit-
tersweet ending. For although Frankie and Buzz grew older,
raised families, climbed corporate sales ladders successfully
and occasionally had lunch together, their families never,
ever engaged in any kind of social intercourse whatsoever.

KNOW THY PRODUCT!
PART 2

Product knowledge is so important that only the dull and ignorant overlook it. Think of all the doltish salespeople you have encountered in your life and how you turned them down. Now think of all the sharp salespeople you met and how they made their deals. We are not asking you to make value judgments in these comparisons, but if you are to make a realistic sales success of your life, you must start by squaring with reality. In our business, excuses simply will not do. Those who make excuses for their failures eventually excuse themselves out of a livelihood in selling.

With this in mind, we wish to relate to you the story of one of the nation's leading real estate leasing agents, his early failure, his later success, and the reasons for both.

Edward S. Gordon is the president of Edward S. Gordon Company, Inc., a real estate leasing firm in New York.

He says of himself, "My success is the result of *discipline* and *good work habits*. Not brilliance! I've pushed many brilliant types out of my firm because they weren't disciplined enough."

Youngish in appearance and in his mid-50's, Mr. Gordon is absolutely obsessed with hard work and discipline.

He grew up in the family wholesale novelty business, but decided to make the move to real estate when he was a young man.

Mr. Gordon is the salesman who, in 1978, sold the nation's largest commercial condominium project to the unlikely partnership of the New York Telephone Company and the Teachers Insurance and Annuity Association. The address: 1166 Sixth Avenue, New York, N.Y. The building consists of 44 stories and 1,430,000 square feet of space. Completed in 1974, it was an instant white elephant, remained empty for four years and *cost the original builders and lenders over $75,000,000 in losses*. And then Ed Gordon stepped into the picture. But Mr. Gordon's *sale* was not the only display of brilliance in the 1166 Sixth Avenue transaction, for he also *leased* 600,000 square feet of the building to International Paper, earning an additional seven-figure commission.

To be sure, many other leasing agents in New York tried to make the deal. But they failed.

What, then, is the difference between success and failure?

The answer: Edward S. Gordon.

Upon entering his office, one cannot help but notice the good taste of his appointments, the numerous framed photographs, engraved plaques and awards that adorn the walls. But amid all the impressive paraphernalia hangs a tattered note.

In Ed Gordon's own words, "The day that note was written, I was three months into the business. I was ready to close my first big deal. All that remained was a final question-and-answer session. But, during the meeting, one of the partners of the client firm left the room for a few moments. When he came back, he handed a note to the second partner. He read it, crumpled it up and threw it away, and said, 'Ed, we'll get back to you.'"

The rookie salesman cleared this throat, looked at the prospective clients squarely and said, "Gentlemen, this deal is in trouble and it has something to do with that note. I'd really appreciate it if I could see it."

The partner hesitated. There was some embarrassed banter back and forth. Finally the partner reached into the wastebasket, removed the crumpled note and handed it to the young and inexperienced Edward S. Gordon.

The note read:

1. *What we want to know from any intelligent real estate agent is the following:*
2. *What is the usable square footage?*
3. *What is the total cost?*
4. *What are the extras and what is the price for them?*
5. *What is the lease term?*
6. *Is it a firm price?*

I can't understand why Gordon doesn't have the answers.

While devastated, the hero of this little tale did not shrivel up and fade away at that point. In his own words, "Right there, I vowed never to walk into another business meeting in my life without having *all* the answers that could be expected of me prepared in advance."

Edward S. Gordon became obsessed with preparation for a sale. Unlike most of his competitors, he went to great lengths to complete his homework before meeting with the clients.

Preparation is absolutely the core of his success.

Once client contact has been made, Mr. Gordon and all his associates abide by the following company rules:

> *Do constant follow ups.*
> *State and restate the case.*
> *Send additional information. Make followup calls.*
> *Write detailed explanatory letters.*
> *All information and reporting must be correct.*
> *Make sure all written presentations look right. The*

right cover, the right paper and the right type.
Do everything that should be done.

The Gordon people *do not* turn over a scribbled blur to
the typist and tell her to make it beautiful. Instead, they *do*
everything that should be done. People like that have very
little competition and make themselves indispensable to the
customer.

In selling the first half of the 1166 Sixth Avenue building to the New York Telephone Company, Mr. Gordon
made it his business to find out what size sales charts would
best fit the phone company's standard easels and what the
phone company's favorite colors were.

Armed with that information, he then went to the same
firm that made up N.Y. Phone's charts and had them make
up *his* charts.

Mr. Gordon maintains: "It's a matter of *creating* a transaction. New York Telephone was perfectly happy where it
was—until I educated them to another possibility."

Not only must the data generated by Edward S. Gordon
Company, Inc., be truthful, accurate and reliable, it must be
perfect! Otherwise it doesn't get out of the office.

The office staff consists of 75 people, and they must all
take responsibility for every facet and detail of their work.
They work longer hours than most of the competition, the
office atmosphere is friendly and businesslike, and all associates are encouraged to earn to the limit of their capabili-
ties. Mr. G. is not interested in middleweight achievers and
one of his associates is being pushed hard by his superiors
because he earns *only* $100,000 per year. To hear Mr. Gor-
don tell it, "My middle guys and gals would be number *one*
anywhere else."

Another lesson we can learn from Mr. Gordon is the
value of a rigorous, continuing education. He's passionate
about learning. In his words: "You can't succeed in real estate or in any other business without knowing all about everything—retailing trends, what cattle are selling for, what's

happening in politics—all other people's business. You've got to suck it all in like a vacuum cleaner."

In addition to espousing discipline and education, Mr. G. tells us, "You've got to derive pleasure from your work or you're sunk. Maybe you have to struggle with yourself to get into the office on a Saturday, but once you're there you had better be getting pleasure out of it." He closed the joint sale and leasing deals at 1166 Sixth Avenue at about 6 P.M. The aggregate value of his work exceeded $250,000,000. He then returned to his office to finish up the details. He did not go out and celebrate or have a drink with the boys. He did what any *good* salesperson would do, keeping both feet on the ground.

His own reaction to a one-quarter *billion* dollar sale? "The deal I just closed was monumental. This was the way to keep the basics of the business. I wasn't going to get carried away."

There is very little we can add to this story except to tell you that there was a mind-boggling glut of office space in this country in the mid-1980's. For example, Houston had 37,000,000 square feet of *vacant office space*. Dallas had 25,000,000 square feet. The nation, 318,000,000 square feet. And the numbers kept rising. Vacant space of this magnitude boded ill for certain lenders, landlords and builders. By the 1990's the real estate debacle had reached epic proportions. Terms like RTC and REO sent prices plummeting. Along with real estate sales and leases. But what an opportunity for salesmen like Ed Gordon. And if we are willing to learn from him, the prospects for sales success are not only increased—they become inevitable.

If this premium on 100% perfection bothers you, let us show you what *near-perfection* will do for you. We obtained this information from our friend David C. Pintard, the president of Stewart Title of Santa Barbara. David is a 100% guy. His 99.9% Table taken from The Stewart Title Quality Awareness Training speaks for itself.

WHAT DOES 99.9% QUALITY MEAN?

One hour of unsafe drinking water per month.

Two unsafe landings at O'Hare Airport each day.

16,000 lost pieces of mail per hour.

20,000 incorrect drug prescriptions each year.

500 incorrect surgical operations performed each week.

50 newborn babies dropped at birth by doctors each day.

22,000 checks deducted from the wrong account each hour.

Your heart fails to beat 32,000 times each year.

1. HARD WORK AND PERSEVERANCE

Some make their fortune by design, some make it by accident, and others by a combination of both. Ask a sophisticated Englishman the secret of success and he will tell you to pursue an attainable goal with great singularity of purpose. Ask an American Fortune 500 company president and he will likely respond: hard work and perseverance. (If he's a real Connecticut Yankee, he will add the word *thrift*.)

But if you ask Sam Bresnik, who recently sold his 1,500 supermarkets to a larger chain with 2,000 stores, he will tell you, "How did I make it? I worked my ass off for 50 years, that's how."

We want to recite the tale of Sam Bresnik because Sam is a genuine success story, the kind we all like to hear about. And we can learn much from his example.

Sam was born in Cracow, Poland, around the turn of the century. The exact date is unknown because the place where the records were kept was blown to kingdom come in World War I. Sam didn't like World War I, never attended school, and wanted to leave Poland for personal reasons. He got married, sired two sons and moved to Warsaw, where he took a job as a janitor for the U.S. Embassy. He offered to work for nothing, explaining to an embassy officer that his goal was to learn English and go to America. The Americans refused to take him on for nothing and paid him a respectable wage in surplus zlotys.

There, he succeeded in learning English. True, he had a heavy accent, which for personal reasons we will not duplicate here.

For those salespeople not aware of it, Polish persistence is a force that makes the burning of the stars pale to insignificance.

Sam came to America with his wife and two sons at a time of great unemployment. He very quickly used up the last of his converted zlotys and could not bring himself to go back to the American-Polish Aid Society for more help. He was ashamed to admit that he had been unemployed, for the first time in his life, for over two weeks. He never wanted to take charity. He only wanted to give it.

One day, out of desperation, he began knocking on doors, offering to work for meals. A little something for himself and a little something to take home to his family.

The answer was *no*. Again and again, *no*.

As noon approached, Sam began to feel faint from lack of food.

He knocked on the door of a sumptuous home—surely they would have *something* for him—and the madame of the house opened the door just enough for her to look out but not enough for him to look in.

"Are you the bookkeeper?" she asked.

"No," he replied. "I am not the bookkeeper. I am only a poor Polish immigrant looking for work. Any kind of work. And you don't have to pay me with money. You can pay me with food. Just a little food for me and my family."

"Go away," the buxom lady said. "We don't need any help."

"My dear Mrs. Lady, I will do *anything*. Wash windows, beat rugs, dust the furniture, mop floors, plant potatoes— anything! But if you turn me away, I could drop dead. I have not eaten in three days." His voice cracked as he spoke.

"Do you know what kind of a house this is?" she asked, through the crack in the door.

"My dear Mrs. Lady, Sam is not asking questions. I am only looking—"

"You sure don't give up, do you?" she interrupted. "Do you know what kind of a *house* this is?"

"No, but I do not ask questions, I only—"

"Well, for your information, this happens to be a whorehouse, and the only help we need around here is a bookkeeper. Do you know how to keep books?"

"Keep books? What do you mean, keep books?"

"Can you add and subtract—multiply and divide?"

"My dear Mrs. Lady—I cannot even read and write! How can I—"

"Here's a quarter," the madam said, thrusting a 25 cent piece into his hand. "Just take it and never come back." Then she slammed the door in his face.

Weakly, he walked down to the corner grocery and bought himself a huge bunch of overripe bananas. He was more concerned with quantity than quality at this low point in his life.

Sam, weakened by hunger and ashamed of his poverty, took his heavy load of near-rotten bananas and walked across the street. He could go no farther. He sat down on the curb and began stuffing himself with bananas.

The food revived him.

He was about to rush home with the balance of his cache when a woman walked up to him and asked for ten cents worth.

Excitedly, he tore off a large bunch from his huge bunch and passed them up to her.

He pocketed the dime.

Then came another lady and purchased five cents worth.

Three hours later, he had made a business of buying, selling and eating bananas.

At the end of the day, he ran home to his wife and shouted, "Ninotchka! Look what I have here! Money and bananas! Tomorrow, we are going to get a pushcart and go in the fruit business. But you will have to help me. With the buying and the selling and making change."

The following day, Sam and his beloved wife went fruit peddling.

The boys went to school to learn to read and write.

As the months went on, they saved their money and rented a store. The boys and Ninotchka were always at Sam's side to help him. In a year, they purchased a market. In ten years, they owned a supermarket. In 50 years, they owned 1,500 supermarkets. They gave mightily to the American-Polish Aid Society. They celebrated the fall of communism by sending a huge barrel of pickled herring directly to the Pope. They sent CARE packages to Poland, regarded Lech Walesa as a hero and sold *SOLIDARNOSC* T-shirts in all their stores.

But eventually the time came to sell out. A large international conglomerate bought out the Bresnik stores for 96 million dollars.

Cash.

As the deal was about to close, with the international conglomerate's board of directors and officers on one side of the table and the Bresnik family on the other side of the table, Sam's attorney, carrying a large bundle of papers, sat down next to his client and said, "O.K., boss, if you'll just sign here, here, here and here—that cinches the deal."

"Sign here, here, here and here? How can I sign here, here, here and here? I can't even read and write."

"You can't read and write?" Sam's attorney asked, incredulous.

"That's right."

The attorney jumped up and said loudly, "Good God! Boss! Think of where you'd be today if only you could read and write."

"I know where I'd be. I'd be a bookkeeper in a whorehouse."

And so (with thanks to Somerset Maugham) ends the story of Sam, a man who despite being illiterate, became a hugely successful salesman, through *hard work and perseverance*.

In spite of his great wealth, Sam has maintained his modesty. Ask him what his greatest achievement has been and he will not utter one word about his many millions. Instead, he will pull a weathered note from his pocket and shove it in your face. It is a note he received from his Polish countryman, Karol Wojtyla. It reads:

Thanks for the pickled herring.

2. GETTING PAID (MEN)

On the matter of getting paid, there are two incidents in the World of High Finance which merit your attention, just as they did ours.

Item No. 1, from the Wall Street Journal: Andrew J. Krieger, former Currency Trader for Bankers Trust Company, made $300,000,000 for his company in 1987, making him probably the world's foremost currency trader. Earlier in 1984, Mr. Krieger had worked at Saloman Brothers, Inc., also trading currency options.

Starting at Saloman, he worked a full day at the office, made trades on his car phone while driving to and from the office, and continued trading each night at home until well after midnight. It was not uncommon for Mr. K. to trade around the clock.

In his first year with Saloman Brothers (1984), he made $50,000 in salary and a bonus of $170,000.

He was then 27.

Another year passed.

Then, Bankers Trust hired him away from Saloman Brothers with an offer of at least $450,000 in 1986.

When his six-year-old son asked him what he did, he said he bought and sold things.

"Like toys?" the youngster asked.

He tried to explain what a foreign currency options trader does, but his son interrupted, "Well, when are you going to do something that helps people, like be a doctor or a fireman?"

When Mr. K. now tells this father-son story, he says he felt rebuked.

However, in 1986, when the other shoe fell, he was paid by his illustrious Wall Street Employer with 1% of his annual earnings. To wit: $3,000,000. His boss made $300,000,000.

He quit.

Publicly, he uttered not one word of anger or disappointment.

But remarkable as it seems, he had been underpaid.

The fact that lesser traders were paid 5% of their gross earnings for doing the same work meant nothing to Mr. K's Esteemed and Lovable Boss. According to the Boss Rationale (a system whereby The Boss Man Thinks for Himself and Makes Up His Own Mind!), the 1% figure was arrived at after asking numerous *competitors* how *they* would reward such an exemplary and unprecedented employee performance.

So much for the Rugged Individualism of the Wall Street Big Shot.

Item No. 2, from the Los Angeles Times in the closing years of the twentieth century:

$10-Million Award Accepted in Firing

Frank V. McCullough, Sr., the Beverly Hills insurance executive fired by Sperry & Hutchinson Co. because he made too much money, agreed Friday to accept a $10 million court award rather than face a new trial of his civil suit against the Green Stamp company.

Jurors in January awarded McCullough $20 million in damages, but Los Angeles Superior Court

Assistant Presiding Judge Jack E. Goertzen decided on Wednesday that the amount was "somewhat excessive" and cut the figure to $10 million.

The judge gave McCullough until 4 P.M. Friday to accept the lower amount or he would schedule a new trial.

McCullough, 64, sued Sperry & Hutchinson over his dismissal on April 14, 1978, as head of its then-subsidiary, S&H Insurance Co., claiming that he was ousted because he earned lucrative bonuses based on a contractual share of profits. He now heads his own firm, Carlisle Insurance Co.

And how did all this come to pass? Quite simply, Sperry & Hutchinson Co. (of Green Stamp fame) hired Frank V. McCullough in 1974 to take over their failing subsidiary, S&H Insurance Co., with the contractual proviso that Mr. McCullough was guaranteed 20% of the subsidiary's annual profits. In 1977, the bonus came to $636,000. The Great and Virtuous Men of S&H asked Frank V. McCullough, Sr., to limit his bonus to $225,000. He refused. But F.V.M., Sr. *did* give one-third of $636,000 (which is $212,000) to *his* employees as a bonus that year.

S&H fired F.V.M., Sr.

He sued.

The termination cost S&H $20,000,000.

The $20,000,000 was then reduced to $10,000,000.

And what did our latest No. 1 Best Seller Hero have to say of all this?

"It was always the principle with me. I really thought I was right and they were wrong. The problem was they didn't keep their word to me. I think in business you should always keep your word."

Which leaves us convinced that the matter of Getting Paid is sometimes worth fighting for.

No. 1 Best Sellers *know* that promises are worthless unless reduced to writing and signed by all parties. If the boss wants the *best* from you, the *least* he can do is sign a fair contract. If you learn nothing else from this book, get your money's worth and memorize the following:

IF IT IS WORTH SAYING,
IT IS WORTH PUTTING IN WRITING.

3. GETTING PAID (WOMEN) (THE DESPERATION CASE - BEGINNING)

We submit the following tale of near tragedy with the full and complete promise to the characters that we would not use their true names or places of residence and business.

Our story begins with a young couple who fell madly in love in college. For her, love was the exquisite fulfillment of a young woman's consuming fantasies. For him, it was about having a helpmate. She: a nursing student on a full scholarship. He: a premed student with grave doubts about his ability to become a doctor.

She pulled him through. Gave up her career plans to become a nurse. Took a low-paying secretarial position at the medical school. Struggled mightily to keep his spirits up. Fulfilled his carnal impulses magnificently. Gave him three beautiful and well-behaved kids. Responded to his grumpiness with cheerful effervescence. Kept the kids quiet. Kept the apartment immaculate. Eight years after they were married and he had completed his residency, he divorced her.

Just walked out.

She sued for support.

He moved out of state.

Married a rich heiress.

Joan Smith's world collapsed.

She wanted to run him over but could not do such a thing. The car would not start.

She locked herself in the bathroom, had a good cry and emerged, red-eyed and devastated, to explain to the children that daddy won't be coming home any more.

The incredible burdens placed on this woman caused her to lose 20 pounds and her university job. Two weeks later, when the rent was due and her savings account was depleted, she decided it was time to act.

She dressed up her children, put on clean jeans, a clean, starched blouse and got in the car. It wouldn't start. She then marched down to her local gas station/garage, herding the children by her side. The garage owner, a tall, thin, one-eyed grump, was known, with little or no affection, by the check-bouncing and miserable people of the community, as Jake the Wrench. But the good people of the community loved him and considered him a mechanical genius. They also called him Jake the Wrench. No relation to Mr. Good-wrench who merely talks about what he will do for you. Jake does the actual work.

Joan met Jake at the gas pump, children in tow, and explained her predicament: "My car won't run and I don't have the money to pay you. Do you have any jobs for a single mother of three so I can pay you back?"

Jake looked at her inscrutably with his one good eye half-closed. "Follow me," he said.

The impoverished family of four followed Jake the Wrench into the foreboding back office, which had all the attributes of a dimly lit and foreboding cavern. The children were silent.

Very silent.

With the gentility and good breeding of his trade, Jake

the Wrench looked at Joan Smith and said, "Coffee?"

Because the coffee urn looked like an offshoot of the La Brea Tar Pits, Joan politely declined. Although she was a dedicated, committed and sensuous caffeine addict, she could not bear the smell of greased coffee and therefore declined. The fingerprints on the mugs didn't spark her addictive proclivities either.

"All right," the Wrench said, while the children held hands and cowered behind their mother, "let's get right down to business." He stepped over to a besmudged, besmirched desk and pulled out the top drawer halfway. "See all those little pieces of paper?"

The Smith family of four nodded their heads in unison although the youngest was too short to see anything at all.

"Well," the Wrench continued, "they're all bum checks. Anything you collect, you get 50%."

Without hesitation, Joan replied, "Deal!" and shook hands with the one-eyed Jake the Wrench. A moment later, she scooped all the NSF and STP PMNT documents out of the drawer. Instantly, she knew she was in business.

Big business.

And big, big sales. But instead of selling a product, she would be selling something much more important: honesty.

She went home, prepared herself a cup of delicious black coffee and arranged the checks in order of value. Biggest amounts on top. Smallest amounts on the bottom.

As she sat down to make her first call, there was a rude banging on the door. The children, well trained, shouted for their mother to answer. When she did, Jake the Wrench stood before her, dangling her car keys in his left hand.

"Car's fixed," he said, squinting, "and don't leave keys in the ignition. Next time somebody might drive off with it."

"Wonderful!" she replied, taking the keys. "How much do I owe you?"

"Nothin'!"

"Nothing?" she asked.

"Wasn't nothin' wrong. Somebody just pulled spark

plug wires. Prob'ly some kid."

"Can I at least offer you a cup of coffee?"

"Nope. Don't drink other people's coffee. Ain't got no flavor." Jake blinked [right-side eye only], turned and left.

In a loud, clear voice she thanked him. She waved him a happy goodbye. Closed the door. Shushed the children. Then sat down to make the first call of the day. Before dialing, she turned on the telephone tape recorder.

The top check was for $1,562.38. The maker, a highly successful businessman with a reputation for treason against the human race, was none other than her husband's poker night friend, Gordon Grinch. A fat little man with a pencil-thin mustache and a huge ego.

In the arcane psychobabble of the psychospecialists who wrote the psychoterminology of such things, Gordon Grinch qualifies as an obsessive/compulsive penocentric entrepreneur in overdrive. Gordon was driven by two demons:

1. Money and
2. Sex.

Joan shushed her children as the phone call was put through.

"Gordon, it's Joan Smith. Harold's left me."

"Well, I'm terribly, terribly sorry to hear that. What can I do to help you?"

"Gordon, you're just about the smartest businessman I ever met in my life and I've got some real big business and personal problems that I have to discuss with you. Do you think you can help me?"

"Well now, you beautiful young thing, there's nothing for nothing in this whole big, great, wild world of ours and—"

"Gordon, I have to see you right away! It's about your reputation and mine."

"Reputation? My God, I hope people aren't talking about us already."

"Well, they could be," Joan said, turning her voice into a sexual powderkeg. "Do you think you'd like that? I'm very, very, very discreet."

"Do you *really* think I can help you?" Gordon asked, lighting the fuse with his satiric voice.

"Gordon, from the way you act and talk you must be just about the sexiest and most potent businessman in Humboldt County, and if what I hear is correct, we've just got to get together. And get it on. I'm a real needy woman."

"When?" he asked as his internal sexual dynamite exploded.

"Right now, Gordon Grinch. Right now!"

"But it's only 10 o'clock! Can't it wait until tonight?" His voice cracked because of the internal turmoil. After all, early morning sex interfered with business.

"Now, Gordon, right now! I'm very needy and lonely and starved for you - know - what. Do you think you can fill that need?"

"At 10 o'clock in the morning?" he protested, leaning forward in his swivel chair and putting his elbows on his massive mahogany desk.

"At 10:15," she said.

"Hey," he laughed, expansively. "I don't know if I can get it up this early."

"You'll do just fine. You've probably got more sexual prowess and good looks than any five businessman like you that I know."

The explosive power of the conversation put a dynamite glow in his cheeks.

He stroked himself. "Hey, you're not such a bad looking dish yourself. Think you can help me get it up?" He laughed loudly. Lasciviously. Patted his potbelly very lovingly.

"Try me. I'll show you the net results of the best sexual intercourse *I've* ever had."

Gordon laughed again. But this time, more loudly. The only words that hit home were: 1. sexual and 2. intercourse.

"Yeah," he said "But where can we go?" At this point

he was swiveling rapidly back and forth. The sexual bomb of great expectations had worked its magic.

"Your office. Right now."

"Yeah, but what about my secretary?"

"Well," she said, "we'll lock the door and get right down to business. You just have no idea how great my needs are."

"Oh but I do! So come on over, baby, and let's get it on! And wear something real sexy."

She hung up the phone discreetly, turned off the telephone tape recorder and took out the tape.

He slammed down the phone, jumped up from his swivel chair and shouted "WHOOPEE," at the top of his lungs. In his hysteria, he stroked himself lewdly and laughed uproariously.

His secretary, Martha, was certain he had just closed another big deal.

"Martha!" he shouted to his secretary, "when Joan Smith shows up, usher her directly into my office. Oh yeah, and be sure to lock the door so we aren't disturbed."

3. GETTING PAID (WOMEN) (THE DESPERATION CASE - MIDDLE)

Fifteen minutes later.

Joan Smith, locked securely in the Great Man's office, stood before his massive desk and looked him straight in the eye.

Dumbfounded, he stared back. But his cheeks went completely pale. When his brain shifter finally connected with his tongue gears, he said, "Hey, what's the big idea with the kids?"

"Gordon Grinch, I want you and your friend Dr. Harold Smith to know that these three kids are the net results of the best sexual intercourse I ever had." She patted her children lovingly and maternally on their heads. "When you see him, please tell him that."

"Hey now," Grinch demanded as the color returned to his cheeks, "what's going on here?"

Joan Smith, newly created NO. 1 BEST SELLER about to close her first deal, flashed the bum check in front of Mr.

Grinch and with purposeful, definitive clarity, said: "You owe Jake down at the garage $1,562.38. But add $10 for bank charges."

"ARE YOU CRAZY?" He shouted.

The children began to cry and clung to their mother.

"YOU GET THE H___ OUT OF HERE OR I'LL CALL THE COPS!"

In steady, determined tones, Joan Smith replied, "Please don't swear in front of me or my kids. And—" she said stepping forward, taking the phone off its cradle and handing it to him, "—here, call the police. I'll be glad to tell them everything I know. Especially the fact that you've locked me up in your office. *That's against the law.*"

Gordon Grinch's lukewarm blood suddenly turned to ice. Once again, his cheeks went sickly pale.

By now, the children were crying uncontrollably.

"This is blackmail," he said, leaning forward, trying to pull the check from her hand.

She pulled the check away. Dropped the phone on his desk.

Above the din of wailing children and Mr. Grinch's fulminating anger, Joan Smith spoke more loudly. "Tilly Jensen's my attorney and she said—" At the mention of Tilly Jensen's name, Gordon Grinch's pale cheeks developed a green tint. Her husband was the local judge.

"THIS IS A PERVERSION AND VIOLATION OF MY CONSTITUTIONAL RIGHTS AND WRONGS!" Gordon shouted. He went into a recitation of Canned Speech No. 489XPQ. The children wailed. Martha, the secretary, had her ear glued to the door. Joan Smith stood her ground.

"FURTHERMORE," Grinch continued, "THIS IS AGAINST MY CIVIL RIGHTS AND INVASION OF PRIVACY!" Whereupon he went into a recitation of Canned Speech No. 490XPO.

The children cried louder and clung to their mother.

"Just pay what you owe, including the $10, and we're out of here," Joan Smith said loudly, clearly, and with great determination. "I'll even throw this into the deal," she said.

"What's that?" he asked.

"A tape of our conversation. I can give it to you or your wife."

Gordon Grinch blanched. Then his rosy cheeks turned gray. His stomach went into mixmaster mode. He was defeated and knew it. And the screaming, crying kids didn't help either. He punched Martha's number on the intercom.

Martha unglued her ear from the closed door and ran to her desk. "Yes, Mr. Grinch, what is it?" she asked. Breathlessly.

"Cut a check for—" he shot a glance at Joan Smith.

"—one thousand five hundred seventy-two dollars and thirty-eight cents."

"Got that, Martha?"

"Yes, Mr. Grinch," she said. Breathlessly.

"AND UNLOCK THE DOOR!" he shouted.

"Yes, Mr. Grinch," she said. Breathlessly.

Upon receiving the check, Joan picked up Gordon Grinch's fancy telephone and called his bank. Told them to put a hold on the funds. Hung up. Marched out with her three crying children. Then drove directly to Jake's Garage. Showed him the check. Went with him to the bank. Cashed it. Split the proceeds. The children were no longer crying. Jake looked at her inscrutably, his one good eye half-closed, and spoke tersely: "Not bad pay for two hours work."

4. GETTING PAID (THE DESPERATION CASE - END)

Ten years later, Joan Smith Collections employed 41 women in six states. All the women were divorcees with children.

Deadbeats were treated with sweet talk in the beginning and flamethrowers in the end.

When Joan successfully sued for divorce and was awarded child-support, Dr. Smith refused to pay. With her growing knowledge of collections and her determination to collect or die, she utterly destroyed her ex-husband's credit.

And how are sales today?

"Fabulous. Just fabulous. We'll never be out of work," she replied. "And we only deal with the weaker sex: men. And rich men at that. The more money, property and stock they own, the more we like it, because we always collect. We're not interested in poor slobs."

"But that's against the law," we said. "That's discriminatory."

"It sure is, and that's the way we like it. That's the way we make a living. If what we do is against the law, I say

that's just great. You should see the number of deadbeat
judges we've nailed. They are absolutely terrible people.
And don't quote me directly, but we've gone after a number
of senators and representatives and made every one of them
cough up. All of them were lawyers. One day we even hope
to get the president. All rich and powerful men are fair
game. We do not discriminate on the basis of race, creed,
color or religion. But my big goal in life is to scalp the
president."

"Furthermore," Joan Smith said, "women are biologi-
cally superior to men. We live longer because we're tougher
and stronger than men. We have an advantage because we
know what makes them tick and they don't even *care* about
what makes us tick. If you don't believe me, then let me tell
you about our male-dominated competitors: not one of their
collection agencies, anywhere in the world, can claim a
100% collection rate. But we can and do. Men have abused
and tormented women from day one and this is our way of
getting back. If they don't like it, that's tough. Let them start
paying their bills and alimony. We have a theory that is
foolproof. We sell honesty. And if we have to use tape re-
corders, camcorders and photos to do it, we do it in spades
and we never fail. I repeat, gentlemen, we sell honesty."

We decided it was time to change the subject.

"Have you found our manuscript helpful?" we asked.

"Indispensable," she said. "Look at these women in
here. They all have big mirrors in front of their desks."

And at the top of each mirror was a sign:

THE NUMBER ONE BEST SELLER

About halfway down the mirror was another sign:

RULES AND REGULATIONS

1. WE SELL HONESTY.
2. FOLLOW THE FOUR BASIC RULES OF SELLING. A.I.D.C.
3. DON'T LET HIM GRAB THE CHECK.
4. DON'T BACK DOWN.
5. DON'T SHOUT.
6. DON'T TAKE NO FOR AN ANSWER.
7. DO CALL THE BANK IMMEDIATELY.
8. DO PUT A HOLD ON THE FUNDS.
9. REMEMBER THAT ALL OUR CLIENTS ARE:
    a) DIRTY.
    b) FILTHY.
    c) SCUMBAG.
    d) DEADBEATS.
    e) THEREFORE, GIVE THEM THEIR MONEY'S WORTH.
10. TALK DIRTY (THE JERKS LOVE IT).

ENTHUSIASM

In our research among the troops, the word *enthusiasm* cropped up repeatedly. The reason for this is well known to our compatriots in the world of selling. Those who lack enthusiasm simply never make it.

We are not talking about the enthusiasm of fanatics, but rather the enthusiasm of successful salespeople. In other words, the enthusiasm sustained by hard work, intelligence, and a positive outlook on life.

For openers, let us give you a definition.

Enthusiasm is taken from the Greek, and in its most literal sense means *to be god-inspired*. Not too many years ago it referred to divine possession or inspiration. The word *enthusiasm* has always had a positive connotation. As used today, *enthusiasm* has come to mean intense emotion compelling action; lively or eager interest in a cause or activity.

So much for definition.

For our purposes, *enthusiasm* is an attitude. It does not come in bottles or pills, but must be generated internally. It starts with your first waking moment and ends when you are fast asleep. You must learn to fling off the covers each morning and spring from your bed enthusiastically. Since most people *die* in bed, it is absolutely essential that you get up and out as fast as possible.

If you are not enthusiastic, we are going to let you in on one of the great trade secrets of the century: you must *condition yourself to be enthusiastic*.

How?

By springing out of bed, getting in front of a mirror and saying:

TODAY I WILL BE ENTHUSIASTIC!

This may seem a little silly on days one through 15, but by the end of one month you will begin to feel the effects of this profound psychological conditioning. After two months you will notice a profound improvement in your attitude and income. You must never again use the words: *Boy, am I tired*! If you are tired, learn to substitute the word *enthusiastic* for *tired*. The patent medicine men may not like it, but it will do wonders for your id, ego and superego. You must train yourself not to complain. You are absolutely doomed to failure as a great salesperson if you are a complainer.

The power of enthusiasm was related to us by a leasing agent in St. Louis, Missouri. In the mid 1990's, business was so bad, the office space glut so overwhelming, that the agent advertised his services for half price. He tried flyers, mailings, newspaper ads, autodialers, free candy for the kids. Business only got worse. The *marketplace* was dead. There simply were no takers. The agent called his crew of four salespeople and passed on the bad news. There was not enough money in the bank to pay the bills. Another month like last month and they would have to close the doors.

The very next morning, a young man walked in the door and asked for a job. He had just obtained a real estate license. The youngster was very enthusiastic. The oldster *almost* blurted out the bad news. But because of his good training, he held back and listened.

"When would you like to start?" the old man asked.

"Right now," the young man replied.

"And *where* would you like to start."

"Right here in this building. From the top floor to the bottom floor."

HIRED!

The enthusiastic young man saved the company. He theorized that if he could show existing commercial tenants how they could move into better offices for less money, he would be successful.

A year later, when business was at least self-sustaining, the old teacher called in his star pupil and asked him for the 20th time: "Tell me again, young man, how did you *do it*?"

The young man smiled and replied for the 20th time: "Simple! By knocking on one door at a time."

Which brings us to our next parable.

We learned a lot about enthusiasm from an extremely successful real estate broker who lives in a very beautiful beach house not far from one of your authors. He is a very nice and reputable guy. He was, in his active years, one of the country's leading leasing agents. When we asked him about his early days in selling, he told us an interesting story.

Our man, Morgan, started off selling vacuum cleaners that trapped dust in a water filter system. Every morning before going out on his appointed rounds, he would have to report to his supervisor and shout:

"BOY, AM I ENTHUSIASTIC!"

"How did you like your work?" we asked.

"I hated it," Mr. Morgan replied. "It was a great product, but they trained us to use high-pressure tactics and I hated it. I hated shouting in front of my supervisor every morning, or shouting at the sales meetings. I hated it because it all seemed so hokey."

"Hmmm," we hmmmmed. "What approach do you use *now* to start your day?"

"I shout into the mirror: *BOY, AM I ENTHUSIASTIC*! But on real bad days when I wake up feeling lousy, I take the Germanic approach and shout: TODAY YOU WILL BE ENTHUSIASTIC!" He paused. Then he looked at us squarely and said, "You know, boys, it may seem a little hokey, but it really works."

Now that we are all flinging off the covers and shouting at the mirrors, we must take you to the next important phase of enthusiasm:

You must learn to be an enthusiastic listener.

When you go for an interview and show a sincere and enthusiastic willingness to *listen*, you will improve your chances of closing the deal enormously.

In fact, here is one of life's great secrets:

You will make more friends in two months by listening and becoming enthusiastically interested in what others have to say than you will in 200 years of blabbing and trying to get other people interested in you.

If you do not believe that, just think of all the compulsive talkers you know and how utterly obnoxious they are. People who talk too much never have anything important to say. Therefore, be an enthusiastic listener. Learn to listen not only with your ears, but also with your heart. Just as parents who listen to their kids raise the best kids, salespeople who listen to their customers cultivate the best clientele.

We can turn to no greater authority on listening than a British-American novelist for whom we have enormous respect. Her name is Taylor Caldwell. In her novel entitled *The Listener*, she wrote:

> The most desperate need of men today is not a new vaccine for any disease, or a new religion, or a new "way of life." . . . . He does not require bigger and better bombs and missiles . . . . His real need, his most terrible need, is for someone to listen to him, not as a "patient" but as a human soul.

And while we are on the subject of great and intelligent listeners, let us quote the Nobel Prize-winning writer Anatole France:

To know what to ask is to know half.

And let's not forget Goode Olde Rudyard Kipling, who tells us:

> *I have six honest servants. They've taught me all
> I know. Their names are Who, What, Where, When,
> Why and How.*

Admittedly, it is not easy to be a good listener and to be enthusiastic all the time. You need a good physical regimen, good diet and a good family life, as well as a good hobby and numerous interests beyond your business.

For those of you who cannot bear the thought of being enthusiastic from your first waking moment, we will suggest an alternate approach. Tell yourself upon awakening that you feel great. If not great, at least darned good.

One of the most successful salesmen we know (who is no spring chicken) told us that he starts every day with the words: "Today I'm not going to be tired." You must learn to do the same.

No amount of enthusiasm will help you if you lack self-confidence. In this day and age, the matter of developing self-confidence is relatively simple. Buy a tape recorder and make your sales presentation into that little electronic miracle. It will not make your mouth go dry or cause a heart flutter. When you have practiced the presentation at least ten times, try it on a real live prospect. You will be amazed at the results. (If you do not have a tape-recorder, try the mirror.)

If you *really* want to develop a great personal style, go to a television recording studio, where they will put you on the tube for a minimal amount of money. Or do it yourself with a camcorder and a VCR. It is amazing the transformation that will come over a shrinking violet once his or her television debut has been made. (But we would be willing to bet that you already have a great deal of self-confidence. After all, this is not the kind of book for shrinking violets.)

If you are intellectually inclined and like to read, keep referring to those books which inspire you the most. Or refer to those passages which inspire you the most. We keep a great many books on quotations, proverbs, aphorisms and the like. When we started this chapter, we came across three quotes in particular that we want to pass on to you. The first is by Samuel Goldwyn, the second by Ralph Waldo Emerson, and the third by Dear Abby.

1st. *No person who is enthusiastic about his work has anything to fear from life.*

2nd. *Every great and commanding moment in the annals of the world is the triumph of some enthusiasm.*

3rd. *An ounce of keeping your mouth shut is worth a pound of explanation.*

VOCABULARY

We encourage you to develop your vocabulary so that you will make more sales. *Intelligent* rejoinder in conversation sells far more than argumentative gobbledygook. Stupid 200-word vocabulary people *never* have anything interesting to say and they always talk too much when they say it. Intelligent people, on the other hand, listen carefully and usually have pretty good vocabularies. The *only* common characteristics among the nation's successful executives are a good vocabulary and a willingness to read. From this comes a good command of the language. Since we *think* in terms of words, and these very same words are used to generate ideas, ideas will be far better with a good vocabulary than the ideas generated by the grunters and groaners. People who make funny noises and who never finish sentences are usually not great salespeople. They may find riches and glory in other areas (such as marriage or accession to the royal throne), but there's just no way they're going to make it selling yachts in Monte Carlo or beach houses on Lido Isle.

Your ability to improve your vocabulary starts with the dictionary. Use it wisely and often. If you wish to improve your verbal acuity more quickly, go to any library or bookstore and get one of their splendid books on vocabulary improvement. Use the books consistently, one at a time, and we guarantee you that your sales will pick up.

Why?

Because words are the most important tools of our trade.

He who speaks bullfizzle really does not make the most sales. He who speaks sense, does.

If you wish to carry the vocabulary improvement program further, for little cost, you can go to your local junior college and take a speech course. No local college in Dimwit, N.Y.? Not to worry. You can do it by correspondence, via tape recorder, video-tape, records, books, and sales seminars. But do it. Your sales life depends on it.

Your improved vocabulary will improve not only your thinking and speaking ability, but also your writing ability.

Now, writing is something your authors know something about. Yes, Virginia, a preposition is something you absolutely can end a sentence with. Provided you know what you're doing. Do we know what we're doing? You bet! Just ask our publisher. Or better yet, ask two of our beautiful, charming, overworked, underpaid and brilliant editors. These junior editors have to keep *everybody* happy and make *everything* readable. Are they interested in our vocabulary? You bet! And so are we.

Because without this joint intellectual effort, we would all fail.

So read. Study. Learn.

Why?

Because a good vocabulary will help you make sales. You must strive mightily to put your point across and be understood. How many people do you know who *do not want to be understood*? Too many, we're sure. How many times have you attended a business, religious, social or homeowners meeting, listened for what seemed an eternity, then scratched your head and wondered what the Great Bore *really* had to say? (Promise not to tell the bore and we'll give you the answer: *nothing*.)

Want another reason why you should improve your vocabulary? Easy. It'll make you more interesting. And interesting people tell interesting stories. Once you have done your share of listening, you may, upon reflection and pause for deep-breathing, speak to your prospect.

The Bible is a prime example of what good story telling can do. The Parables are known by many and remembered by most because they are in story form. You would be hard-put to find someone in the Western World who did not know the gossip about Samson and Delilah. Even though the story has been related countless times, it still survives from generation to generation because people delight in hearing stories. They begin this lifelong love affair with tales by listening to nursery rhymes and fairy tales when they're mere tots. Infants and children can even be sold on the idea of going to bed, so long as they're first told a story.

The successful salesperson, in short, is the person who has mastered the art of verbal seduction. Which is why he or she gets paid a lot. Furthermore:

1. Giving a gift is not a bad idea.
2. If you show honest interest in others, they will probably show honest interest in you.
3. Arouse the prospect's interest by telling him (or her) what you are going to do for him (or her).
4. Develop your vocabulary and your storytelling ability.
5. Go to prospect trade shows. If a prospect show interest in your product, be sure to show interest in your prospect.
6. Educate yourself continuously on your product or service.
7. Never knock the competition. If you do, you will create negative interest and lose the prospect forever.
8. Never argue. If you win the argument, you lose the sale.

9. Here's what our buddy Albert Camus had to say about listening:

Great ideas…come into the world as gently as doves. Perhaps, then, if we listen attentively, we shall hear amid the uproar of empires and nations a faint flutter of wings, the gentle stirring of life and hope.

Sadly, the world is nothing more than a not-so-happy breeding ground for those dodos who do not want to be understood. What they really want is an audience. Since the dodos could never make it in front of a *real* audience, they have to settle for a *captive* audience. Whether it is the boss or those crybaby louts in diapers at the water cooler, these ninnies do not want to be understood. They are so hung up on themselves that they want to hear themselves talk. They have big ids or big egos, or both. But they are not looking for clients to please. They are looking for victims to bore to death. And they are selfish. Selfish people should not go into sales.

The whole point of language and vocabulary is to understand and be understood. It's a give and take, not a take and take.

And just as the purpose of language is to communicate, the purpose of communication is to tell the truth. The plain and honest truth. Here's one of the great trade secrets of the last 6,000 years:

Do it our way with honesty, good intentions and a good vocabulary, and you will make more sales than you have ever made before in your life.

Possibly the strongest tool in your sales arsenal is *credibility*. And it takes a good vocabulary to get your credibility across.

In closing, we would like to remind you of the following: Shakespeare used about 38,000 different words in his magnificent writings. The Bible, about 8,000. Guess who's the No. 1 Best Seller in that readership race.

The point: don't go overboard on your vocabulary. Speak like an intelligent person, not like a thesaurus.

(P.S. When thou converseth with customers, thou shalt not use dirty words! Never! For a foul mouth loseth deals.)

THE MIRACLE - PART 1

Class is really over and you don't have to read this chapter if you don't want to. But since you have already paid the price of admission, why not stay for the whole show?

Let us start off by reminding you that Our Beloved Country went from being the world's largest creditor nation to being the world's largest debtor nation in seven short years. Mercifully, the lunatics who did this are by and large gone. By some miracle, the lunatics who've replaced them may yet get us out of this mess. But most likely not. Most of them, Democrats and Republicans alike, are attorneys. We do not know of *one* who is a professional salesperson.

As No. 1 Best Sellers, it is our business to bring buying and selling parties into agreement *as quickly as possible* without inflicting pain or suffering. If we do that, we get paid. If not, we starve. Conversely, attorneys are the only professional people in the world who get themselves paid handsomely by committing the Mortal Sin of Perpetual Delay. More delay equals more money.

In the competitive and unforgiving world marketplace, the heads of major Japanese and Western European companies simply will not do business with the Chief Honchos of American companies if The Great American Man brings along one or more attorneys to the Big Meeting. Do *they* know something *we* don't know?

You bet.

They know with absolute certainty that the most successful U.S. companies are run by former salesmen. And the very worst? By former attorneys.

With very few exceptions, attorneys, by training and temperament, are committed to the principle of *fighting and winning without taking undue risks*. Whatever the outcome of a deal, attorneys believe with great passion and commitment that *they must be paid*!

No. 1 Best Sellers, on the other hand, *always* try to please the customer. If they don't, *they never get paid*!

Attorneys believe in adversarial relationships. Salespeople believe in customer satisfaction.

What does all of this have to do with a crackpot book on selling? Plenty. The fate of this nation hangs totally on our ability to *produce* and *sell*. That goes for every other country too, but for most of *us* it is an article of faith that we must do what is morally right. *We* want to be decent salespeople with the right product delivered to the right customer at the right time. We know there are going to be problems aplenty along the way, but with what *we* know, *we* are going to make all the wrongs turn out right. Or break an arm and a leg trying. With all our faults and failures, our atrocious and bloodcurdling international efforts, all our ugliness, violence, crime, prejudice, drugs and hypocrisy, we still are a bunch of soft-headed saps when it comes to saving the world (or parts of it) from famine, suffering and disease, and *we* know, better than most, how to solve these tragic problems. The majority of the American public (including a considerable number of attorneys) will not stand by idly while millions suffer and die needlessly. We are certainly far from perfect, but there are few who have done for humanity what *we* have done for humanity.

There has never been a country like this in world history. And if we fail, there may never be another. We absolutely need your help in keeping the Ship of State on an even keel. As of late, the captains have been letting her list port or starboard in a manner that leaves us a bit seasick.

The solution?

Millions of No. 1 Best Sellers who believe in miracles.

You are indeed one of our Immortal Friends. *You* went out and *bought* the book. All our *relatives* called and wanted a copy for *free*.

So much for the Drooping Limbs of our Family Tree.

But *you*! *You* are really and truly a friend! You never even called and asked for a discount. Therefore, Dear Friend, believe us when we tell you we believe in you. You have given us good reason to believe in your friendship, your beauty and, above all, your intelligence. And as friends, we have one more request:

Fling off those blankets in the morning and shout a happy, joyous greeting to the Great Wide World with the first blink of your eyes. Then go forth and perform the miracle of No. 1 Best Selling! Do it for us because we've done it for you. (And possibly to you.) And if all of us do it, we will make this Great Marketplace Country of ours No. 1 in *everything*. There will be no stopping us. For now and forever.

And how will future historians refer to *our* efforts? They'll call it a *miracle*, of course.

THE MIRACLE - PART 2

Try to make every human being you meet feel important, needed and helpful. Alfred Adler, the great psychologist, said after a lifetime of study that the most important human need is the need to feel important. Learn to fill that need in your customer and success is sure to follow.

THE MIRACLE - PART 3

Forgive us if we've been a little hard on attorneys. If you think *we're* tough, go read what they write about themselves. Try Louis Nizer's *My Life in Court*, or *The Terrible Truth About Lawyers* by Mark H. McCormack. Or a great little book about lawyers written by a writer: *The Suing of America* by Marlene Marks. (We must admit Marlene is a friend, neighbor and she's a very fine writer.)

But look at the lawyering problem this way: the next time you are sued, consider that the suing lawyer is just trying to generate business. There's no validity to the lawsuit. If not for lawyering, the jerk would probably be out stealing hubcaps. Or trying to fix tickets. Sue him or take him to the Bar Association for malpractice and malicious prosecution and his fellow lawyers will fall all over themselves to find the Degreed Hubcap Thief completely innocent. Where this society has made a big mistake is in allowing lawyers to judge lawyers at the Bar. All the Bar Associations should be manned and defended by *doctors*.

At the same time, although it is hard for your Big-hearted Authors to make such a generous admission, we must say: *lawyers have their place!*

The word *gutter* comes to mind, but our munificence encourages temperance. We really don't think that's very nice. So we'll say: the *Courthouse*. Or, The *Law Office*. Or, the *Back Room*. But not the *Head of the Company*! And certainly not the head of the sales force.

Why?

Because (most of) the CEO's with backgrounds in law (or finance) view business problems as inherently legal (or financial). And with that kind of training, they tend to get around problems by the clever manipulation of the Laws (or numbers). There is a fierce, burning desire in the bosom of every law student to one day stand up at the Law Association Banquet Table and scream: "Hey, Gang, look what *I did* to: (1) beat the rap! (2) skirt the law! or (3) massage the numbers!" But you will never hear the words: "Hey, Gang, look what *I sold* to make the customer happy!"

Attorneys, by training and temperament, are always trying to impress their peers with their clever legal maneuvers. They simply don't make good business leaders.

The Japanese, who are one of our major competitors, have a different approach. Many of their Great Industrial Leaders are *not attorneys, but engineers* (approximately 75%). *They* see business problems as glitches in the money-machine that are capable of solution through engineering and science. All for the glory of Japan, Inc. Japan, they tell their people, is a *family*.

But Japan has a weakness. Its companies' business practices are largely predatory. America would have an advantage over the likes of Japan if only the salespeople took the reins of power from the attorneys. Using the technique of satisfying rather than battling its customers, the U.S.A. could reaffirm its place as sales force to the world.

Remember, if industry is the successor to religion, selling is the successor to prayer. And success in selling is best made where commitment to the customer is practiced with religious fervor.

Our Darling Government, in an effort to help us understand customer service and the seriousness of customer gripes, paid $434,000 to Technical Assistance Research

Programs, Inc., of Washington, D.C. for a study entitled *Consumer Complaint Handling in America*. The upshot was that 70% of customer complaints were not handled to the customer's satisfaction. The other 30% made a serious, religious, effort to satisfy complaints, and developed a much stronger brand loyalty after taking good care of the customer.

The report went on to say that government bureaucracy is as bad as business. We quote directly: "The data, therefore, suggest that it may be to business's self-interest to solicit complaints."

How's that for $434,000?

And if we hear any one of you guys complain about the price of this book, we're going to bang you on the head with a copy of that report.

THE MIRACLE - PART 4

There is a great wailing and gnashing of teeth in this country concerning what the Japanese are doing to us. They lost the war but they sure knew how to win the peace. And the marketplace. Although there is at least a shred of truth in the accusation that they don't play by the rules, along with the Germans, they may take over the World Marketplace without firing a shot. In all fairness to our former foes, their Commercial World Conquest, if won on a level, competitive playing field, is O.K. In that case, we can all say: *They earned it.*

They work hard. They respect their elders and teachers. All their salesmen are as singleminded as *kamikaze* pilots. And they send the very best and brightest of their youth to U.S. universities for a Straight A scientific education. B's are out. They will not do anything to embarrass the family back in Hokkaido. So for the moment, we've got a problem. All those hard-working guys out there are whipping the socks off us. They stick together. Most of the time, they win.

Why?

Brains. Partly.

But there are other reasons. Many other reasons.

From our cubbyholes, we wish to pass on *one* very cogent reason.

The Japanese spend 5% of their GNP on fuel and *we spend 11.2%.* (You don't believe us? Then have your accountant explain it to you.)

What this means, effectively, in the world marketplace, is very simple: IT GIVES THE JAPANESE A 6.2% EDGE ON EVERYTHING THEY SELL! In more academic terms: IT MEANS THE JAPANESE HAVE 6.2% MORE TO SPEND ON PRODUCT DEVELOPMENT *AND* SALES EFFORTS, RELATIVE TO GNP. Which makes our job in the sales field wretchedly more difficult than it should be. It gives *them* the high ground in the war of sales.

There are a number of other reasons why the Japanese are beating us in the marketplace. For openers, they don't play by the rules. They lie, cheat, steal and kill for love of closing the sale. They are absolutely predatory in their trade practices. Once the territory is established, they fire all the salespeople. Especially if those salespeople are Afro-American or Latino. Don't believe it? Then believe this: when a Japanese businessman or politician says, "We'll look into it," he means: "ABSOLUTELY NO!" Maybe we and our politicians should look into *it* a little more closely.

As for Japanese Fair Trade, a pound of rice in Tokyo costs seven times as much as a pound of rice in Los Angeles. And in the car market, they sell us about 2,000,000 a year. How many American cars do they buy yearly? How's 70,000? Vicious and predatory trade practices such as the aforementioned make our selling job hellishly hard in Japan. It appears from the record that they hate, loathe and despise us—but they do so with a smile.

We've got to learn to smile back.

And make many, many more sales over there.

One reason for their success to date: those guys take the long-term view. If no sale is made today, how about tomorrow? Or next week? Or five years from now?

Our view tends to be short-term.

There is a great downsizing taking place in the boardrooms of American industries, and the first gang to be axed is the sales force. Then comes the slaughter of the work force. And lastly, the executives. Although this hacking and cutting may boost productivity figures for a short while, the truth is that corporate bloodletting is not too healthy for long-term growth.

Now, if we as No. 1 Best Sellers are going to help ourselves and turn our nation around,we must always take the long-term viewpoint.

Without that viewpoint, the miracle is not possible.

THE MIRACLE OF COMPETITION

Say what you will and believe what you will. But one basic fact remains: we are essentially a free and outspoken people. Our form of government allows us to say just about anything. That gang of kooks we call *Americans* openly and freely expresses a rainbow of opinion on just about everything. We are believers. We are workers. And we are producers. When one of Our Gang goes forth in the world to sell, sell, sell, that salesperson wants the product to be the very best, the cheapest, the most reliable and the most satisfying thing the customer ever purchased. We are the people who want to do it right.

And we will compete!

Given the products, the tools, the services and the latitude to go out there and do the job right, we will prove to be worthy competitors in the local and world arena. We may not be first (Western Europe has the largest cumulative Gross National Product in the world marketplace), but we will always strive to be best.

The fanatic critics of ours have never been successful in competing for the hearts and minds of our (or their) countrymen because they are rotten, mean-spirited salesmen.

They believe in blab.

We believe in delivering the best.

Are the rabid critics a bit crazy?

You bet they are.

But that's the way we work it.

Let the jerks mouth off and do their lousy, lying sales job because few sensible people will buy it anyway. But, would it be asking too much of the Darling Fascist, Socialist and Communist Dictators of the world to reciprocate by letting us sell them a free exchange of products, ideas and services?

Of course not!

And don't count on a dictatorial change of heart.

Dictators are always cowards and perverts at heart. Terrible salespeople. They always live a lie. They just *love* our money but *hate* everything else about us.

None of the dictatorial countries have anything resembling a sales force anywhere. And they do not believe in competition.

But we do. And we believe mightily that our force of No. 1 Best Sellers deserves a fair chance to compete in every marketplace in the world. Because where we go, the ideas of fair play, decency and honesty will follow. The shrewd Yankee horse trader did not attain world prominence by being a treacherous sneak. He did it by delivering the goods. He had something the Barbary Pirates and their ilk *never* had. And it boils down to one word: *trust*. Without it, the machines won't run and the whole system breaks down. But with *trust*, machines run more smoothly. The planes fly a little higher. The blue chip stock market goes through its bumps and grinds and edges eternally upward. Well-chosen real estate retains its value. In recession times, when trust disintegrates, values plummet. But when there's trust, most of the time, our country and other democratic countries are strong.

Please don't think this discussion doesn't belong in a book on selling. Because *good* selling has to do with engaging the competition on a level playing field.

If extreme rightists and extreme leftists can peddle their wares openly *here*, why can't we do the same, openly, *there*?

Please listen to us, World. As No. 1 Best Sellers we know that a product invented in the U.S.A., with components manufactured in Japan, Taiwan, Korea and Hong Kong, that is then shipped to Mexico for assembly, for resale to Canada, for transshipment to Poland, better work right when turned on in Warsaw. Because we know with certainty that it is infinitely more important to *compete* in the marketplace than to *kill* on the battlefield. Or to blow up buildings in New York, Rome or Oklahoma City.

On this matter even the attorneys and psychiatrists agree with us.

Now that we have conquered Eastern Europe and Russia by selling them our cultural icons called Coca Cola, Levi's, Mickey Mouse and Herbalife, we have got to invade all those nasty dictatorships in Asia, Africa and Latin America, with a refreshing gang of No. 1 Best Sellers.

The survival of civilization depends on it.

We must sell them, at no cost, everything we know about the level playing fields of democracy.

You don't believe it?

Then look at where *they* are and compare it to where *we* are.

MLM

Multi-level marketing (MLM) has become one of the great sales techniques of modern times. The object is not simply to sell customers, but also to develop and train other distributors. If you can find a reputable MLM company and convince a few hundred *people to become distributors* and locate the ultimate customers, you may become a very successful distributor yourself. You not only get commissions on what you sell, but also on what your distributors sell, and also on what the distributors' distributors sell, etc. *ad infinitum.*

And how do you find out if an MLM company is reputable? You ask. The source of your information is the:

DIRECT MARKETING ASSOCIATION (DMA)
1120 Avenue of the Americas
New York, NY 10036
Phone (212) 790-1400 or (212) 768-7277

DMA is a governing association for upholding a code of ethics for *honest* MLM selling. If in doubt, *call them first.*

All MLM salespeople are referred to as distributors and work not as employees, but as independent contractors.

We recently came across some material put out by an

MLM sales organization of questionable virtue. Where and how they came up with their figures, we do not know. But the hustlers behind this outfit sure had a lot of fancy statistics to bandy about. And they called their hustle *networking*. This, so it seems, puts them on a level with ABC, CBS and NBC.

The network's stats went something like this:

1. Only 2% of the populace are self-starters with discipline.
2. Americans will only achieve 33 1/3% of their potential.
3. How many people don't know what they want out of life? How's 23%?
4. 67% of the populace knows what it wants but doesn't know how to get it.
5. 20% of the individuals in any business organization do 80% of the work.

So how does that grab your apple?

Not too well?

Same here.

The hustle continues with gross claims that go something like this: "Now look, if you can…(please connect the dots properly and fill in the rest of this for your Charming Authors, we know you can do it) . . . .
. . . .
. . . . you'll
be a millionaire. Millionaire? *Multimillionaire*!"

(Thank you for your assistance.)

The crazy thing about all of this is that among reputable MLM companies it is a great way to attract people into sales.

But beware.

There are good MLM companies as well as bad ones.

Some of the bad MLM people will tell you, if you put a penny in the bank and double the account every day for a week, you will come out with $1.28 on day seven. (If you *really* want to know, it's 64¢ on day seven and $1.28 on day eight.)   If you double it for a month, it comes to $5,368,792.12. Do it for a year and, using $100 bills as the medium of exchange, it comes to more than the entire known weight of the universe.

Some distributors enter MLM with religious fervor. Others with unadulterated greed. But the problems for the fanatics are not those of hard work and perseverance—the problems are those of human greed and cupidity. MLM is so attractive to zealots and true believers *not* because it offers *honest work*, but because it looks like a way out of the rat race and a way of beating the laws of economics.

It can't be done that way. Success in MLM must be accomplished as in any other successful venture: through hard work and perseverance.

Therefore, let us mention *good* MLM cases which are both realistic and inspiring.

We know of a kind and soft-spoken gentleman in New York who has a Ph.D. in Electrical Engineering, holds many patents and has written books on his subject of expertise. His name is Professor Alex Mirer. When he left Russia a few years back to try his fortunes in America, he could not find work in his chosen field. Today, he and his wife are successful Amway distributors. Their sons are also gainfully employed. The younger, a programmer. The elder, a medical doctor.

And what does Professor Mirer have to say of all this: "Al, Burt, I tell you it is a miracle! It is a country of miracles!"

In addition to this positive, enthusiastic attitude of Alex and Tatiana Mirer, allow us to quote directly from his most recent letter:

"I was (and I am) pleased very much by mentioning my name in your new book. I understand that this can not add too much to my glory, but the fact that you just remember me makes me happy.

"We all are doing well…and I want to say again, what we repeat every day when we get up every morning, during the day and at night when we go to sleep it is always on our lips: *Baruch Hashem [Praise the Lord]* and God bless America…God bless America…"

But our favorite MLM company is Herbalife International. Rather than bedazzle you with stories of achievement at the very top, let us introduce you to an average sales story about a couple of average No. 1 Best Sellers who were introduced to Herbalife about 15 years ago. Their names? John and Lori Tartol.

John received a Bachelor of Science degree in Finance from the University of Illinois. He then went on to complete a year of law school at the University of San Diego but never graduated. As he was an accomplished musician, the lure of music overtook his life, and for seven years he played keyboards for some of the best rock groups in the country.

Since insanity is the major ingredient for all things in the highly competitive arena we call the entertainment business, John found himself plagued by the dual problems of an overweight mainframe and severe stomach distress. So serious was his intestinal disquietude that he drank antacid liquids from the bottle and bought antacid tablets by the carton.

Although John was ever the good provider, Lori was the brains of the outfit. She still is. When she saw an ad in the L.A. Times for part-time people who wanted to make an additional $500 per month through part-time sales, she answered it.

The product: good health.

The company: Herbalife.

With a touch of skepticism they attended an Herbalife meeting, took the plunge and bought scads of vitamins for nutritional balance, the Herbalife Weight Management System for weight reduction, Herbal Aloe and NRG for improved energy and a natural herbal product for that gas in the gut. Result: no more tacky tummy, improved drive, and for John, a weight loss of 12 pounds in 10 days.

The Tartols threw that cloud of skepticism in the trash and became full-time believers. They attended further Herbalife meetings and discovered the only infection you could get from *that* crowd was enthusiasm.

"O.K." John said to his beautiful wife, "I'm going to put the keyboards in storage and we're going to devote our complete lives to this for six months."

Lori made four sales in their first hour of committed selling. At first, John and Lori came in for a bit of chiding and ridicule from family and friends. How could a law school dropout with mixed feelings about the music industry possibly make it in vitamins?

Undeterred, they enrolled in Herbalife's excellent training courses. But the great personal motivator for the Tartols was that they knew from personal experience they were helping *others*. John's father lost 72 pounds, and as a result of the weight loss, his blood pressure returned to normal. Sister Mary lost 40 pounds in two months. Sister-in-law Nancy lost 70 pounds in six months. Father-in-law George lost 20 pounds in two months and was helped enormously by Herbalife APR (Arthritis Pain Reliever). The family skeptics threw their doubts in the trash and became Herbalife distributors. They all love what they do and they all do it very well.

John's theory is quite simple: Keep the sales machine moving and never let it stop. He subscribes to all the daily newspapers, opens them up to the want ads each morning and proceeds to call everyone who has placed an ad under Positions Wanted. He creates a dialogue, listens carefully and asks the job-seeker if he or she is interested in making an additional $500 to $1,500 per month, part-time with no change in lifestyle or occupation.

Without the banter, John's enthusiasm flags. But with good, interesting, helpful and meaningful conversation back and forth, his enthusiasm stays up. He asks questions and listens, listens and listens. *He never makes lavish promises.* It is a matter of strict company and personal policy *not* to make big time promises. If the distributor can make $500 to $1,500 per month part-time, that further and continuous climb up the ladder is certainly possible.

If good health and truth and enthusiasm and helping others are your thing, your chances of becoming a No. 1 Best Seller in this arena are pretty darn good. Part of the Tartol theory is to sell a new customer (and hopefully gain a new distributor) every 72 hours. Of course, every 24 hours is better. Constant work keeps their attitude fresh and wholesome.

Should you attend an Herbalife Extravaganza, chances are you will see John there. He speaks to groups around the world. From individual people on the streets of Paris, France and Moscow, Russia to a crowd of 40,000 at the Herbalife Extravaganza in Atlanta, Georgia, John is always selling his products.

Delegates from 30 different countries around the globe attended the Extravaganza where the attendees spoke 17 different languages. The Extravaganza constituted the largest gathering of people tuning into simultaneous translations on earphones that the world has ever seen, heard or known.

When John lectures, he tells his audience the following:

1. The key to success requires the distributor to be consistent (talk to at least 10 prospective customers every day).
2. Be enthusiastic. Enthusiasm is to sales what God is to the angels.
3. Give a simple presentation which is duplicatable.
4. Follow up with clients and distributors.

The Tartols travel extensively and love what they do. The pleasure they receive from their work comes from a number of sources. First of all, they feel comfortable dealing with people who have common interests. Secondly, people they meet from all over the world, in all walks of life, are given an opportunity to blossom into No. 1 Best Sellers. The new distributors lose weight, gain health and vastly improve their self-esteem.

When the Tartols went to France a few years back, they had two strikes against them. Strike 1: they spoke no French. Therefore, they had to approach at least 50 people daily to find 10 who spoke English. Strike 2: they could not advertise (it's against the law there).

Not to worry.

They went to Paris suburbs of St. Cloud and found the owner of a health club. They sold him $1,000 worth of Herbalife products on the spot. Two days later, Michael Palmsteirna, a Scandinavian in France who spoke pretty good English, called to reorder. He is currently making $40,000 per month as a distributor. (We have no idea what he makes from the health club).

When John and Lori went to Russia, the language barrier and the laws were meaningless. Their Russian hosts told them their very lives were in danger.

Not to worry.

They made their standard presentation to a number of budding Russian free-enterprisers, then left the country. The Russian Herbalife distributors in turn trained an enthusiastic young man named Leon Weisbain. Leon was not only a Russian, but a Siberian Russian. When his countrymen asked from where he hailed, he responded, "Siberia."

"Siberia? How long were you in Siberia?"

"All my life," Leon would reply.

"All your life? What did you do?"

"Nothing," Leon would reply. "I was born there. I wasn't in a prison camp. I was born there."

"Too bad," the questioner would mutter as he walked away. "And so young. Tsk, tsk, too, too bad."

When he was a bit younger, Leon applied to medical school and was accepted. The chaos that ensued after the collapse of the U.S.S.R. drove him out of Mother Russia entirely and into the sunny warmth of Israel. In Israel, his first and only job was picking oranges for $400 per month. But he fell off a ladder and ended up disabled. The severity of the fall almost took his life.

While recovering from his injuries, he decided there must be a better way.

Back to Mother Russia.

As the chaos stabilized, Leon stumbled across an Herbalife distributor who had been trained by John Tartol.

Before committing himself, Leon Weisbain *tried the product*. The Herbalife supplements restored his health to the point where he was truly convinced of the merits of Herbalife. When *that* happened, he threw himself whole-heartedly into the Herbalife program. Leon was not only amazed and intrigued by the improvement in his health but also by the duplicatable simplicity of the program. He was certain he had stumbled across a wonderful opportunity.

He signed up.

He blossomed.

He later met John Tartol in person and the two young men became fast friends. They now cooperate on training programs and Leon can *on his own* draw a crowd of 10,000 people for a Russian Herbalife Extravaganza.

After three years in the business, Leon Weisbain became one of the top three Herbalife distributors in the world. So much for that old canard, "Yeah, but it's too late," or better yet, "Yeah, but what if everybody does it?" Distributor Leon Weisbain is currently making two million dollars a year selling Herbalife products. He just bought a Mediterranean villa for $1,700,000 all cash. No more Siberian winters for Leon.

Please do not take this write-up as an endorsement of Herbalife. We simply write and tell the truth. We were in no way encouraged, discouraged or paid to write this chapter. What truly amazes us about the No. 1 Best Sellers of Herbalife is that they are encouraged and trained to make as much money as possible for themselves. Amazingly, there are some high-tech firms who pay their salespeople on a declining sales commission scale and want their salespeople to make as little as possible. And certainly nothing in excess of $100,000 per year. For example, these professional dreamkillers pay 1.0% commission on the first million in gross sales, 0.5% on the second million, 0.25% on the third million until the salesman quits and goes into his own business. Don't believe it? Ask Ross Perot. It astounds us to hear that the president of IBM thinks salespeople are becoming obsolete. Don't tell that to Bill Gates or Warren Buffett. Or John Tartol. Herbalife International, a firm built on sales and salespeople, has likely produced more millionaires than any company in world history. And all from ads asking people if they would like to make an extra $500 to $1,500 per month. The people who answer emphatically *yes* make it just fine.

A few other interesting facts about the company that sells us our vitamins and supplements.

Fact 1. All the middle-aged secretaries at world headquarters look, talk, walk and act like healthy teenagers.

Fact 2. Walk into their legal department and you think you're at a weight-lifters convention.

Fact 3. Herbalife International has been in business since 1980, is a member of the Direct Marketing Association and has hundreds of thousands of customers and successful distributors in over 30 countries. They buy the product. They use the product. They sell the product. Would they do this if they did not *love* the product?

Now that we have expounded on the good news, we have a few words of admonition for John Tartol.

Don't let all of this good stuff go to your head, John. Because we know for a fact that if it were not for Lori, you'd be out there on the road, doing a gig and beating your brains out while banging on those keyboards.

P.S. After 15 years on the job, John and Lori work just as hard today as they did on day one and make in excess of $70,000 per month.

RECOMMENDED READING

Sadly, there are very few good books on selling. But there are a lot of mediocre ones. And a small number that are downright rotten and stupid.

Read them all.

Then you will appreciate what your Long-Suffering and Mentally Disturbed Authors have gone through in bringing you this act of Literary Lunacy. Not only did they have trouble sitting in the same room together, but they argued about *everything*. What one liked, the other one hated. Professional jealousy. Finally, their wives insisted they communicate through the mail. Even then they would read each other's stuff and mutter things such as:

"Stupid!"

"Crazy!"

"Revolting!"

"Boy, are you going to get it from the editors!"

Plus other choice literary tidbits.

What all of this proves is that authors who carry their creative juices in cracked cups can also be No. 1 Best Sellers.

Yes, Virginia, there really is a Santa Claus. You can be

crazy and creative in our business and still come out on top. But what distinguishes our brand of lunacy from that of life's losers is our ability and desire to read.

You don't *have* to read but you *should*. Why? Because reading will keep your creative thoughts percolating. To paraphrase our buddy Mark Twain, a man who can read and won't is as bad off as an illiterate, and if we taught people to speak the way we teach them to write, everyone would stutter.

Read.

Because if you *read*, it will force you to *think,* and thinkers are creative.

So here's our list.

1. *How to Win Friends and Influence People* by Dale Carnegie.
2. *Think and Grow Rich* by Napoleon Hill.
3. *The Battle for Investment Survival* by Gerald M. Loeb.
4. *How to Buy Stocks* by Louis Engel.
5. *Acres of Diamonds* by Russell H. Conwell.
6. *The Richest Man in Babylon* by George S. Clason.
7. *The Warren Buffett Way* by Robert G. Hagstrom, Jr.
8. *Learn to Earn* by Peter Lynch.
9. *How to Make a Buck and Still be a Decent Human Being* by Richard C. Rose & Echo M. Garrett.
10. *Successful Telemarketing* by Bob Stone and John Wyman. [The subtitle is *Opportunities and Techniques for Increasing Sales & Profits.*]

Another very fine book is *The Winning Performance: How America's High-Growth Mid-Size Companies Succeed* by Richard E. Cavanagh and Donald K. Clifford, Jr.

In a nutshell, this is what they say:

> *The best-run mid-size companies don't talk much about the bottom line. They forget about business school truisms. They talk about improved products and the future. "Wealth creation is kind of a byproduct." The key to success is usually an innovative product and an absolute commitment to quality, not price. A highly motivated sales force is essential to success. And success is never smooth. It's usually bumpy. But what they don't do is resort to massive layoffs during a downturn because when the upturn comes, they're going to need all those good people.*

Another literary gem is *The HP Way - How Bill Hewlett and I Built Our Company* by David Packard. In this book, Mr. Hewlett and Mr. Packard claim they were not just looking narrowly for money and profits. They also wanted:

> *A company which focused on fields of innovative contributions for their immediate society and the entire world.*

A dedicated and justly compensated work force that operated in an environment which fostered individual creativity.

A companywide commitment to community involvement.

An openness to change.

A will to win and,

Recognition for the virtue of hard work.

These books will lead you to other books.
Read them all.

Actually, as already stated, these are just *some* of the sales books out there. If you are genuinely interested in reading a good and sensible book on sales psychology, we recommend *Influence: How and Why People Agree to Things* by Robert B. Cialdini. When Professor Cialdini tells us that successful salespeople exploit six basic behavior principles, we believe him. The six are:

1. Consistency.
2. Reciprocation.
3. Social proof.
4. Authority.
5. Liking.
6. Scarcity.

We believe him for two reasons.

First, he is an experimental social psychologist on the faculty of Arizona State University and has devoted his career to a study of "compliance practitioners." Whether the practitioners are good guys or bad guys, Professor Cialdini tells us the "effective persuaders" (salespeople) manipulate us most of the time *by appealing to our better nature*.

Second, he gained his experience by signing on as a trainee salesman for cars, encyclopedias, vacuum cleaners, real estate and dance lessons. He also did apprentice work in advertising, public relations and fund-raising. He has a good grasp of the psychology of selling. And when he tells us *truth* is the only relevant moral test of a sale, we believe him.

And so should you.

WHO SUCCEEDS AND WHO FAILS?

We do not have an exact predictor for success and/or failure, but we sure have some strong hunches. We have seen a whole gang of disciplined dimwits make it, while we have seen a whole troop of undisciplined bums-with-brains go down the tubes. But the greatest successes are generally those with brains *and* discipline. And the people *we* consider successful are the ones who maintain their principles and humility with or without money. But what do writers know? They're all sort of crazy. Therefore, we went to experts, and came up with what follows.

Our research led us to a lovely, beautiful and charming psychologist by the name of Marilyn Machlowitz. Your authors were attracted *immediately* to such a Slavic-sounding name, and were delighted to discover she had written a book in English. The title: *Whiz Kids: Success At An Early Age*.

Among the gems in Ms. Machlowitz's writings:

1. Success is never neutral.
2. We love it in ourselves but hate it in our friends (or others).

3. We cultivate heroes and still celebrate victims.
4. Young success is *bad* and sets tongues to wagging but old success is *not quite so bad*.

"In these seeming paradoxes," she tell us, "lies the essence of success."

According to Marilyn Machlowitz, some people seem destined for success, and although others *seem* to do everything right, they never quite make it. Some are flashy, others humble. But the single most common characteristic among the so-called successes was the fact that they all were, are and will continue to be *workaholics*.

The young ones bristle at the suggestion that they made it overnight. One 17-year old claimed he started his ascent at age 10 and his success was "slow and gradual."

Success has cultural and temporal overtones also. In the '60's and '70's, "questioning of the success ethic was *de rigueur*." (Which means that the whole thing was started by a tough-talking Frenchman). In the '80's, ambition became *chic* and the *entrepreneur* a hero. (Which means the whole thing was started by a sweet-talking Frenchman with style).

The '90's are what we call the crazy times. Early on, sales of houses, cars, computers, books and bonnets went down the drain. Peugeot and Daihatsu withdrew from the American car market. The Yugo automobile went up in smoke. And video became bigger than ever. For the hedonists, fun was infinitely more important than transportation. Liberals took over politics and conservatives took over the airwaves. Unemployment went through the roof. The country then created more millionaires and billionaires than ever before.

So much for the fickleness of the mob and the tenor of the times.

All successful people, we read, were impatient. Surprisingly, many successful people did not consider themselves successful. The self-image actually lagged behind the achievement. Some successful people failed on occasion.

But the failure was viewed as a lesson and not a tragedy. The all-important word *next* "is never far from their lips," according to Ms. Machlowitz. The people she interviewed and wrote about demonstrated "a high rebound factor, great resiliency."

The common element among all those studied was "a goal set and accomplished."

The key word here is *discipline*.

In the beautiful lady's own words on success: "It's never too late or too early. The hard part is figuring out what you want to do."

(We figured that one out a long time ago and it can be reduced to six words: Become a No. 1 Best Seller.)

But there's more.

In our research, we discovered that the *only two common characteristics* among successful people are:

1. They all have good vocabularies.
2. They all read (approximately 19 books per year for ladies and gentlemen earning over $100,000 per year).

O.K., kids. Now run out and find another 18 books like this and your income this year will take off like a rocket.

HOW TO INVEST

First, buy a house.

Second, carry insurance on your life, health, home and car.

Third, save your money. It is the greatest key to success ever devised by man, woman or child.

O.K.?

O.K. But then what?

We are sure our critics will accuse us of being a pair of narrow-minded, uptight religious bigots for what we are about to tell you. Why? Because we tell the simple, Biblical truth. If the critics could just spend a little time with us, they would learn that Prelutsky and Winnikoff are, in fact, very broadminded practitioners of religious eclecticism. In other words, your Charming Authors believe in taking the best from *everyone*. Old Testament, New Testament, it really does not matter. P and W will even take info from the heathens if they have to. But here, in *this* book and chapter, they want you to take a sound bit of advice and pull a page from the Holy Scriptures of *both* the Christians and the Jews. For it is written, without partiality or prejudice, that although *Jesus Saves, Moses Invests*. And what does all this deep and profound religiosity have to do with HOW TO INVEST? Plenty. First, you won't get anywhere if you don't learn to save. And secondly, *good investments are better than cash.* To prove our point, we discussed this chapter with one of our few rich friends. He told us when he made his first million after 20 years of hard work, perseverance and thrift, he paused to figure out how much he'd be worth had he simply saved his money and never invested. How's $60,000? $60,000 is a lot of money, more than most of the bellyachers at the water cooler will ever save. But it's not a million dollars. The saving-investment machine has a reciprocating engine. And it won't work unless you put it together and fuel it with great regularity. Therefore, we encourage you to:

1. Save.
2. Invest.

Then as the machine, controlled by *your* brain and *your* hard work, begins to crank out more and more riches, picking up speed over the years, you may, if you so desire, make nice, big, fat donations to the religious denomination of your choice.

And if you hear anyone say ugly things about your Pious Authors, tweak *him or her* by the tail and say a little prayer for all of us.

At this point in our discourse, we think there should be a comment (or two) on what you should do with all your honest, hard-earned investment capital. If you have done everything right, the odds are 99 to one you will have money to invest in five years. In ten years, it is a 100% certainty. This kind of a time span is *never* mentioned in the investment books, but most success stories by No. 1 People take place over the long term. Everyone out there knows this simple fact, but most people refuse to believe it.

It is advisable to start your investment plan early in life and think first in terms of decades, later in terms of generations. If you can take the long-term view, success is sure to follow. To succeed, you must have *long-term discipline*!

To back this up, let us consider a 20-year economic study of 1,500 American families. The study was made by the National Science Foundation. At the end of year 20, exactly 1,083 families completed the study and disclosed their finances. The concluding data showed a total of 88 families were rich, with an *average* net worth of $1,200,000. Another 90 families in the study had failed completely. In a few cases, ill health and accidents had caused these failures. Most of the failure families, however, had incredibly negative attitudes toward their work, as well as low self-esteem.

As cautious writers attempting to instruct and entertain *truthfully*, we question the NSF figures. Based on a sampling of 1,500 families, approximately 6% became wealthy. Based on 1,083 families, the figure jumps to about 8%. These statistics seem a little skewed on the high side, but it is possible that the original sample selected only success-oriented families. In any case, the success stories all had two traits in common: (1) a willingness to work long, hard hours and (2) *a long-term viewpoint.*

Interestingly, the economic winners tended to be more emotionally and spiritually stable than the economic losers. The winners tended to be regular churchgoers, very good parents, imaginative, optimistic, creative, truthful and, in many cases, quite humble and *less concerned with their success than were their jealous neighbors.*

None of the winners were alcoholics or pill-poppers.

The winners were neither fanatics nor bums on the job. *They were steady*! In many cases they started out doing what they considered detestable work. They *tended* to work *without complaint.* But 20 years later they all seemed to be doing what they enjoyed most in their chosen fields. All the success stories had loyalty to:

1. Family.
2. Company (or boss) if employed by such.
3. Staff and employees if self-employed.
4. Customers.

Our own research indicates that in the area of investment, you must always be aware of the fact that *you* earned the money and if *you* want to succeed, you must rely totally on the decisions made by *your* mind. Remember, *you* are the business! And what *you* do will make that business succeed or fail. If you rely on what *they* say, do, or tell *their* customers, you are economically doomed. *They* absolutely do not know. Because if *they* absolutely did know, *they* would not tell *you* about it. Just as you should *never* play poker with strangers, the only thing you should *never* take from advisers is advice.

Without exception, all the rich, successful people we know and interviewed for this book told us, in one way or another, *the best way to succeed is to get rich slowly*!

In our travels, we came across an extremely astute young man with numerous advanced degrees and a perceptive insight into money and such. He advises pension funds on how to invest their billions. First of all, he told us, it is advisable to be consistent. Stay the course. No matter what the temptation to jump into the fast track, stay the course. Never bet on a lottery or look for get-rich-quick schemes. For every winner among them there are millions of losers.

But what you *must* understand about the swinish multitude and the media (which engorge them with financial garbage) is that they love the unusual. They love to tell and be told about the quick win. The media will never print the number of lottery losers alongside the number of lottery winners. The game of riches is so heavily stacked against the quick killing that the odds, if not millions to one, are billions to one. So don't bet on *them*. Bet on *you*.

Sound strange?

Well it's not!

If you have come this far with us, we think you deserve the best financial advice in the world.

So pat yourself on the back and congratulate yourself: you are getting a wealth of priceless information for the simple cost of this book. Or for free, if you borrowed the book. In either case, *you* made the decision to read. And if you feel good about this kind of enlightenment, just keep up the good work.

We recently came across a group of so-called successful men and women who got together in a posh banquet hall to celebrate the 75th birthday of a beloved economics professor. All the attendees had at least an M.B.A., and quite a few had Ph.D.'s. Most worked for large corporations. A few had gone into their own businesses. *A comparison of notes showed that the most financially successful were those who picked a specific field of endeavor and stuck with it.* The financial losers were all over the board. The losers talked up a storm about investments in boxcars, oil tankers, vineyards, wines, Scotch whiskey, limited partnerships and other assorted tax shelters, which lose over 90% of the time. (Uncle Sam has put a whole bunch of overpriced and overdue coffin nails into the Tax Shelter Box, so they're not worth anything anyway).

The losers all lacked *discipline*!

Among the losers, it must be noted, there was a tendency to buy frills. In plain English, the losers just *had* to spend their hard-earned cash on junk. If our Freudian friends are right, material things never satisfy fully because they are not infantile desires. The novelty of the new toy wears off quickly. But love endures. Affection endures. Trust endures. Honesty endures. Tenderness endures. And kindness endures. Although the fictional part of our heritage tells us the losers are happy and the winners are miserable, *our* little survey showed the winners were, for the most part, people who believed in—and practiced—the virtues. Among the losers, there was a tendency to buy frilly and freaky lingerie. *He* just *had* to have a leather jock strap. And *she* bought it for him. What's more, she overpaid! In the end, it was thrown to the rear of the closet or tossed out in the next spring cleaning. The losers were compulsive spenders. The winners were affectionate savers. And the winners all had *discipline*!

Will anyone ever write a treatise on how to go from riches to rags in one day? Or from millions (or thousands) to zero in ten seconds flat? We doubt it. But we don't need a treatise. There is not an economic creature on the face of the earth who has not suffered loss at the hands of a swindler. The common thread between most swindles: they promise amazing *short-term* gains. We scratch our heads and ask why everyone can't be as nice to us as the swindlers before the swindle? And so viciously cruel after? A No. 1 Best Seller will learn something from these errors. The No. 1 Best Seller must learn that it is an act of sickness and perversion to swindle, lie, cheat, steal, ensnare or otherwise prey on the decent intentions of Trusting Humanity. A No. 1 Best Seller sells with compassion and with the very best interests of Trusting Humanity in mind when making the sale. The No. 1 Best Seller knows not to swindle or be swindled.

The No. 1 Best Seller takes his lumps and develops the mentality of a winner. The No. 1 Best Seller works hard and concentrates on the long term and helps his/her client do the same.

For reasons that are not quite clear to us, those with the loser mentality waste enormous amounts of time and energy boiling their feeble mental cauldrons with the foul-smelling ingredients of anger, hatred, gossip, craziness, and revenge. Then they bathe the mess in an offensive perfume to cover the stench. The loser is frequently an addict. Whether the addiction is food, blackjack, dope, drink, smoke, gambling, lies and/or lechery, the loser/addict refuses to recognize two simple facts: (1) the addictive substance is *always* in control, and (2) the addict is *never* in control.

Losers always feel sorry for themselves, wallowing in tragic tales of how external forces have made their lives a mess. They are always right and the world is always wrong.

For the unrepentant loser, excuses are the order of the day. The loser will never stand up at the all-important meeting and say, "I'm sorry, I made the mistake. I did it.

I'm a loser" *The loser always blames others.* But it is ultimately the destiny of the loser to fail. Tragically, they often take innocent victims along on their ride down the tubes.

The loser mentality, it must be noted, is always looking outward for someone else to make him or her rich. The winner mentality, like a British diplomat, pursues an attainable goal with great singularity of purpose. The winner always looks inward to make life a financially successful venture. To do otherwise is to court and tempt the seductive Goddess of Disaster. How do we know this? Because we have been there and it has cost us dearly. Very dearly. But unlike the eternal losers, we are never going back for more.

If this book teaches you nothing more than to make the right choice between success and failure, consider the price of admission to our Best Seller Club an absolute bargain.

Go forth carefully, courageously and with *discipline* into the minefields of economic uncertainty, and we know you will make it. You may curse us for getting you into this mess and you may hate us for making you work and think so hard, *but you will not fail.* You will not fail (1) yourself, (2) your loved ones, (3) your buyers and (4) your boss.

Be a good German and put the following sign above your mirror:

TODAY YOU WILL NOT FAIL.
AND NO FAILURE WILL BE
ALLOWED TOMORROW EITHER.

Judging from the way those guys build and sell cars, we are sure they know something.

Not all companies and not all bosses are very good. However, assuming your boss is not totally maniacal, you will be well paid for your superior production as a No. 1 Best Seller, and you must decide what to do with the money. We urge you not to psych yourself into thinking *someone else* will handle your hard-earned sales rewards better than *you* can. Do not in any way, at any time, for any reason invest in another person's business. Always invest in your own business. Always invest in a business where *you* have control.

If you decide for some *very* good reason to invest in someone else, get the names and addresses and social security numbers of the entrepreneurs and get a *credit check*. For your own safety and sanity: GET A CREDIT CHECK! For just a few dollars, you can check anyone's credit with a reliable credit-reporting company. Unfair? You bet! Therefore, tell the entrepreneur you will give him *your* name, address and social security number so he can get a credit check on *you*! Fair is fair.

If you are embarrassed by such things, have your attorney do it for you. After all, not all attorneys are bad. If you have a good one, as we do, he can be a big help. (While on the subject of attorneys, use them for legal work only. Never allow them to make business decisions for you).

As for the type of investment you should make, we are partial to real estate. But the best investment is your own business.

We conclude this chapter with a strong recommendation to again study, read, examine, learn, and profoundly examine a situation before you invest. Then proceed with *discipline*.

If someone calls you with a take-it-or-leave-it type deal, *always* leave it. We give you this investment tidbit for good reason. If the No. 19 Worst Seller tells you, in confidence and hushed tones, that he doesn't want his deal to get shopworn and that he has the deal of a lifetime, cut him off. *Any* deal that is not exposed to the marketplace is probably a scam. The con artist is always trying to gain your confidence. Where most legitimate deals contain merely a shotglass of juice, the con man will promise you 40 gallons if you act *right away*. Please tell him what we want you to tell him. (Refer to Canned Speech No. Y86 for the exact wording.)

Since we are relativists and not absolutists, we know

there are situations where snap decisions *must* be made. If you are a proven expert in the field of the investment, you are entitled to make such decisions. If not, exercise extreme caution.

To rehash, if you are contemplating an investment:

Read.
Study.

Make it *your* business to *know* what you are doing.
Then invest.

Our friend Frank Johnson, noted for his Ding-Dong Fame earlier in this book, became a highly successful stock broker for his customers, his firm and lastly, himself.

How?

He read, studied, then invested.

Frank investigated quite a few investment strategies. For example, one was called the *fixed-mix*. The fixed mix puts a set percentage of investment capital (otherwise known simply as *money*) into each of several asset categories. For instance: foreign and domestic stocks, bonds, and real estate. In 1987, after 22 years of fixed-mix investment, one management firm reported an average 10% annual return. Just a bit better than the 8.9% annual return for the Standard & Poor's 500 stock index, and better than the 7.4% annual return for most professional money managers.

He could have just bet the market, or put his cash in a mutual fund.

But our well-read hero opted for something else.

His own investment policies were based on a lifelong *discipline*! He read *hundreds* of investment books. And he created his own even more successful investment strategy.

His two favorite books on investment were and still are:

1. *The Battle for Investment Survival* by Gerald M. Loeb.
2. *How to Buy Stocks* by Louis Engel.

In the Engel book there are a few paragraphs on *dollar cost averaging*. As a young man, the concept caught Frank's eye and imagination.

Basically, dollar cost averaging tells us that if your grandfather plunked down $13,500 on RCA stock at the height of the market in 1929, it would not even be worth that amount, including dividends, in 1956 (27 years later). *However*, if your family invested $500 per year in RCA for 27 years without fail, the investment total would have reached $72,122.83. With Dow Chemical stock the 27-year value reached $185,432.06.

So intrigued was our Sales-Hero with this information, he made a little study of his own. To wit: if a buyer of stocks had dollar-cost averaged $6,400 over a 64 months, and had purchased $100 worth of Dow Jones Industrial Average each month for the 64-month period, even beginning the investment period just one day before the October 29, 1929 stock market crash, the $6,400 would have grown to $7,157.50 during that terrible Great Depression period. The DJIA, on the other hand, *declined* 89% between 1929 and 1932 and was down 73% in the 64-month period.

Frank took this information and put his first 20 clients on a dollar-cost-averaging program. When he had just 20 clients, the office gang laughed at him. We will not tell you exactly what the office gang said because you have heard it before. However, now that our friend Frank is servicing his *third generation* of clients, who number in the thousands, he is treated a little more respectfully. The young brokers wonder how he does it. They tell each other that it's too late for them to start a program like that.

Heard it before?

So have we.

But the simple fact remains: unless there is a blizzard howling or an earthquake growling, the best time to start an investment program is *now*! Right now! This very moment! To delay is to kick your id-ego-superego circuitry into a frenzy of disarray. We do not mean you have to run out immediately and spend your money. We mean you have to get to the library and study, study, study the investment medium that has the most appeal to you. Then invest. And once you have started the program, *stick with it*. Without *discipline*, you are

DOOMED!

In 30 years, when you have found a bit of financial security in an insecure world, when you are comfortably seated in your favorite chair, sipping your favorite drink on your favorite island, think of your Charming Authors and have yourself a little laugh. After all, as you will then know, if they can do it, anyone can do it.

P.S. Mr. Frank Johnson, Senior Member of the No. 1 Best Seller Club, is an honest man. When we showed him our manuscript and told him we wished to include the matter of *dollar cost averaging* in this book, he asked us to caution our readers that past performance is no guarantee of future performance. Then he delved into his meticulously kept files and pulled out two case histories. Client No. 1 invested $500 annually in Dow Chemical stock beginning January 3, 1972, and withdrew on December 30, 1987. His overall cash investment was $8,000 and his final withdrawal was $37,858. Client No. 2 invested $500 annually in RCA stock beginning January 3, 1972 and withdrew on December 30, 1986. Her overall cash investment was $7,500 and her final withdrawal was $31,199. Both clients reinvested their dividends.

(We confirmed the above data with our astute friends at The Plexus Group. They told us we were right on the money. Thanks, guys.)

THE NITTY-GRITTY

Not long ago, we were called into a meeting with our senior editor. "Guys," he said, "You have to write more seriously and cut out all the nonsense."

"You mean stick to the nitty-gritty?" we asked.

"I hate the term nitty-gritty," the editor said. "You have already missed a series of deadlines and we simply have to go to press with this book."

"You're not going to sue, are you?" we asked.

"I'm thinking about it," the editor replied. "My father and sister are attorneys and you haven't exactly been fair to attorneys in your writing."

"In that case, don't sue and we'll make it up to you. We'll tell them about all the cruel, stupid, perverted bosses who cut the territory in half every year but keep the quota constant."

"Look," the editor said, "just tell us the truth."

"Then let's tell our readers about Ben and George and Sam."

"Good," the editor said. "Go to it."

And so...Here beginneth the Saga of Ben Winnikoff.

Ben Winnikoff is the elder statesman of the Winnikoff family. Unlike writers, he really knows something. He has been in sales all his life.

His line: paint.

His territory: Northern California.

His only failing? He has a strange sounding name.

When Ben started out in paint sales, he was a very young man. Except for the interruption of World War II, at which time he served his country with honor and success against the greatest tyranny the world has ever known, he has always been a paint salesman. He always made quota. But in 1961, at age 45, he was fired by his employer. The news of his firing spread through the company like wildfire. Some of the women in the office broke down and cried.

Although shaken by the experience, Ben found another job immediately, with the Frank W. Dunne Paint Co., San Francisco, California. He developed the company's sales to U.S. government agencies.

Although he retired officially from the Dunne Co. on December 31, 1986, he still works two or three days a week because the company refuses to let a good man go.

His *previous* employer tried on one occasion to lure Ben back, but he turned them down.

When we told him about this book and asked for some comments, he volunteered the following:

1. Have a *good* relationship with your company.
2. Your best teacher is another salesman. Preferably, an old-timer. Whether that salesman is good or bad doesn't matter. The good guy teaches what you must do. The bad guy teaches what you must *not* do.
3. Persistent, steady calling on all customers and prospective customers is very important.
4. Follow your gut feeling.
5. Make no lavish claims.
6. Never lie.
7. Make no promises you can't keep.
8. Never go to the purchasing agent first. Always last. Find the user first, discuss his problems, see

how you can help with a solution. *Then* go to the purchasing agent.

9. As a general rule, when a dispute arises within the company, always defend the customer. Conversely, with the customer, always defend the company.

10. Try to sell the world's best product and know it thoroughly.

We have a lot of respect for Ben. He is past retirement age but has the energy of a 20-year-old. (You don't believe us? Ask his wife Rose.) He keeps himself in great shape with lots of exercise, vitamins, good health habits and a very sensible diet. When we stay at his place for a weekend, we come away feeling like rejuvenated rabbits. But what we like best about Ben is his dogged professional devotion to selling. In his own words: "You know, guys, selling is one of the few professions where there's no forced retirement age. I plan to go on forever."

And so does Rose.

This ends the story of Ben Winnikoff.

And thus beginneth the Saga of George Finch.

George was a stock broker. Although he has taken up permanent residence in that Big Brokerage House in the Sky, we sure have some fond memories.

George's specialty was elderly widows and spinsters. His silver-gray hair, neatly trimmed mustache and craggy good looks served him well. His gruffness and labored speech belied a heart of gold. He loved his customers and listened attentively to their numerous daily complaints. He defended their interests with fierce loyalty. One of his accounts called him George the Lionhearted.

When one of the dowagers had a problem, she called George. A dirty joke she just had to tell someone? Call George. Problems with grown kids, money, neighbors or domestics? Call George. When one of the lovely ladies was threatened by her fourth ex-husband, she blithely got on the phone and called George. He was on the scene in a flash. And although he saved the elderly damsel-in-distress, he got himself shot right through the lung.

George's assailant went to jail *briefly*, and George Finch, Hero, got a life sentence of wheeze-filled speaking.

Was he sorry?

"OF COURSE NOT!" he said, his wheeze nearly reaching a bellow.

Many years ago, we invited George to dinner because of a stock we had purchased. The stock was called Wizard Boat Company, Inc., of Costa Mesa, California, and we had purchased 100 shares at three dollars per share.

He fumed, railed and wheezed at our stupidity.

"BUY QUALITY!" he shouted. "BUY QUALITY!"

He was right.

We lost 300 bucks.

And thus ends the tale of George Finch.

Now that we have discussed two genuine heroes of Best Sellerdom, let us give you the nitty-gritty on a fictional character.

Here beginneth the Saga of Sammy Sales.

Sammy sure was a hard worker. He started his career as a typewriter salesman. His boss, Barry Hardnose, was an absolute ogre. Barry was vice-president of sales. Barry denigrated *everybody*.

But Sammy persisted with his efforts, despite the negativity of his boss.

Sammy read a number of sales books.

Within a year, he was truly No. 1. He kept flawless records. So good was his record-keeping that not only did Barry Hardnose use Sammy's files with religious fervor, but so did Growling Harry Snought, President of The Company (and Barry Hardnose's brother-in-law).

And he persisted.

The business prospered.

At Sammy's insistence, the company got into word processors.

They changed the name of the company from Snought Sales to Tick-Tock Tech.

What the Fearless Leaders lacked in imagination, they compensated for with intimidation, anger and desk-pounding. And they *never* met with customers. Never!

Eventually it came to pass that there was a recession in the land. All the charts and graphs pointed down. Straight down. Sammy Sales became concerned, but he did not panic. He sent a memo to Barry Hardnose and requested, for the first time in his ten years on the job, a two-minute meeting with the Officers and Directors of Tick-Tock Tech.

After a one-month blizzard of internal memos and special meetings, the Fearless Leaders of T.T.T. agreed to let Sammy have his two minutes.

But not one second more!

Even before Sammy got his two-minutes worth, though, B. Hardnose pounded his fist on the massive conference table and shouted, "WE'RE CUTTING YOUR TERRITORY IN HALF. BUT YOUR QUOTA WILL REMAIN THE SAME! IT SEEMS TO ME, SAMMY, YOU'VE BEEN FALLING DOWN ON THE JOB!"

Without batting an eyelash, Sammy threw one sheet of paper on the table and said, "Here's my plan for getting this company back on its feet."

"Your WHAT?" B. Hardnose bellowed. "WHO DO YOU THINK YOU ARE? WHY, YOU'RE JUST A LOUSY SALESMAN!"

"And FURTHERMORE!" the President and CEO of T.T.T. screamed . . . . . (At this point in the drama, please insert Canned Speech XPQ19. Or leave it out. We all know it by heart. It ends:)

"...YOU'RE FIRED!"

Sammy winced a bit, internally. After all, he had a family to think of, as well as mortgage and car payments. But he had not lost his composure. He looked Mr. President right in the eye and said, "Thank you, gentlemen."

On his way out, one of the Directors shouted, "AND WHO ARE YOU CALLING A GENTLEMAN?"

The point: A No. 1 Best Seller never fears for the loss of his or her job. NEVER!

But, then, what happened in the saga of Sammy Sales?

First, the T.T.T. Big Shots voted themselves a raise, since business was so bad and getting worse.

Second, they hired a brilliant attorney to fabricate a prestigious legal document entitled: *THE GOLDEN PARACHUTE.*

Third, they signed the document at a company banquet held in the city's most expensive restaurant.

Fourth, they congratulated themselves, ate too much, drank too much, smoked too much, and compared themselves to the signers of *THE DECLARATION OF INDEPENDENCE.*

Then, T.T.T. went down the tubes.

Meanwhile Sammy, the recently fired salesman, had started a modest little company called Sammy Sales.

S.S. specialized in selling word processors.

S.S. started a newsletter.

S.S. gave seminars.

S.S. knew that loyalty goes two ways, up and down the ladder.

S.S. employed lots of people and took good care of them.

S.S. became a great success later.

But best of all, Sammy was rid of the Snoughts of this world forever. And ever. And ever.

We asked Sammy for a closing statement. And this is what he told us:

"Look, guys, all my life I heard this stuff about selling the sizzle and not the steak. Of course it's a lie, but it's a cute lie. So a lot of people believe it. But in the *real* world—*my world*—I found out long ago that the whistle doesn't pull the train."

Sammy, we are proud of you, we thank you and wish you continued success.

And thus here endeth the last of our sagas. . .

Suddenly at this point, we were confronted by our editor. He read our material.

"Is this what you had in mind?" we asked.

"Not quite. You're getting there, but—"

"Then let us throw in a little more sales stuff and where to go for help."

WHERE TO GO FOR HELP

No matter what you sell, there is help available for improving sales. High tech help has its place and if used wisely, can boost business enormously. In this age of technomiracles, the crux of the argument is simple: if you have the right skills, time and technology are your friends; if not, time and technology are your enemies.

We note two brief examples because they help prove our point:

No. 1: Elizabeth, The Beauty Makeover Computer. Elizabeth Arden uses it to put a prospective customer's face on a video screen, then brushes in an electronic palate of lipsticks, rouges and eyeshadows. Whenever Elizabeth is installed, sales go up about 400%.

No. 2: Florsheim shoes uses a computer catalog to display their entire line of about 250 shoe styles in full color. With a few taps on the keyboard, the shoes can be sold and delivered to the customer's home in a matter of days.

And if you already have a computer, here's a list of software that can help enormously.

Software	Producer	Function
Marketfax	Scientific. Marketing, Inc. Costa Mesa, CA	marketing communications management
Prospecting	Key Systems Inc. Louisville, KY	prospect and client tracking
Sales Edge	Human Edge Software Corp. Palo Alto, CA	training, prospect tracking
Saleseye	High Caliber Systems Inc. New York	prospect tracking
Sales Manager	Market Power Inc. Rough & Ready, CA	managing sales force
Sales Planner	National Microwave Inc. Irvine, CA	customer letters, reports
Scamp	Profidex Corp. New York, NY	sales management
Sell! Sell! Sell!	Thoughtware Inc. Coconut Grove, CA	training organizing

WHAT TO SELL

Having a problem deciding which selling specialty to choose? First, have a look at the Bureau of Labor Statistics figures for this decade's service employment:

Job Category	Number Employed
1. Sales	7,395,000
2. Mechanics & repair	3,723,000
3. Teachers (K-12)	2,884,000
4. Technician & support	2,821,000
5. Engineers	1,644,000
6. Nurses	1,349,000
7. Accountants & auditors	1,083,000
8. Cooks	856,000
9. Waitresses & waiters	576,000
10. College instructors	443,000

Now that you have reviewed the numbers, we must also tell you that manufacturing jobs went from about 34% of (non-farm) employment to 16% from the 1950's to the 1990's.

The primary reason for this manufacturing employment decline is not because the U.S. is going down the tubes, but because of strong productivity gains by manufacturers. Workers today are far more productive than they were 50 or 100 years ago. Don't believe it? You witness increased productivity every time you check out of a store that uses bar codes and optical scanners. The U.S. is producing more than ever with fewer workers. True, the U.S. has lost jobs in areas such as tool and shoe manufacturing, but employment is way up in new fields such as microprocessors, chips, software, biotechnology, gene therapy and communications products. High tech is here to stay. And the crux of the technological argument is simple: If you have the right technological skills, technology is your friend; if not, technology is your enemy.

And how does this affect you? Simple: although the competition will be fierce, *every person on the above list is a potential customer*! Pick your specialty, work with passion, and you will never be unemployed.

For instance: Let us assume you enjoy reading about biotechnology but never graduated from high school. There are about 200 financially viable firms in the field. Write a *good*, short letter to all of them and tell them of your interest. *Then tell them you will go to work for them for free*. No salary, no insurance, no car, no liability, no risk. Just straight commission selling. One of the 200 will hire you because they know the importance of marketing, motivation and greed. Your authors know you can do it! Furthermore, they know YOU WILL NOT FAIL!

HURRAH! HURRAH! THE END! THE END!

Dear Abused Reader:

The hour grows late. The authors grow old. But we're not that old. We're *nervous*. We want this book to succeed. After all, WE HAVE BEEN WRITING THIS BOOK FOR 20 YEARS! How's that for discipline?

And why did we stick with this project for 20 years?

There are actually many reasons. But since this is a closing chapter, we'll give you just two:

1. *We* believe in what *we* are doing.
2. *We* hope *you* believe in what *you* are doing.

We hope you believe, as we do, that selling is an honorable profession and that all the good, decent, honest, hardworking people of this world belong to one another. That what we do is essential for the continuing progress of civilization.

We have tried, with the finest selling techniques we possess, to please (1) you, the customer/reader, (2) our brilliant editors and (3) our scintillating publisher.

When we entered our last editorial conference, the senior editor was actually very kind and helpful.

Getting right to the point, Author Number One asked: "You're not going to sue us?"

"No, of course not," the editor responded. "In fact, we're going to give you another contract extension."

"How nice."

"How nice."

"One of the problems you have," the editor said, "is your point of view is inconsistent. Your verb tenses are inconsistent. You are repetitious. And, in some respects, you've offended large segments of the reading public."

"Such as?"

"Such as?"

"Attorneys."

"That won't hurt sales—" Author Number One said.

"—it will improve sales," Author Number Two concluded.

The editor smiled and said, "Look guys, what distinguishes a great work of art from mere writing is the ring of TRUTH."

"You think we've been lying to you?"

"Not at all, but in my years of editorial experience, I've noticed that writers tend to get a little tired and lazy at the end of a book. Very often, things fall apart in the last chapter. And it's my job to shore things up a bit. It is my duty to make the entire book ring true."

"And how do you propose we do this?" W. asked.

"Al, what was your first BIG deal?" the editor asked.

"The 712."

"And what was the 712?" he asked.

"The sale of 712 acres just south of Sun City, California."

"Was it easy?" she asked.

"No."

"Was it simple?"

"No."

"Was it interesting enough to write about?"

"Absolutely."

"Then I'll make a deal with you: if you'll write of that experience, and write it well, I'll let some of your more indecent chapter headings remain in the book."

There was a long silence.

Finally, Prelutsky, who didn't have to write the last chapter, said:

"Deal."

"Deal," the editor said.

Since Winnikoff was stuck with the last chapter, he hesitated. But finally he muttered: "Deal."

We shook hands all the way around to seal the deal. And as the editor walked out, he said, "Oh, and one last thing—"

"What's that?"

"Make it a good ending."

And so here beginneth the somewhat truthful saga of Winnikoff's First Big Deal. Only the names have been changed to protect the innocent, prevent lawsuits, and pound home the pertinent points of the selling process.

It came to pass that in the year 1965, Winnikoff quit his technical writing job at the Bunker-Ramo Corporation and went to work for a real estate firm called OlandO. Mrs. W. was in a state of shock because the new job paid on a straight commission basis. Bunker-Ramo had paid weekly without fail and was an excellent employer.

OlandO was an unknown.

The three owners of OlandO were extremely gracious and charming salesmen with their customers. They *tried* to be nice to their sales force. And they were terrible to the secretaries.

OlandO, which was some profound acronym dreamed up by a 4-year-old daughter of one of the owners, *pretended* to be an old line land research firm, but in simple fact was just a bunch of beautiful, charming and fun-loving crooks. We will not go into a detailed explanation of this childish blather, but if you are seriously interested in the origin of company names and trademarks, check with your local kindergartners. They will set you straight.

The facade was impressive. The research materials utterly, totally and completely perfect. The bank wrote a fairy-tale recommendation. The Los Angeles City Council ordered a scroll in OlandO's honor. Some big-name customers gave glowing testimonials. (Some of which later proved to be false and misleading.)

For OlandO's benefit and profit, Winnikoff sold 160 acres in the green-belt of Riverside County for $380,000. Sales time: less than 30 days.

The fun-lovers were impressed. They wined and dined Winnikoff. Once. But they patted him on the head and slapped him on the back frequently. They had 712 acres for sale for $3,500 per acre. $2,492,000 full price.

"Winnikoff, how would you sell this?" they asked with a pat on the head.

"Well," W. said, "I'd make up a brochure—a nice brochure—and mail it out to every prospective buyer in Southern California. If they're interested, they can send us back an enclosed, postage-prepaid return card."

"Well, who would you send these to?"

"Every doctor, dentist and attorney—"

"But those lists are expensive," they objected.

"Every doctor, dentist and attorney in the phone book."

"And who else?"

"Every Beverly Hills household north of Sunset Boulevard."

They did it.

They also hired a retired economics professor to write a book on the 712. When the book was completed, OlandO fired the old professor. Then they hired an editor to include all the favorable information in the book and exclude all the unfavorable information. Then they printed 100 copies of the book. The book was chock-full of slick color photos and reams of impressive statistical material.

Five thousand mailers were sent out. The secretaries were driven to exhaustion.

There were about 500 responses.

Of the ten salesmen in the office, Winnikoff was consulted most frequently for advice. "One thing I would suggest is a credit check on all the prospective buyers."

This reduced the prospect list by about 90%.

The owners of OlandO then gave each salesman ten copies of the *book*. The other nine salesmen gave out their books on the first day. Winnikoff merely let a prospect *look* at the book. He held onto all ten as long as he could.

The OlandO Company Policy No. 48Q3TZ required salesmen to go out in teams of two. Winnikoff was teamed up with Dirk Snark.

To say the least, Dirk was a jerk. He hated everybody. He was hostile. He was obsequious *before* the sale, but not very nice *after*. A bootlicker with the bosses. A tyrant with the secretaries. He also smoked heavily, drank heavily, and had a poor memory.

Therefore, he took memory lessons. The Memory Professor taught *memory by association*. Dirk remembered the name *Donald Douglas, as a prospect,* by association with the name *Donald Duck*. But during their second meeting, when Dirk referred to the prospect as *Mr. Duck*, the sale was lost. The same thing happened with *Mr. McDermid*, who became *Mr. McTermite*.

Thereafter, Winnikoff wrote out the prospect's name, in CAPITAL LETTERS, on a folder, keeping it in full view of Dirk Snark.

The activity in the office was fervent. The atmosphere, electric.

Without revealing their true costs or interest in the 712 acres, OlandO had tied up the property from a distressed seller for $1,350 per acre ($961,200) and put it back on the market for $3,500 per acre ($2,492,000), even before they had consummated their purchase.

Potential profit: $1,530,800.

They promised W. that no matter who sold what portion of the deal, they would pay *him* a 5% commission, or

$124,600 when it was all sold. (Because OlandO was bubbling with generosity, they even upped the figure to $125,000.)

Winnikoff accepted the challenge.

Except for Winnikoff, all the salesmen had passed out their 712 Books during the first week of the sales program. Since Winnikoff kept one copy of the 712 Book in his briefcase and the other nine copies in his car, one (or more) of the OlandO salesmen smashed one of his car windows and removed the other nine copies, which speaks volumes about the mentality of OlandO's salesmen.

Then, an inquiry card came in from Jack Forester.

Jack was an extremely wealthy Beverly Hills investor. OlandO hired a *detective* to check him out. The detective's report was pure hokum.

Al Winnikoff and Dirk Snark were sent to interview Mr. Forester. According to OlandO's bosses, Al and Dirk had the lowdown on Jack, and a sale was therefore inevitable.

Not quite.

Now for a digression. Please bear with us; the digression has a point, and we will return to our story shortly:

Al W. had dealt for many years with another wealthy Beverly Hills investor by the name of Harry Dove.

Al W. and Harry Dove were complete opposites.

Harry was rather short, feisty, tough to do business with, and not highly educated. Harry was an early riser. 4 A.M.

Al, on the other hand, actually stood 6 feet 4 inches. He was extremely polite to *everyone*, easy to do business with, and had received an excellent liberal arts education from the University of California (Berkeley). He was, is and will forever remain a late riser. 8 A.M.

Harry's 4 A.M. calls to Al went like so: "Meet me at Bob's Big Boy at 6 for breakfast." Click!

Winnikoff, bleary-eyed and numb, would get up and go. Every time. He never made excuses. He just went.

But there was something else between the older entrepreneur and the younger salesman. Something else clicked.

They actually *liked* each other. They disagreed on politics, investment strategies, land values, the stock market, religion, cars, and a host of other life details, both large and small. But still they clicked.

So when Jack Forester sent in his OlandO inquiry card, Al W. called Harry Dove and asked, "Harry, do you know Jack Forester?"

"Know him? I play poker with that—of-a—!"

"Is he any good?"

"No! He's not good! He's a rotten poker player!"

"Does he make straight deals?" W. asked.

"If he makes deals the way he plays poker, he should go to jail!" Mr. D. replied. "And he's got a *terrible* temper!"

"Harry, I have to know. Is this guy honest or should I avoid him?"

"I guess he's O.K."

The supreme compliment.

"Harry, I thank you."

"Don't thank me. And what's more, if Jack Forester goes into a deal, count me out!"

"Will do."

Click!

Click!

When Dirk Snark and Al Winnikoff finally went to see Mr. Forester at his palatial home, they were impressed with the surroundings.

Mr. Forester himself was a short, brusque gentleman with a big cigar. Unlike his poker-playing buddy Harry Dove, Jack Forester was an extremely well-read, analytical, gregarious and urbane gentleman of eclectic tastes. He was also an attorney licensed to practice in New York and California.

When the salesmen sat down with Mr. F. in his comfortable den, they were offered drinks.

"Scotch on the rocks," Dirk said,

"Do you have any milk?" Winnikoff asked.

"Of course," Mr. F. replied, the faintest hint of a smile

crossing his lips.

When the three gentlemen were comfortably seated and drinking, Al W. handed Jack Forester a copy of the 712 Book.

"Very impressive," Jack said. "A little slanted, but very impressive."

Suddenly Dirk Snark got in the act. "I understand you were in the Army Air Force during World War II."

"Yes, I was."

"Well, boy, that sure is a coincidence because so was I—" (Dear Reader, we are not going to relate Mr. S's wartime exploits. You have all heard them before. For those who need more info, refer to Military Canned Speech 48QZP.)

When Dirk Snark finished with his war stories, Mr. Forester turned to Al W. and asked, "When can we go look at the property?"

"You name it," W. replied.

"Well, you'll have to clear that with me! I've got a very busy schedule!" Dirk said. He then downed the last of his Scotch.

The following day, Tuesday, Dirk Snark left a note for Winnikoff telling him they would meet at the Forester residence at 9 A.M. Friday morning to take Jack to see the property. Winnikoff duly noted the time and place in his appointment book.

Then, with a cautious look on her face, one of the secretaries took Winnikoff aside and told him the Forester trek was really going to take place on *Thursday* at 9 A.M.

"Thanks," W. said.

With his blood near the boiling point, Winnikoff called Snark at home and demanded an explanation.

Snark went berserk. His duplicity was so obvious that Winnikoff said, "Look, Dirk, I don't think you can make that deal alone—"

More berserk phone talk from Mr. S.

"— and furthermore, if Jack Forester senses a lot of

friction between the two of *us*, he'll never go through with it. Now either you start behaving like a respectable human being or——"

After a lengthy conversation, Dirk Snark agreed to go along with Winnikoff's suggestions.

They met on Thursday at the Forester mansion and Jack made the introductions.

1. Phil Corbett, C.P.A. and lifelong Forester friend.
2. John Gard, jeweler and lifelong Forester friend.
3. Robert Tome, attorney at law and lifelong Forester friend.

Jack Forester took one look at Winnikoff's 1960 Peugeot 403 and had himself a good laugh. He tossed Winnikoff the keys to his brand new 1965 Cadillac Coupe de Ville and said, "Here, kid. You drive. At least we'll have air conditioning."

The trip from Beverly Hills to Sun City and back took most of the day. They got stuck in the mud on the 712 and had a great time and a lot of laughs getting out. Mr. Forester bought them a sumptuous dinner toward nightfall.

After returning to Beverly Hills, Mr. Forester and crew shook hands with the two OlandO salesmen. Mr. F. told them he had a lot of checking to do but promised he would call in two weeks.

For the next 13 days, Winnikoff spent his days and nights checking everything he could for miles around the subject property.

True to his word, Mr. Forester called on the fourteenth day.

Winnikoff and Snark were all ears.

"We'd like to go down there with you tomorrow again," he said. "And we'd like to show you some other properties we're considering."

"Is 9 o'clock all right?" Winnikoff asked.

"Fine."

"We'll see you then."

The second expedition was a bit more tense than the first. For although Jack Forester and Company had done a great deal of homework, nothing else truly compared with the 712 acres.

Except for one parcel of land which *did* compare favorably with the 712.

On the way home, Jack ordered Al to pull over to the side of the road near the southeast corner of Highways 60 and 395.

"This section's for sale," Jack Forester said, "and if we drive on it we're not going to get stuck in the mud. It's like a beautiful mound and I think it's the prettiest piece of acreage for 20 miles around. And it's only $3,000 per acre." He turned to his cronies and said, "Phil, what do you think?"

Phil loved it.

"John, what do you think?"

John loved it.

"Bob, what do you think?"

Bob was ecstatic.

"Dirk, what do you think?"

"You call this acreage? This is garbage. This is the worst piece of property in Riverside County. Why I remember when we used to go out on a bombing mission and my commander used to give us a steak dinner, why I felt just like a lamb being led to slaughter and—

(Dear Reader: put in anything you want at this point. But Dirk Snark's speech ended as follows:)

"—and I'm your friend, Jack. Take my word for it. I've been in this business 30 years and I'm an honest man. I wouldn't steer you wrong! Trust me!"

At this point, Jack Forester poked a finger into Al Winnikoff's ribs and said, "Al, what do you think?"

"It's beautiful."

Dirk Snark turned ashen.

"Is that all?" Jack asked.

"It's probably the prettiest piece of property for 20 miles

around."

"Is that all?"

"Look, Jack, let me tell you what I know about the acreage business."

"Tell me," Jack said, poking Winnikoff's ribs again.

"Well, any *good* piece of vacant ground has to have four elements: (1) water, (2) drainage, (3) utilities and (4) roads. Now, there's no water on this property but you can probably sink a good well for very little money."

"How much?" Jack Forester asked.

"With casing, about eight dollars a foot for maybe 300 feet."

"So that's $2,400. How many wells do you think we'll need?"

"Ten, maybe."

"O.K. What else?"

"The drainage," Winnikoff said, "is near perfect. You won't get stuck in the mud here."

Dirk Snark was at this point livid.

But Al continued. "There are no utilities *on* the property, but there are plenty of power and phone lines running the perimeter of the property. And as for sewers, there are none. But I suspect the percolation would be good for a private septic system."

"Then you're saying the utilities are no problem?" Jack asked.

"That's right."

"Now what's the last thing you mentioned?" Jack asked.

"Roads. You've got two miles of major highway frontage on the north and west boundaries of the property. You can't get much better than that."

"So you're recommending we buy this piece instead of your piece," Jack Forester said.

There was a long silence while Winnikoff took a deep breath. The only sounds in the car were the hum of the air conditioner and the outside traffic.

Finally Winnikoff said, "I didn't say that."

"Then what are you telling me?" Mr. Forester demanded, shaking his cigar furiously.

"I'm telling you that once you have all the facts, you should make your own decision."

"Is that all?"

"No," Winnikoff said, "because although this is a great piece of land, it has a stigma attached to it."

"A *what*?" Jack Forester asked.

"A stigma."

"What are you talking about?" Mr. F. demanded.

"Well," Winnikoff continued in his slow, California drawl, "the Riverside Raceway is less than a mile to the east of this property. And when they race, you can't hear yourself think. And on race days, the traffic backs up for miles around here."

"You think that's a problem?" Mr. Forester asked.

"That's only part of the problem."

"What's the rest of it?"

"Well, March Air Force Base is about three miles to the southeast, and when those B-52's come roaring out of there, you—"

There comes a time in every dedicated salesperson's life that the gods smile benevolently on his or her efforts and lend a hand in furthering *The Close*. It was at this precise moment in Winnikoff's career that a B-52 flew out of March Air Force Base and shook every bolt in Jack's Cadillac to the core. The racket was so intense the Gang felt they had lost the fillings in their teeth. Speech was futile. Lips moved, but no sounds seemed to come out.

Dirk Snark's complexion returned to its normal shade of green.

A hint of a smile crossed Jack's lips. When the B-52 was gone, Jack turned to Al and said, "O.K., kid, let's go."

But our saga does not end here.

For although Al and Dirk got Jack, Phil, John and Bob signed up, there was still much to be done.

When the hard-core, rough homework had to be done,

Snark disappeared and OlandO's founders proved to be absolutely worthless. In fact, they were worse than worthless. For they hounded their salesmen daily to get everything signed, to get the money in and close the deal, and ethics be damned.

One of the problems which arose was the matter of water bonds. The preliminary title policy indicated that water bonds had been issued in 1906 and the 712 acres was to receive an allotment of so many acre-feet per annum.

Jack wanted it in writing. He wanted the actual bonds.

There *were* no bonds. And even if there *were*, no one could find them.

Jack called Al late one Friday afternoon and said, "I want to see you right away about these water bonds."

"I'm sorry, Jack, but I'm on my way to Slushy Meadows with my kid."

"You *what?*" Jack Forester asked, incredulously.

"We're going away on a Boy Scout outing over the weekend."

"Are you crazy?" Jack Forester shouted in the phone. "What's more important? A two-and-a-half-million-dollar deal, or the Boy Scouts?"

Al paused, then did the right thing. "The Boy Scouts."

Click!!!!

The following week, W. straightened out the matter of the bonds. It was very complex, but he straightened it out. It involved a retired judge who, as a young attorney, had incorporated the water district, put a complex bonded indebtedness on the landowners and never distributed the paperwork in 1906. But Al Winnikoff got his hands on that paperwork by taking the old judge out to dinner and explaining his problem. The kindly old gentlemen made copies of everything for the young salesman at no charge. He then called Jack Forester and apologized for the delay from 1906 to 1965.

Before leaving the retired judge, the salesman asked, "Isn't 59 years some kind of a record for completing the legal paperwork?"

The old man smiled. "Maybe that's why they made me a judge," he said.

Later, when A.W. explained everything to Jack, Mr. Forester, himself a lawyer, pulled out a photo of a tombstone.

"I took this picture in Exon, England," he said. The epitaph read:

GOD DOES DO WONDERS NOW AND THEN—
HERE LIES A LAWYER WHO WAS AN
HONEST MAN

"What do you think of *that*?" Jack Forester asked, jabbing Winnikoff fiercely in the chest.

"Well, it's interesting. But before I go, may I ask a small favor?"

"What's that?" Mr. F. asked. He was as tall standing up as W. was sitting down.

"Please don't jab me in the chest."

"Why not?" Mr. F. barked, jabbing Mr. W. in the ribs and spilling cigar ashes all over Mr. W's jacket. "What's wrong with you young guys today? You've all gone soft!"

"Well, I've got these bruises all over my chest and my wife—"

"Your wife!" Jack Forester barked. "Let me tell you something, Winnikoff—" there was just a hint of a smile on Jack Forester's lips—"anybody who lets his wife and the Boy Scouts run his life *deserves* a few battle scars."

"But what if you poke a hole in me and I bleed to death?"

The hint of a smile never left Jack Forester's lips.

It was after 9 P.M. when Winnikoff returned to the OlandO office.

The OlandO reception committee was waiting. They went berserk when Winnikoff entered the door. The gist of their blustering-boss-anguish went something like this:

OlandO owner Number One, eyes bulging: "Do you know how long this deal has been dragging on?"

OlandO owner Number Two, veins throbbing: "How dare you [blah-blah-blah-]? You've dragged this thing out for almost six months now!"

OlandO owner Number Three, fist shaking: "You *promised*, by God, you *promised* you would have signed partnership papers and checks *today*! And you *lied* to us! Why, if we knew you would do this to us we never would have let you [blah-blah-blah-]."

And who was there as a cheering section?

You guessed it.

Dirk Snark.

When the heated anger of the bosses subsided slightly, D.S. stormed in with, "How could you let that stupid, ignorant, two-faced, mealy-mouthed—of-a—run you around like this?" Dirk Snark asked.

"Well," Al W. replied, "Jack Forester always said nice things about you."

"Why did I ever let you take over? I should have handled this myself!" Dirk Snark exploded.

"Dirk," Winnikoff said, "do you know who the smartest and most important person in the world is?"

"*I am*!" Dirk Snark replied heatedly.

"No," Mr. W. said.

"I suppose you think you are!" OlandO Number Three chimed in.

"No," W. replied. He paused, waiting for a quiet moment.

The hyenas grumbled and snarled. Ugly creatures thriving on chaos.

"No," W. said again. "*The smartest and most important person in the world is your customer*."

The hyenas went wild. There was much anguished howling, screaming, barking and snorting.

Then Dirk shouted above the roar of the pack, "What makes you think that stupid, ignorant— of-a——is so smart?"

"*Because he's got the money, he's a decent guy who knows how to control his greed, and once you lose sight of that you're in real trouble.*" Mr. W. replied. Then he threw the signed and notarized partnership agreement on the desk, along with some hefty checks, and departed.

When Winnikoff arrived at his apartment, Dirk called. "They're going to fire you when the 712 deal is over," he said.

"Thanks."

To say that Winnikoff was ill-abused and terribly depressed during this period of his life would be an understatement. He did not sleep well and lost weight.

When the 712 deal closed, he demanded payment and handed in a letter of resignation. For six months, Mr. W. had requested a signed contract, and OlandO 1, 2 and 3 made repeated verbal promises and excuses but never delivered the paperwork. Not only did OlandO refuse to pay him the promised $125,000, they also went to vicious extremes to get him fired from his *next* job.

After talking to 12 lawyers, Mr. W. took matters into his own hands and settled for $17,250.

He was so depressed by this that he went back to technical writing and got out of sales completely. In about three months he finally recovered, going out on evenings and weekends to peddle his *own* land deals. None of which ever lost money for his partners and investors. However, when one limited partner once sold out his interest to another limited partner, there *was* a loss of $1,750 by the party of the first part. Proof of the fact that no one is perfect.

Over a period of 30 years, Mr. W. has had over 200 partners. Not one of his partners has ever sued or threatened to sue him.

During the down times, the *only* person with whom Albert Winnikoff discussed his depressing problems was his wife, Lillian. They eloped in 1952 and he loves her as much today as he did during the courting days of the 1940's.

Which goes to prove that although sales are made and lost, love endures.

(Here endeth the somewhat truthful Saga Of The 712.) If you learn nothing more from this book than this basic TRUTH, consider your lesson well-learned and your time and money well-spent: And the TRUTH is: IF IT'S WORTH SAYING, IT'S WORTH PUTTING IN WRITING. (If they won't put it in writing, they're crooks. Plain and simple.)

Meanwhile, back to the publishing world...

Our editor seemed pleased with this write-up and turned us over to Mr. Gunn, newly appointed head of the Marketing Department.

"I'm a salesman too," he said. All gush and gums. "But I really want to help you boys."

"How?"

"Well, please don't tell my employer—I—ah ha—have a little business going on the side—ah ha—with a promoter friend of mine and he—ah ha—wants to put you two on the road. Seminars, pep rallies, booster meetings. Things like that."

"Not interested."

"Not interested?" Mr. Gunn asked incredulously. "Why you could get rich from the promo alone."

"We're not interested because most of that road show stuff is hype and most of the late night TV get-rich-quick schemes are just dirty, ugly scams."

"How can you possibly say such a thing? Some of my best friends are in that business!" Mr. Gunn said.

"Look, Mr. Gunn, anyone who has a normal greed gland is O.K. in our book, but anyone who tries to break the law of economics is automatically a crook in our book," Mr. Prelutsky said.

"But you two are naturals. You would be a smash hit!"

"Whose smash?"

"Whose hit?"

"But what will I tell my dear, dear—ah ha—friend?"

"That we're not hucksters."

"That we're writers. Honest writers at that. We believe what Khalil Gibran said in the *The Prophet: Work is love made visible*."

"Well!" Mr. Gunn said, exhaling his indignation. "I can't say I wasn't warned! All writers are crazy!" He walked away and left us with our truthful work of art.

We let our a sigh of relief.

"Done?"

"Done! And well done at that!"

"Now what?"

"Wrap it up!"

So as we careen down that bookish highway called THE END, let us tell you we are happy, happy, happy. If you don't know why, please check with your local psychiatrist. He has an answer for everything. But we don't. We *think and hope* we've been of great help to the reader, but we will never know for sure.

Why?

Because your success or failure in sales is totally, strictly, absolutely and completely up to you. Sure *we* can help. But *you* have to produce.

And if you have a down day or a down hour or some down time, don't let it bother you. It does not matter: Put more forcefully: IT DOES NOT MATTER. IDNM. Whoever and whatever and wherever you are: IDNM. Your future is in your hands. In your heart. In your brains. In your soul.

Work hard, do the job right and make yourself indispensable to your customers. For the true No. 1 Best Seller, it is more important to make a living from what you give than what you get.

Allow us to again quote our buddy Joe Girard:

"The truly great salespeople in this world are more anxious to provide benefits to their customers than they are to receive large commissions."

Do it our way and fear not for the economic returns tomorrow. TNOBS who sticks to business is never unemployed.

If you are a waitress or stewardess abused by the boss or patrons, bear in mind: IT DOES NOT MATTER. IDNM. Why? Because if you can juggle all those heavy trays, keep the coffee mugs, wine goblets and water glasses full at all times, while catering to the surly, screeching abuse of your tormentors, think of how successful you can become while satisfying kind and rational customers who appreciate your service instead of those hungry lunkheads at the dinner table. Remember: IDNM. If you are a laid- off aerospace engineer, technician, clerk or card-filer, you had to know *something* to get the job. So why not apply that know-how to *this* job and become a No. 1 Best Seller. IDNM. If you have failed or are homeless or a victim of downsizing, IDNM. Getting back on your feet and becoming TNOBS in your league is what truly matters. For in good and decent and kind and generous sales there is a home for you.

If you have lived your entire life without a home, do not curse the sun or rain or moon or stars. IDNM. Think of the man who lived 40 years in the wilderness with a theory and vision of his own. It was a vision he shared primarily with His Lord. For the man we call Moses spawned not one, nor two, but three great monotheistic religions and sold 10 of God's Commandments not only to the barbarians of his tough lifetime, but to the barbarians of all time.

[There is an apocryphal story of the Lord's first offering of five commandments to Moses.

"How much?" Moses asked.

" For Thee and Thy people they are free," the Lord replied.

"In that case I'll take ten."]

Please be a believer. For among those you love and who love you in return, you breathe the gentle, sacred fires of life. And from that fire we all know in the warmth of our souls that success conquers defeat and love conquers all. Therefore, go forth Gentle People and do not curse the darkness. IDNM. Go forth and light a candle. (Or, if you are computer literate, go forth and flip a switch.) Do the positive things and you will quickly learn the negative things do not matter all that much.

One of the TNOBS gang has told us on numerous occasions that the wheel of fortune, like the coin of the realm, is round and if you stick with it, your number will sooner or later come up. And how do we know these things about you and your number? We know that you are sitting and reading *our* words and ideas at this time (in your hands) and putting *them* into *your* brain. Therefore, please reciprocate and become the very best you can become, i.e. TNOBS. And when you do, the deal between us will be well made. And we will all profit.

Now that you have come this far in the discourse, we tell you with absolute 100% certainty that you will make it in sales. Anyone who can plow this far through the magical mystery of letters, numbers, words and ideas of a book— and especially *this* book—is destined for success. Don't stop now. We are here and you are out there. We can help, but you, TNOBS, must do it. And the fact is that you are more than 99% of the way there. And all TNOBS's go for the 100% close. So don't stop now. For the end (of this book) and your new beginning (in life) are at hand.

For further confirmation of this fact, allow us to quote Winnikoff's dear departed mother-in-law. A smart and good lady who was wont to say:

"Every man for himself and God for us all."

Now, would the Almighty lie to you?

Of course not.

And how can we be sure that you will perform the selling miracle? Simple. After all these thousands of words and hundreds of pages devoted to telling our customers the truth, do you think we would start lying to you now?

Of course not.

Still in doubt?

Forget the doubts.

IDNM.
Because.
You are TNOBS.

OUR PRAYER

In closing, we hope we have appealed to your better nature in going forth to do the world's very important work of selling. We pray and would be particularly gratified if our words strike a responsive chord in gentle, learned people of the world, like English and history majors who wonder what they will do with their lives and diplomas after graduation. With sensitive school dropouts and concerned former nuns and clergymen. With single mothers and unemployed fathers. With clerks and cooks and dishwashers surviving on minimum wage. With all those who truly believe that the customer is the smartest and most important person in the world. With abused but tender and loving souls who *know* they can do it, but are afraid to put forth the incredible effort and make the first step. To all of you, we say do it and do not despair. Because TNOBS cannot lose if the customer wins.

IDNM that you are black, green, yellow, white, gray or red. Young, old, rich, poor or somewhere in the middle. Or if you have made terrible mistakes in your life. Whether you are a Republican, Democrat or Independent, we know you can make it in sales. After all, *we* made it in sales. And if you're *our* kind of people, we need you.

The world needs you.

Therefore, friend, let us all pray that as you put this book down, you do the following: Look in that mirror, notice that irrepressible glint in the eye of the beholder, and then go forth to elevate the status of our profession with good and continuous deeds.

Finally, we wish you Good Health, Good Fortune, Much Love and Godspeed in the attainment of your goals.